The Making of Auschwitz

The Author

Ian Baxter is a military historian who specialises in German twentieth-century military history. He has written more than sixty books including: 'Poland – The Eighteen Day Victory March', 'Panzers In North Africa', 'The Ardennes Offensive', 'The Western Campaign', 'The 12th SS Panzer-Division Hitlerjugend', 'The Waffen-SS on the Western Front', 'The Waffen-SS on the Eastern Front', 'The Red Army At Stalingrad', 'Elite German Forces of World War II', 'Armored Warfare', 'German Tanks of War', 'Blitzkrieg', 'Panzer-Divisions At War', 'Defeat to Retreat: The Last Years of the German Army At War 1943–1945', and, most recently 'the Sixth Army and the Road to Stalingrad'. He has written over 100 journal articles including: 'Last Days of Hitler', 'Wolf's Lair', 'Story of the V1 and V2 Rocket Programme', 'Secret Aircraft of World War Two', 'Rommel at Tobruk', 'Hitler's War With His Generals', 'Secret British Plans To Assassinate Hitler', 'SS At Arnhem', 'Hitlerjugend', 'Battle Of Caen 1944', 'Gebirgsjäger At War', 'Panzer Crews', 'Hitlerjugend Guerrillas', 'Last Battles in the East', 'Battle of Berlin', and many more. He has also reviewed numerous military studies for publication, supplied thousands of photographs and important documents to various publishers and film production companies worldwide, and lectures to various schools, colleges and universities throughout the United Kingdom and Ireland.

The Making of Auschwitz

The Largest Killing Factory of all time

Ian Baxter

Pen & Sword
MILITARY

First published in Great Britain in 2025 by
Pen & Sword Military
An imprint of Pen & Sword Books Limited
Yorkshire – Philadelphia

ISBN 978 1 03612 139 6

A CIP catalogue record for this book is
available from the British Library.

Typeset by Mac Style
Printed in the UK by CPI Group (UK) Ltd, Croydon, CR0 4YY.

The Publisher's authorised representative in the EU for product safety is
Authorised Rep Compliance Ltd., Ground Floor, 71 Lower Baggot Street,
Dublin D02 P593, Ireland.
www.arccompliance.com

For a complete list of Pen & Sword titles please contact

PEN & SWORD BOOKS LIMITED
47 Church Street, Barnsley, South Yorkshire, S70 2AS, England
E-mail: enquiries@pen-and-sword.co.uk
Website: www.pen-and-sword.co.uk
or
PEN AND SWORD BOOKS
1950 Lawrence Road, Havertown, PA 19083, USA
E-mail: uspen-and-sword@casematepublishers.com
Website: www.penandswordbooks.com

Contents

Foreword

Writing another book about Auschwitz had never really been my intention but over the years of constant research and writing about the holocaust, I found there had been an overwhelming need to write about the camp again. This need arose purely from my interest in how a concentration camp like Auschwitz evolved from incarcerating political detainees to becoming the largest mass murder factory of all time. The origins of this tragic concentration and death camp are quite well-known, but what is less known is how this camp evolved through the various construction phases and planning decisions that made the site the epicentre of the Nazi killing machine.

The making of Auschwitz was only made possible by the creation of a special construction office which would oversee planning, various projects, and the adaptation of existing buildings, including new structures and constructing a completely new site which would be later known as Birkenau. This camp with its new barracks and buildings soon developed into something the Nazis had never embarked on before – the mechanized extermination of thousands of men, women, and children. Grisly as this was, the SS had in fact created a killing factory on an industrial scale. However, these murderous activities could only ever be achieved by an efficient construction office supported by outside expert companies, all of which were vyng for financial reward.

In the camp's short existence by the late summer of 1944 almost one million people had been murdered. Yet, in spite of the war being lost and Red Army forces approaching the borders of Poland, the construction office was still required to continue drawing plans to extend Birkenau further with more buildings and barracks. But, as Red Army troops approached, *SS-Reichsführer* Heinrich Himmler reluctantly ordered Birkenau's killing facility to be shut down and the apparatus used to kill hundreds of thousands of people removed or destroyed. When it was reported that units of the Soviet 322nd Rifle Division were approaching Birkenau from the direction of Krakow in late January 1945, SS personnel were ordered to incinerate all important documentation relating to their crimes. Vehicle loads of documents including various reports and other associated documentation relating to the Auschwitz complex were burnt in ditches in massive pyres of paper. However, in the panic that had ensued to leave the camp, the SS had in fact missed the construction archive, which had been locked away in a different building. As a result, when the Russians liberated Auschwitz on 27 January 1945, they found masses of intact technical paperwork including construction blueprints. However, it was not just Auschwitz where the evidence was found, but Gross Rosen concentration camp, 40-miles southwest of Breslau. As the Russians advanced it was here that the *Bauleitung* transferred huge amounts of documents including maps, plans, blue prints, technical drawings, models, cost estimates, letters between construction firms including Topf and Sons, furnace technical plans and installation reports as well as transfer deeds relating to the crematoria. There was also financial and photographic domentation as well as furniture, drawing boards and other apparatus for architects and designers, all of which were sent to Gross Rosen for safety. But as further battles on the Eastern Front intensified the Red Army captured the besieged city of Breslau then advanced units drove towards Gross Born where the camp was liberated on 14 February 1945. It was here that much of the evidence relating to the construction of Auschwitz-Birkenau was unearthed.

Since the liberation of both camps, this paper trail to murder had been locked away until after the Cold War ended, and is now accessible to researchers and the general public. It was these captured papers from the construction office which made this book possible. Using hundreds of plans, budgets, letters, telegrams, contractor bids, financial negotiations, work site labour reports, requests for material allocations, and the minutes of meetings held in the Building Office among the architects themselves, with camp officials, and with high-ranking dignitaries from Berlin, it illuminates to what extent the Nazis went to planning genocide on a mass scale.

Many of these documents derived from what was initially called the Bauburo (construction office), which initially oversaw the conversion of the Auschwitz main camp from what had been a Polish army barracks until October 1939. The office was only small and set-up on the ground floor of the camp *Kommandantur* and named the *KL-Bauleitung* (Concentration Camp Construction Board). It comprised of six men, and consisted of four sections: Registry, Commercial, Material Warehouses, Accounting, and Reporting and Planning.

Quickly the office expanded to nine persons and was later renamed the *SS-Neubauleitung in Auschwitz O/S* (New Auschwitz Construction Board, Upper Silesia). As further plans for development of Auschwitz grew, which included Birkenau and the surrounding sub-camps, the construction office quickly enlarged, becoming more complex with a mixture of divisions and roles including a chain of command and preferred German specialised construction companies. As a result, the *Bauleitung* further grew and in November 1941 it became the *SS-Zentralbauleitung der Waffen-SS u. Polizei Auschwitz O/S* (Central Construction Board of the Auschwitz Waffen-S and Police, Upper Silesia). However, in spite of its size, and the fact that it was engaged in virtually all aspects of construction, the *Bauleitung* had no authority to sign-off and pass various plans and ideas. In fact, in regards to quality of construction the office was answerable to the *SS Hauptamt Haushalt und Bauten* (SS Main Office for Budget and Construction, later known as the *SS-Wirtschafs und Verwaltungshauptamt*: WVHA – SS Main Economic and Adminstrative Office). As part of the SS garrison at Auschwitz the office was also subordinated to the camp commandant, and had to obtain his authorization on construction plans and projects. Strange as it was, the commandant would then have to gain further permission by the Oranienburg headquarters near Berlin. It was at this office that some of the most important projects were created and planned including the ordering of the crematoria.

From the inception of Auschwitz to its gradual development, the *Bauleitung* grew and evolved too. Even prisoners with technical knowledge were employed by the planning offices, including civilian draughtsmen. Over the course of four years the office had specific departments comprising of design, construction, planning, finance, workshops, supervision, hydrology and storage, including roofing, painting, carpentry, ground work, metal work, electrical and even glazing. It basically covered all aspects of construction and was the executor and inspector of all the projects that were undertaken at the camp.

The documents and various papers that derived from the *Bauleitung* tell us a great deal of what happened at the camp, including the problems and technical issues the engineers and architects had during the camp's evolution. Step by step, these documents, comprising of blueprints, architecual drawings and correspondence, show how the office came to plan and execute the horror we call Auschwitz today. It reveals how crucial it was for the SS to employ civilian expertise to install the various structures including sewage systems, chimneys and to provide building shells. One of the best known firms contracted at Auschwitz was Topf & Sons from Erfurt, which was a company that had diversified into silos, chimneys, incinerators for burning municipal waste, and crematoria. As with a number of private companies involved in assisting the SS at Auschwitz, it used its considerable expertise to assist the Nazi regime to make mass execution an efficient, industrial process.

There were some 46 private firms involved in the varied projects, plans and construction of Auschwitz. All of them received financial reward from the SS for their work and even received bonuses if completed early. Assisting the private firms were foreign workers and prisoners, which formed prisoner *Sonderkommandos* to carry out the work. Many of them were drafted to dig out the drainage ditches and foundations, transport various building materials, build various structures and erect new buildings of death. Even Russian PoWs between 1941 and 1942 were forced to build some of the structures under German supervision in appalling conditions.

There was also a penal company of prisoners that were given some of the hardest jobs on site, and many of them, including Soviet PoWs, perished.

For more specialised jobs such as bricklayers, carpenters, electrical engineers and electricians, their jobs were often perfomed by foremen and skilled workers and were under direct supervision.

During the camp's existence, the *Bauleitung* architects and draughtsmen produced many maps and plans including technical drawings, models, and cost estimates, as well as photographic documentation of the build. Through the planning and construction stages there were also vast quantities of letters and correspondence indicting not only the SS in their intentions of building a mass murder factory on an industrial scale, but also implicating the private companies as well.

These documents also tell us that Auschwitz was not as efficient as first thought. Although the SS callously boasted of the numbers they killed during its operation, the machinery which the *Bauleitung* had constructed for murder was often unreliable due to poor quality. In fact, there were constant technical issues with the four Birkenau Crematoria. Builders often had to economize during the construction of both Crematoria II and III, and they were less solid constructions. The retort ovens also did not meet the requirements. As a result of being overworked, the internal lining of the chimney and the connecting flue to the incinerator of Crematorium II collapsed and it was temporarily taken out of commission so that engineers could re-line the chimney. The construction report outlined that this was due to thermal expansion variations in the building materials used, which had led to the damaging of the thermal insulation layers. Since the crematoria only had a short warranty period, both contractors, Topf & Sons plus Huta, argued with the *Bauleitung*, trying to blame each other for the technical issues. Although they all agreed to divide the costs for repairs, reports confirmed that between April and the end of September 1943, Crematoria II, III, IV, and V only worked for two months at full capacity. Only a quarter of their maximum capacity was used due to technical issues. From late December 1943 until April 1944, Crematoria II and III ran without any major technical issues, but were not operated at full capacity. In mid May 1943 Crematorium IV furnace started to crack due to being overworked. Also the natural ventilation was noted as being unacceptable and dangerous. It was considered that Crematorium IV's incinerator needed replacing. However, the building was still deemed effective as a gas chamber. As for Crematorium V, it was deprived of most of its furnaces due to cracking and technical issues. It was eventually decommissioned and kept in reserve as a gas chamber, but was brought back into operation for the Hungarian action in the summer of 1944. In service, the building operated as a gassing facility and used the nearby open-air cremation pits to burn the murdered victims due to the fact that the crematorium furnaces were inoperative.

Despite the problems the *Bauleitung* and Nazi hierachy faced with the main killing apparatus at Auschwitz, the crematoria played a pivotal part in the camp's operation, especially during 1943. Documents quoted in this book together with maps, diagrams, correspondence and imagery give evidence of the lengths the SS, engineers, architects and private companies strove in order to satisfy their blood lust and greed.

(The views or opinions expressed in this book and the context in which the images are used do not necessarily reflect the views or policy of, nor imply approval or endorsement by, the United States Holocaust Memorial Museum – USHMM)

Introduction

This book, commemorating eighty years since the liberation of Auschwitz-Birkenau, is the story of the construction of the camp, and its evolution into the largest mass murder factory of all time. Using hundreds of captured German documents and architectural plans that were not destroyed from the 'Central Building Authority of the *Waffen-SS* and the Police, Auschwitz, Upper Silesia', headed by *SS-Sturmbannführer* Karl Bischoff, the book is a unique historical source of how the architects came to plan and accomplish the horror we now call Auschwitz today.

Drawing on key documents from the Building Office archive, this in-depth study of Auschwitz uses plans, letters, telegrams, work site labour reports, and minutes of meetings. It reveals how the SS needed civilian knowledge to install electrical, sewage, heating systems, and build chimneys and other structures, both wooden and brick. It reveals how various outside contractors were involved in cooperating in genocide, and shows just how eager they were to produce goods for the SS for financial reward.

It shows Topf & Sons from Erfurt, a company proud of its production of first-class incinerators, sending promotional material to the SS about its double-muffle furnace, which was designed to burn only corpses. For the building of Crematoria IV and V for instance, there were no less than nine civilian firms that participated in their construction. Each company was given a specific role and job in the construction process. The shells were constructed by Huta of Kattowitz and Riedel & Sons of Bielitz. The roof was designed by Konrad Segnitz of Beuthen and built by Industrie-Bau AC of Bielitz. The chimneys were built by Robert Koehler of Myslowitz. All these firms had time sheets and included reports on the work undertaken and costs involved, with many of them on bonuses to complete the work on time.

The book illuminates the step-by-step transformation of the camp's development, and the blueprints and various drawings prove beyond any reasonable doubt what happened at Auschwitz eighty years ago. The construction of Auschwitz lasted a number of years and was never fully completed. In the course of its planning and construction phases between 1940 and 1944, many architectural technical drawings of various sites and buildings were drawn-up by SS draughtsmen. Even prisoners with technical knowledge were employed by the planning offices, including civilian draughtsmen. When these plans were approved they were presented to the contractors to carry out the building work. Just after the construction had begun on Birkenau in 1941 and the decision was made to transform the site into an extermination camp, architectural plans were presented to include the new crematoria and gas chambers. Many of those drafted to erect these new buildings of death were both German and foreign workers, including the inmates themselves. Even Russian PoWs were forced to build some of the structures under German supervision in appalling conditions.

By the summer of 1943 Birkenau had been transformed into a murder camp, but building and planning to further extend the site continued. Even a rail line was built in the camp in order to facilitate and speed up the extermination process for Hungarian Jews the following year.

The construction of the camp continued remorselessly until November 1944, when Himmler gave the order to halt the construction of the complex, and dismantle the extermination facilities in order to conceal their murderous activities. When the Red Army arrived on 27 January 1945, most of the camp was still left intact. Although the SS had incinerated the camp's archives just before the arrival of Soviet troops, they had forgotten to destroy the construction archive, which was kept in another building. As a result, the Russians had found many of the technical drawings and various documents, including construction blueprints that clearly detailed the extermination facilities.

This is the story of those that planned and constructed the death camp and is proof of the Nazi extermination policy. With detailed captions and text together with rare photographs, the book is an important study and incredible insight into those that masterminded the murder of almost 1.1 million people.

Chapter I

Auschwitz I Stammlager 1940–1941

Following the conquest of Poland in early October 1939 the Nazi regime had already planned on the large-scale annexation of the country, both geographically and racially. Almost immediately Adolf Hitler and *SS-Reichsführer* Heinrich Himmler carved up large areas of Poland into the Reich, and made plans to clear-out Poles and Jews from these newly incorporated areas, replacing them with Volksdeutch or German settlers.

Some 3.3 million Jews lived in Poland, more than any other country in Europe. The Nazi regime was determined to unleash more-or-less unrestrained fear and terror attacks, especially in the newly incorporated areas. These actions were aimed against the Jewish community and what they termed was the threat of subversion by Polish nationalist, Jewish Bolshevists and those regarded as enemies of the state.

In order to contain the 1.8 million Jews in these occupied areas plans were drawn-up to imprison them in Ghettos from where they would eventually be deported to new and existing concentration and slave labour camps. Already, immediate action had been planned through SS channels and government officials in the expansion of the concentration camp system through Poland, especially in the unincorporated areas. This region was initially known as the 'General Government of the Occupied Polish Areas', but in 1940 was renamed the 'General Government'. It comprised the Polish province of Lublin and parts of the provinces of Warsaw and Krakow. Throughout the 'General Government' it was planned that those that were sent there would be incarcerated and set to work as stonebreakers, and construction workers for buildings and streets. It was envisaged that these Poles would remain as a slave labour force, and it was therefore deemed necessary to erect 'quarantine camps' in order to subdue the local population and work them as slaves. Initially, it had been proposed that the 'quarantine camps' were to hold the prisoners until they were sent to the various other concentration camps in the *Reich*. However, it soon became apparent that this was totally impracticable. Instead it was decided that these camps were to function as a permanent prison and those that were sent there would work.

In order for the many thousands of Polish political prisoners and Jews to be sent to these camps a Nazi delegation had to be dispatched to the 'General Government' in order to survey viable sites.

Between January and February 1940 two commissions, one led by the *Schutzhaftlagerführer* of Sachsenhausen, Walter Eisfeld, and another by the new inspector of concentration camps, Richard Glücks, journeyed to southern Poland to search for suitable sites. On 21 February Glücks reported to the *SS Reichsführer* in Berlin that the former labour exchange and artillery barracks near a small district town called Oswiecim had been deemed suitable. Himmler immediately began negotiating with the German Army, who evidently had control over all the former Polish military sites. Once the army had agreed to transfer the former Polish barracks, Himmler notified Sachsenhausen to order another commission to this little town called Oswiecim, led by *SS-Hauptsturmführer* Rudolf Höss, who had been chosen to lead a commission to this new site in southern Poland.

With Höss's five-man delegation, they drove by car the long journey to Upper Silesia. As they motored across the countryside they spoke at length about the recent inspection reports on the site. During the journey they stopped in the city of Breslau to confer with Erich von dem Back-Zelewski's aide, Arpad Wigand. In January Wigand had already led his own commission to the former Polish barracks at Oswiecim and found the site suitable for developing into a transit camp. Over lunch Wigand explained to his guests that they should take into consideration that the site should serve as a regional dumping ground for all Polish political prisoners. He added that the camp should also be looked upon as a holding pen so all these undesirables can be transferred at a moment's notice to camps in the west as slave labourers. The camp, he said, had been envisaged by the *Reichsführer* as a quarantine camp for labour exchange. Höss agreed with Wigand about the proposals, and together they adjourned to the sitting room to discuss matters on the size of the camp, and how best to accommodate some 10,000 prisoners.

The town of Oswiecim itself was situated in a remote corner of south-western Poland, in a marshy valley where the Sola River flows into the Vistula about thirty-five miles west of the ancient city of Krakow. The town was virtually unknown outside Poland, and following the occupation of the country Oswiecim was incorporated into the *Reich* together with Upper Silesia and renamed by the German authorities as Auschwitz. Prior to the war, the town's population was 12,000, including nearly 5,000 Jews. The surrounding countryside in the foothills of the Tatra Mountains, whose peaks remain covered in snow all year round, lies in a humid often foggy swampy valley. During winter the weather is harsh and the whole area could often lie in snow until late March, or even early April. In spring the whole area would be revived and could look very beautiful, especially when the warmer weather produced a mixture of wild flowers through the sprawling meadows.

When the German officials arrived inside this little town on 18 April 1940, the small committee of SS officers drove for five minutes from the hotel they were staying opposite the town's main station to the location of the former Polish barracks. Upon their arrival they wasted no time and set out to inspect the site. They noted that the accommodation that consisted of eight two-storey and fourteen single-storey brick barracks framing the north and south sides of a large exercise yard could readily be transformed into a prison camp with extra buildings. The location for the site was also deemed well situated, for Auschwitz had very good railway connections and was isolated from outside observation. Although the water supply was polluted and there were mosquitoes everywhere, the delegation could see plenty of potential. They would be able to transform these swamped infested marshes along the Vistula and Sola Rivers into what they envisaged as a valuable outpost of the *Reich.* Armed with extensive reports of the area and hand-drawn sketches, they left the quiet little town of Oswiecim the following day, 19 April, bound for Berlin. When they arrived in the *Reich* capital Höss and his committee chaired a meeting with Glücks, discussing the suitability of the site. After the meeting Glücks went to see Himmler, telling his boss that *SS-Hauptsturmführer* Rudolf Höss had agreed that the former Polish barracks in Oswiecim was well suited for a camp. He told him that the site would be isolated from the outside world, and easily expandable and accessible by rail. The *Reichsführer* saw good reason to set up the camp and immediately instructed his Inspector of Concentration Camps '*to get things prepared*'.

A week later, on 27 April, Höss received confirmation that Himmler had approved plans to go ahead and commence construction and adapt the new site at Auschwitz. It was also agreed that it would house around 10,000 prisoners. *SS-Obersturmführer* Walter Eisfeld, on the other hand, who had first visited the barracks in January, was not in agreement about the camp and told the *Reichsführer* that in his view the area and surrounding terrain posed great difficulties, not least the materials required to build the barracks into a fortified installation. After much deliberation, added Glücks, he had decided to decline Himmler's offer for the position of Auschwitz commandant. Höss, however, was Glücks' next choice and after submitting his name to Himmler, on 29 April he was asked if he were interested in taking up post at Auschwitz as camp commandant. On 4 May 1940, Höss was officially named as commandant of the new camp.

In order to construct and transform the new camp and adapt the twenty brick barracks for the inmates the new commandant, Höss, had been given a construction budget of two-million Reich Marks (RM). With this generous allowance he would be given the task of cleaning the existing barracks for the guards, rebuilding the two barracks outside the fence into officers' quarters and a hospital for the garrison, build a barrack for the *Blockführer* at the gate, construct eight guard towers around the perimeter of the camp, construct a hayloft, install a crematorium in the abandoned powder magazine building, and tidy the three storey house on the edge of the existing camp in order to make it habitable for him and his family. Initially, Höss took up residence in the hotel overlooking the Auschwitz station whilst his family home was prepared.

To transform the existing site, the commandant first required a labour force. He asked the Reich Security Head Office or RSHA to let him have political prisoners, but they refused on the grounds that they did not want them working on the new site. Instead, *Rapportführer* Gerhard Palitzsch found thirty German criminals, whom he had selected from Sachsenhausen for their various technical skills, and had them transported to Auschwitz to begin work. The town council of Auschwitz was also required to submit a number of workers to be assigned to the camp. Within days the town's mayor gave Höss some 300 local Polish Jews, and under the close supervision of the newly-recruited camp foreman, or *Kapos*, they escorted the Jews along the main road to their new place of work, Auschwitz.

With the full support of the SS Main Economic and Administration office, Auschwitz was funded and planned. The office that was charged with the construction and conversion of the new site was known as the *Bauburo* (construction office). The office was only small and they immediately set-up their desks and drawing boards on the ground floor of the camp Kommandantur and named it the *KL-Bauleitung* (Concentration Camp Construction Board). The Bauleitung was charged with adapting the pre-war Polish barracks, which included buildings for the concentration camp as well as adjacent buildings for the SS.

During late April, May and early June, and armed with plans from the *Bauleitung*, construction of the camp progressed, but relatively slowly due to lack of materials. In fact, in late April a cost estimate of 15,000 RM was calculated for a potential camp crematorium. This was proof that even during these early days of the camp's evolution there was a higher-than-normal mortality rate among the workers.

Whilst further plans were drawn-up for a crematorium, a fence with second-hand barbed wire was erected around the perimeter of the camp, and gradually new buildings began to be constructed as more funds were released. The first phase of building was to convert the existing army barracks into prisoner blocks. Yet, the new commandant was more interested in having a steel gate built at the entrance of Auschwitz. In a meeting with the *Bauleitung* a new steel gate was quickly planned, drawn and later forged in a hurriedly built workshop with a frame built. Over the course of a day or so workers erected this new gate. Blazoned along the top of the gates frame the inscription read '*Arbeit Macht Frei*' – 'Work Makes You Free'. As at

Dachau concentration camp, in the eyes of the commandant the words marked a new journey for all prisoners that passed through these gates, and hard labour, he believed, would somehow bring the prisoners a spiritual freedom. However, in his mind all prisoners that entered through these gates were enemies of the state and their forced labour was justified as punishment.

Throughout the early phase of building more SS men were recruited as guards and by 20 May, fifteen SS men arrived from the Cavalry Unit stationed in Krakow, and were soon installed as part of the camp's guard garrison. During June an additional 100 SS men were sent to reinforce the guard garrison, along with SS officers and SS NCOs of various ranks.

The Auschwitz transit camp was gradually taking shape, but was far from completed. With the construction work barely begun, Höss received a message from the Inspector of the Security Police and the Security Service headquarters in Breslau impatiently enquiring when the camp would be ready to take prisoners. On 14 June a passenger train steamed into Auschwitz station from Tarnow prison carrying 728 political prisoners. However, the camp was far from completed. For a number of weeks there had been difficulties in cordoning off the camp because of serious problems obtaining barbed wire. Frustrated and unhappy about the situation, Höss immediately dispatched thirty inmates to strip an abandoned prisoner of war camp for Polish prisoners for the desperately needed barbed wire. The prisoners were accepted at the gate and they were instantly set-to work under the control of the *Kapos*. For these hapless Poles the sight of the brutal *Kapos* was the first deep impression of how the camp was going to be run.

Constructing the camp was plagued with many difficulties as there was a serious lack of building materials and other important provisions. Although the camp budget had covered all costs for the work, there was nothing to purchase. Even the newly commissioned camp's thirty-nine-year-old architect August Schlachter and his deputy Walther Urbanczyk, who had been entrusted with building the new construction office in the camp, found it almost impossible to obtain proper supplies. In spite of requests by Schlachter to obtain the building materials, Höss and his administration was still unable to assist, and ignored the architects' requests until they found a solution to the growing problem.

Throughout July and early August work continued on the camp, and this included the modification of the former powder magazine store, which started about 5 July. Its primary use was to be a crematorium, but it was initially used for delousing purposes and the incineration of prisoners that died in the camp. Before the crematorium was in operation those that died were transported to Gliwice and incinerated in the municipal crematorium. The conversion of the crematorium was undertaken with the full authorization of the SS Construction Management. In fact, even before Höss had taken up his new post at Auschwitz the installation of a crematorium had already been decided. J.A. Topf and Sons of Erfurt, a company with a section specialising in the manufacture and installation of crematorium furnaces headed by the chief engineer Kurt Prüfer, had been commissioned to undertake the first drawings. The plans showed the first furnace to be installed and gave full details of the internal structure. Schlachter himself had already obtained extensive information on the technology used in the double muffler system and the coke-heated furnace. Together he discussed this new equipment with Höss and the camp officials, and plans for its installation were agreed with SS headquarters in Berlin noting it was a 'method to make the environment more hygienic'.

The conversion of the building into a crematorium in July was undertaken relatively quickly, considering the lack of building materials. The installation consisted of one entrance on the northwest side and included a furnace room with two incinerators and a charnel house. The concrete roof was flat and the building was surrounded on three sides by earth embankments with openings for the window of the coke plant. There were two windows in the furnace room, which were installed to cool down the inside temperature of the building. An external chimney had been built and was connected to the furnaces by underground flues. The entrance to

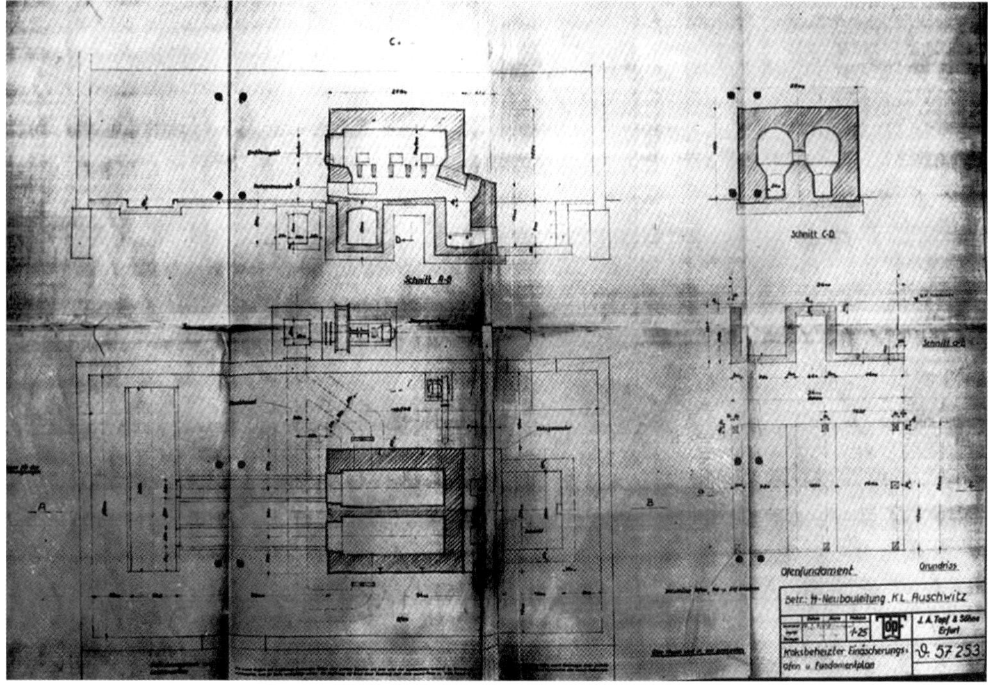

This Topf & Sons drawing is dated 6 June 1940 and refers to the crematorium's first furnace to be installed. It gives details of the internal structure. The drawing shows the furnace with two cremation chambers (also known as muffles) heated with coke by two hearths. However, the lateral pulsed air installation appears not to have been fitted to the furnaces. (*Auschwitz-Birkenau State Archive*)

the crematorium was camouflaged by a very large concrete wall that enclosed the courtyard with two enormous wooden gates. In order to conceal the crematorium from view, a one-storey building housing the SS hospital was constructed nearby, along with the camp workshops and the barracks of the political department.

Besides the transformation of the former powder magazine store into a crematorium, work continued on various other buildings both inside and outside the camp. Building materials, however, were still in short supply so Höss had to steal what he needed. Fortunately for him there had been an attempted escape from the camp by one of the prisoners in early July, and as retaliation for helping the prisoner escape, many of the Polish civilians living in the vicinity of the camp were removed from their homes and deported to forced labour camps. Höss was therefore able to order teams out into Auschwitz town to demolish all the empty houses for wood, bricks and anything else he could find useful. But still this did not alleviate the overall problem. Grudgingly he was compelled personally to drive across southern Poland and even into the Sudetenland searching for any materials he could find.

On 17 August, two days after the first transport from Warsaw arrived at Auschwitz bringing yet more male prisoners to the camp, a disgruntled Höss received a letter from his architect Schlachter outlining clearly the seriousness of the lack of building supplies. Without adequate materials, he said, the whole construction programme would grind to a halt. Schlachter requested that he supply him with sixteen rabbit cages, and it was then that Höss realised how serious the extent of the problem had become. A list of items for nails, wood, fencing and other materials was drawn up and sent to Höss, who in turn sent the list to Berlin. But still nothing happened, until a few weeks later when a surprise visit was made to the camp in September by Oswald Pohl, who headed the WVHA (*SS-Wirtschafts - und Verwaltungshauptamt)* SS Main Economic and Adminstration Office. Pohl also managed the *Hauptamt Haushalt und Bauten* (main bureau [for] budget and construction', which was part of the Reich's Ministry of the Interior). He oversaw all SS construction projects and building enterprises through both these offices.

Pohl envisaged that Auschwitz would play a fundamental part in the concentration camp system in Upper Silesia and had already earmarked the economic future for the camp. He saw that the nearby sand and gravel pits could be easily incorporated into the SS-owned German Earth and Stone Works. It was therefore imperative for Pohl that the camp was running efficiently and the construction programme was maintained with highest priority and within the budget.

Höss's meeting with Pohl was cordial, and as they walked around the camp flanked by other staff members from the Economic Office, the commandant repeatedly told him about the serious lack of building supplies and delays in construction. Pohl told Höss that he would certainly rectify the problem because he had decided to double the capacity of the prison by adding a second storey to the fourteen one-storey barracks.

Two weeks later, on orders directly from Pohl's offices on 4 October, the first trainloads of materials arrived at the camp. Höss was back in business and he could now complete the bulk construction of the site, which now included, at Pohl's behest, adding second storeys to the one-storey barracks.

The labour force that continued building the camp lived and worked in appalling conditions, in spite of Höss's frequent tours of the camp. By October 1940 there was a mixture of inmates that consisted of Jews, members of the intelligentsia, and resistance and political prisoners, together with Polish Catholic priests. All of them were struggling for survival and yet nothing was done to alleviate the dire conditions. Under-equipped, lacking protective gear, and malnourished, the inmates went about their place of work, constantly being mentally and physically abused by the guards.

Despite the terrible conditions which the inmates and those that were building the camp had to suffer, there was one particular building that Höss was keen to get ready; it was the house in which he was to live with his family. The house was the pre-war house of a Polish non-commissioned officer. The rebuilding of the villa began in the spring of 1940 and would not be completed until 1941. The refurbishment of the house included a new bathroom and central heating system. By the summer of 1940 the house was deemed habitable, in spite of the fact the exterior of the building was still in need of painting and that the garden needed to be completed.

The house, or the commandant's residence, but commonly known at the Auschwitz camp as the Höss villa, was an imposing two-storey building situated on the corner of the camp. The front of the building with its large windows and small terrace overlooked the Rajsko to Auschwitz road. There was a little untended garden to the front with a small brick wall and gate to the main entrance to the house. On the opposite side of the house, reached by a concrete path, was the tradesmen's entrance, which consisted of a flight of concrete steps leading to the side door with a porch, and overlooked the garden. The garden itself was predominantly situated to the side and rear of the house and consisted of a number of trees and shrubberies from the previous occupants, but this overgrown area of land would soon be transformed for the commandant's family to play and relax. In the garden other buildings were planned and drawn including a summer kitchen, greenhouse and garden log shed.

During the first phase of the villa's modernization a fence with barbed wire was erected around the perimeter of the garden and the house in order to divide it from

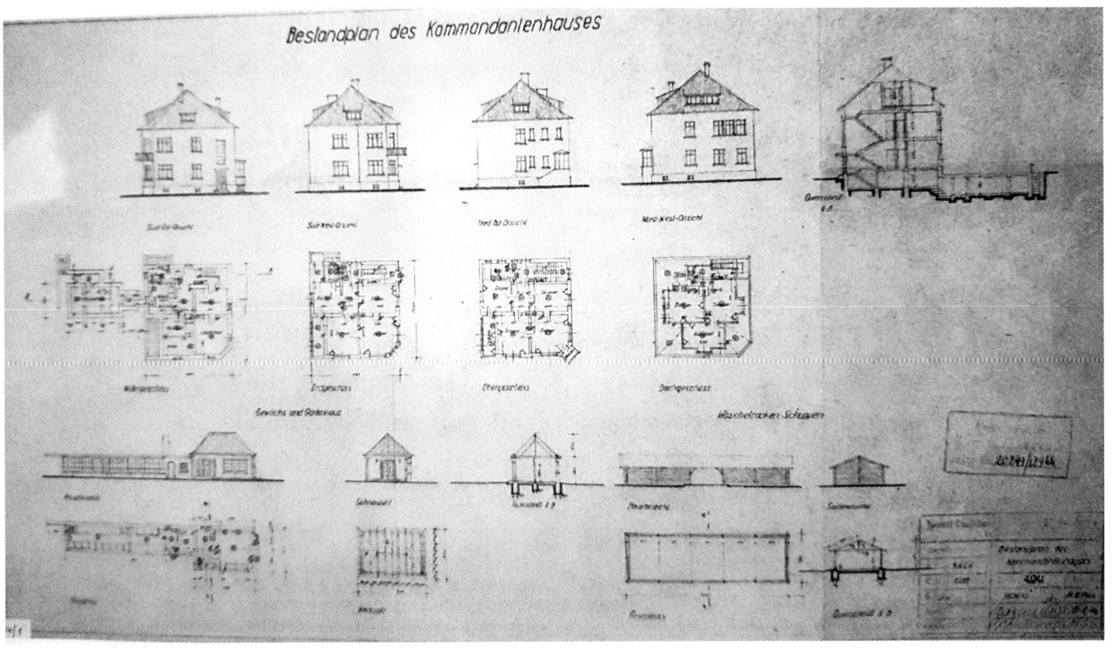

This drawing shows the commandant's house, drawn September 1944 by Haftling 121643 (Jerzy Trzcinski), which shows the electrical installations. It also outlines plan views of the other buildings, including the summer kitchen, greenhouse, and garden log shed. (*Auschwitz-Birkenau State Museum*)

the main camp. In fact, only 100 metres away from the garden was the crematorium of the camp. In November new high concrete fencing was constructed and topped with barbed wire to replace the old fencing around the entire boundary of the camp. The new fencing was also installed at the rear and the sides of the Höss villa, making the camp completely separated from the house and virtually invisible from the garden, except for the roofs and chimneys of the new Commandant's Office and Administration buildings. The fence to the rear of the house, which hid the Commandant's Office, Administration offices, SS guardhouse and the newly constructed crematorium, was further hidden by a large mound of earth placed behind the fence, and trees were planted. Höss had been particularly insistent on trying to conceal the villa from the camp as much as possible, and made it known that he wanted his family to live in absolute privacy.

During this period of rebuilding of the villa, there were plans drawn-up to modernize and convert other private houses in the area for the SS officers and non-commissioned officers and their families. Much of this construction, however, was not carried out until 1942. Most of the houses that had been selected for rebuilding required modern heating and water supply systems.

Another building drawn, planned and eventually adapted for the SS was an unfinished pre-war theatre, which was situated on the south west side of the camp.

However, this huge structure, which was to include a large stage for an orchestra, and a basement area for a bowling alley and beer cellar, was never actually completed as a theatre, but the Germans temporarily used it as as warehouse to store various items.

During this time, other building projects were also put forward, including a design for a new grand *Kommandantur* building complex. Designs were put forward which included a ceremonial hall complete with a podium overlooking a large gallery to deliver speeches.

Yet, in spite of these grand plans the *Bauleitung* were gathering in their construction office, there were still pressing issues to complete the camp. During the first week of October 1940 the first snow showers fell at the camp and there had so far been little preparation for the winter, but construction had to continue in spite of the thermometer plummeting to below zero. The inmates that had to work in these arctic conditions had no winter clothing or any other adequate protection. Every day they were forced to work in the icy driving rain and sleet, often without a break and continuously being subjected to appalling brutality.

In the midst of these difficult times, in November Höss was ordered to Berlin for a meeting with his boss, Himmler. Armed with a progress report on the construction of Auschwitz he journeyed the 500 or so miles to Berlin. Upon his arrival in the *Reich* capital an air of victory still prevailed over the bustling city. Germany was master of Poland and the population were still revelling in the victory over France.

The meeting with the *Reichsführer*, according to Höss's diary, was relaxed and cordial as the commandant gave a detailed progress report on Auschwitz. Using various maps, blueprints, diagrams and drawings put together by the *Bauleitung*, he discussed at length the construction and materials required for its completion. During their conversation Himmler spoke almost incessantly about his bold plans for Auschwitz, enthusiastically outlining his fantasy whilst his adjutant, *SS Sturmbannführer* Heinrich Vogel, watched them poring over plans and reallocating the lives of many thousands of ethnic Germans and Poles. Himmler's plan was to Germanize Upper Silesia with agricultural workers and use Polish labour in large agricultural enterprises that would be put to work building towns, villages, roads and draining ditches. Auschwitz, he declared, was at the heart of this policy. He would banish from the earth the gaudy Polish farmsteads and raise in their place firm, well-managed German farms. In his eyes this would embody German peasant culture and become an historic foundation for future generations. From this German settlement, he said, a model town of Germanization would be born with various villages erected. He envisaged that these Germanic villages would have a bell tower at the centre of the new settlements, surrounded by a village hall, an inn, a school, a Hitler Youth home, a kindergarten, and buildings for the local farmers. He even intended to design villages comprising of a number of settlements with the main village in the centre and the satellite villages bordering them. By concentrating these settlements together, it would ensure social cohesion and allow both the farmer and land to prosper.

Himmler looked upon himself as the supreme architect of the German East and made it known that the areas now in the expanded *Reich* would soon be flourishing with German settlers. Auschwitz, which was just outside the General Government, was now German soil and would be transformed and Germanized.

When Höss returned to Auschwitz he once again set to work overseeing construction and creating many of the necessary structures and principles under which Auschwitz would function for the future. With a new year beckoning, he was resolute in creating a camp that was efficient and that embraced all the necessary requirements Himmler had envisaged in a concentration camp.

By early December work had progressed in spite of the considerable harsh weather. The wooden and barbed wire fence that had previously surrounded the camp had now been completely removed and replaced by a concrete one. The prefabricated guard towers too had been placed on order with a firm and were to arrive early the following year. The whole site, when completed, was to have a very large camp kitchen, utility, theatre, registration buildings, a *Blockführer* office, commandant's office, camp administration offices, SS hospital, a fully operational crematorium, Gestapo offices, medical block, and a large water pool reserve for fire emergencies. It was also intended to have twenty-two two-storey buildings converted into prisoner quarters. Plans were drafted and approved for a prisoner hospital, and offices and quarters for some of the camp's prisoners. The majority of these buildings were constructed in redbrick, ran in straight rows throughout the camp, and were given block numbers for identification purposes. The *Blockführer's* guardhouse, however, was a wooden structure and this was built just outside the main gate. Another building under construction outside the main perimeter was a very large redbrick building, known as the registration building. Here, new prisoners would be catalogued, receive their camp registration number and have their photograph taken, before being escorted by armed guard through the main gates to serve their sentence.

Most of the buildings that were built at Auschwitz and those planned for the future served merely to house and provide the basic needs for the prisoners, guards and SS staff that ran the camp.

SS-Brigadeführer Richard Glücks, stands carrying a briefcase with other SS men on an official visit to Gross-Rosen. Glücks was responsible for the forced labour of the camp inmates and was also the supervisor for the medical practices in the camps. It was Glücks who had recommended to *SS-Reichsführer* Heinrich Himmler on 21 February 1940 that Auschwitz should be chosen as a concentration camp. Glücks also accompanied Himmler and a number of directors of IG Farben on 1 March 1941 for a visit to Auschwitz, where it was decided that the camp would be enlarged to hold up to 30,000 prisoners. Furthermore, he discussed with Himmler about an additional camp that should be constructed nearby which could be capable of housing some 100,000 PoWs. He also discussed about building a factory in the Auschwitz area where camp prisoners could be placed at IG Farben's disposal. (*USHMM*)

SS-Obersturmbannführer Rudolf Höss photographed at the end of July 1944. It was in early 1940 that Höss was dispatched to assess the viability of establishing a concentration camp in western Poland. His report led to the creation of the Auschwitz camp and his appointment as commandant. (*USHMM*)

A photograph of the *Bauleitung* (Concentration Camp Construction Board) offices. These offices were later renamed the *SS-Neubauleitung* in Auschwitz O/S (New Auschwitz Construction Board, Upper Silesia). As further plans for the development of Auschwitz grew, which included Birkenau and the surrounding sub-camps, the construction office quickly enlarged, becoming more complex with a mixture of divisions and roles including a chain of command and preferred German specialised construction companies. As a result, the *Bauleitung* further grew and in November 1941 it became the *SS-Zentralbauleitung der Waffen-SS u. Polizei Auschwitz O/S* (Central Construction Board of the Auschwitz Waffen-S and Police, Upper Silesia). (*Auschwitz-Birkenau State Museum*)

The house, or the commandant's residence, but commonly known at the Auschwitz camp as the Höss villa. It was an imposing two-storey building situated on the corner of the camp. The front of the building with its large windows and small terrace overlooked the Rajsko to Auschwitz road. The rebuilding of the villa began in the spring of 1940 and was completed by 1941.

Two photographs taken in 2007 by the author showing the rear of the Höss villa. The garden itself was predominantly situated to the side and rear of the house and consisted of a number of trees and shrubberies from the previous occupants. It would be in this garden that the commandant's family would play and relax. In the garden other buildings were built and included a summer kitchen, greenhouse and garden log shed. (*HITM – courtesy of Auschwitz-Birkenau State Museum*)

Photographed in 1941 showing *Kommandos* of bricklayers constructing the camp kitchen in Auschwitz I. The labourers are under the strict supervison of Kapos who can be seen wearing armbands. The new camp kitchen was initially drawn and planned in August 1940. (*Yad Vashem Archive*)

Construction of heating facilities in the camp during the construction work in 1941 of the *Lagerweiterung*. As the labourers are seen preparing the foundation for the heating, two engineers observe the progress. (*Yad Vashem Archive*)

During the winter of 1941 prisoners are seen returning to the camp following a day of work outside the site. Prisoners performed various kinds of labour inside and outside the camp boundaries, often under appalling conditions. Illness and mortality rate was often high. (*Yad Vashem Archive*)

Prisoners with a steam shovel digging at the entrance of the camp during the winter of 1941. (*Yad Vashem Archive*)

Two photographs showing the eastern row of buildings in the camp during its expansion construction phase in the winter of 1941. (*Yad Vashem Archive*)

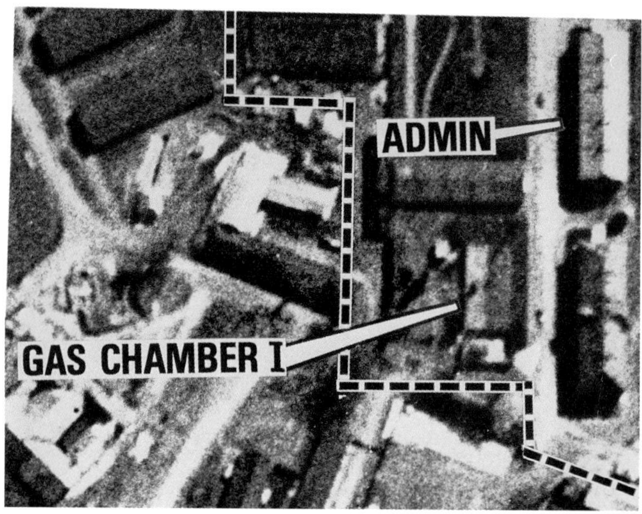

An enlarged aerial reconnaissance photograph of Auschwitz I showing the administration building and gas chamber. In drawings showing the camps crematoria, architects marked it as the *Altes Krematorium* (old crematorium) with plans to build a new crematorium next to it. The camp's crematorium was a former powder magazine building and was modified in early July 1940. The building was used initially to incinerate dead prisoners. The crematorium functioned as a cremation installation from November 1940 to July 1943. Its gas chamber, however, was used intermittently sometime at the end of 1941 to 1942. The installation was closed down sometime in 1943 and its three furnaces dismantled and the chimney removed. It was later converted into an air raid shelter. (*NARA – National Archives and Records Administration*)

A photograph taken by the author in January 2006 showing the north-west side of Crematorium I in the main camp in its present state with a new rebuilt chimney for reconstruction purposes. Note the steel-faced, gas-tight door with peephole. Overlooking the crematorium was the SS hospital of the camp. The first floor windows gave direct view of the roof of the crematorium, and it was quite possible that witnesses could see SS-men pouring Zyklon-B crystals through the traps during gassing operations. During these periods of gassing it was forbidden for any persons to look out of the windows. It was largely the close proximately of these buildings that led to the SS converting the crematorium into an air raid shelter for the SS hospital in September 1944. (*HITM*)

Chapter II

Evolution of Auschwitz 1941

By January 1941, Auschwitz began to slowly enter a new crucial stage of its evolution. Although the bold plans envisaged by Himmler seemed encouraging for the successful continuation of the camp's progression, there were still delays in its construction. To add to these problems, the Economic Office in Berlin put forward new enterprising ideas for the camp's development. One of the proposals mentioned when Pohl visited in September was about using Auschwitz's sand and gravel pits for the German Earth and Stone Works enterprise. It was suggested that this enterprise would ensure the future growth of the camp, but it came at a price; Auschwitz would have to be enlarged purely to house a permanent slave labour population.

The significance of the plans meant that more prisoners were needed to be shipped to the camp quickly. Already there were around 8,000 Polish prisoners, and the list was growing daily. However, construction was still behind schedule and the camp did not have adequate space or time to accommodate them properly. Another concern was the spread of typhus and other infectious diseases breaking out. Conditions in the latter part of 1940 had already seen the situation deteriorate with disease and death, and this was anticipated to get much worse if the camp was not completed.

Throughout January work continued tirelessly in the snow-covered camp trying to get the two-storey brick barracks completed so that it could meet the demands for the rapid expansion of Auschwitz. At the end of February Concentration Camp Inspector Richard Glücks arrived at the camp and was guest at the Höss villa. During his brief stay he reiterated once more that the *Reichsführer* had taken particular interest in Auschwitz, warning that the whole area would soon be transformed. He made it clear to the commandant that Himmler intended to make a visit and this would probably be the most important visit he would ever receive. The future of Auschwitz did not just lie with grandiose plans in agriculture, he said, but with industry as well.

On Saturday, 1 March 1941, Himmler with his delegation arrived at Auschwitz in the afternoon by car. The *Reichsführer* brought with him District Party Leader

Bracht, Glücks, governors, the high-ranking SS officers and political leaders of Silesia and the leading corporate officers of the giant industrial chemical conglomerate IG Farben, which was proposing to build a synthetic-rubber factory near Auschwitz. Evidently the *Reichsführer* had flown from Berlin to the industrial city of Gleiwitz, where he was met by Provincial Governor Fritz Bracht, von dem Bach-Zelewski and Glücks. After lunch they drove the thirty or so miles to Upper Silesia to inspect Auschwitz, and then toured the local countryside with the commandant.

Once inside the camp Höss accompanied Himmler, Bracht, Karl Wolff, and the others around the site. Walking past the administration buildings, the crematorium, and the prisoner barracks they saw first-hand the herds of undernourished prisoners with shaved heads, wearing tattered blue-and-white striped uniforms, being worked under the supervision of the *Kapos*. The prisoners wore badges, a different colour for each category of prisoner – politicals, homosexuals, Jehovah's Witnesses and ordinary criminals. Although looked upon with distaste, they were nonetheless regarded as a valuable commodity, for they represented a resource for the *Reichsführer*'s new vision.

Walking around the camp Höss guided his boss to the first blocks of barracks, the kitchen, the carpentry and joining shops, supply rooms and they looked at the various buildings under construction. The whole camp was a hive of activity. A number of the redbrick buildings were only half completed and were enclosed by huge amounts of wooden scaffolding, much of it improvised. As they strolled past various gangs of inmates vigorously working, the commandant spoke to Himmler and the delegation about the general purpose of each building they inspected.

Once they had completed their inspection, Höss waited until only he, Himmler, and Erich von dem Bach-Zelewski were all in the car alone before the commandant complained to Himmler about the present conditions of the camp. Höss knew he could speak his mind, he had done so numerous times with Glücks, and he never feared any type of reprisal if he complained, or even questioned an order. Those that knew him, especially in higher authority, were well aware that he unequivocally believed in the Nazi vision and was criticizing not the system itself, but how it was implemented. So, as they drove out of Auschwitz and begun touring the local area, the commandant spoke to Himmler about the lack of building materials, the lack of staff, and the problems he was faced with by the continual shipment of prisoners, which was overcrowding the unfinished camp. The *Reichsführer* quickly rebuked Höss, telling him, 'it was his business and as an SS officer there should be no problems'.

Just outside the town of Auschwitz Himmler, Höss and the rest of the delegation arrived in a marshy tract of land in the Auschwitz district of Zasole, adjacent to the parent camp. Standing on the land accompanied with maps and various architectural

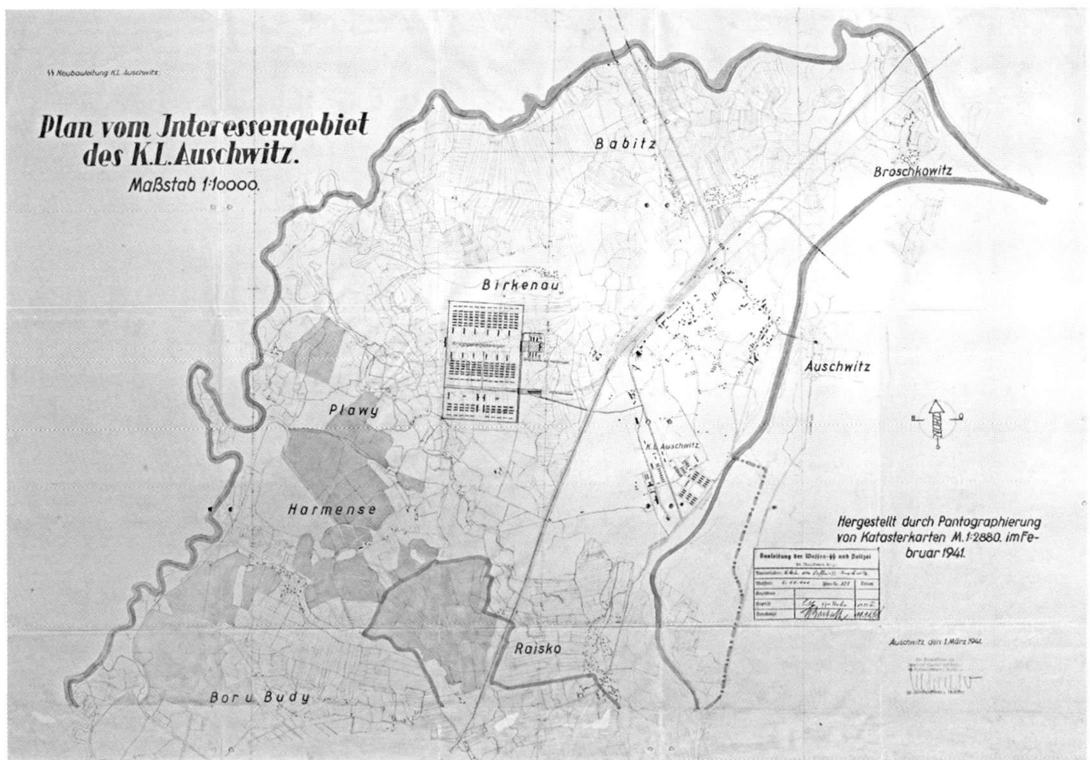

The site chosen to become the Birkenau camp. The final drawing was drawn on 1 March 1941, the day Himmler visited the area, but the March drawing had been superimposed in ink on an earlier map which was sketched, probably in late February 1941, in preparation of the *Reichsführer*'s tour. This drawing shows the railway siding, marked in red, which initially was drawn towards the railway station. (*Vad vashem*)

drawings, Himmler suddenly announced that the area they were standing on had been chosen as a new potential site.

Auschwitz, he exclaimed, would be soon expanded, and here a huge satellite camp would be constructed, far greater than anything else planned or envisaged. This new camp, he said, would house a population of at least 100,000 prisoners. Höss and Fritz Bracht were quick to raise objections, as were a couple of other officials, who spoke out about the drainage and sewage problems and the materials needed for such a mammoth project. The proposed site itself was built on marshy land with the ground slightly higher than the Vistula and Sola rivers. This meant that rain, melting snow, and floodwaters were unable to effectively drain into the river, nor could it soak into the earth. But Himmler just grinned and sarcastically declared, '*Gentlemen, this project will be completed; my reasons for this are more important than your objections!*'

Later that afternoon, over dinner at the SS mess hall, Himmler spoke once more about his grandiose ideas of transforming what he saw was the Auschwitz complex.

In front of his bewildered audience he announced that he not only proposed to establish a huge satellite camp, but also intended to increase the Auschwitz camp population from the anticipated 10,000 inmates to a staggering 30,000. He made it clear that the massive increase in prisoner population was urgently required for labour availability, which was key to the progressive development of the region. The *Reichsführer* envisaged that gangs of slave labour would be used to improve the dykes along the Sola and Vistula, and would also be put to work demolishing sites in the town for new building developments that were planned. In order to undertake these new building developments, he said, all Jewish and Polish residents living around the camp were to be evicted and incarcerated in a camp in the neighbourhood of Auschwitz and used as unskilled construction workers. By evicting these people, it would allow the town to be available for the factory staff of a new massive enterprise that Himmler was eager to see built in the local area – IG Farben.

Officials from this massive chemical cartel had come to Auschwitz with Himmler to decide finally whether a factory should be built in the area. For sometime IG Farben had shown interest in the region around Auschwitz, and particularly welcomed using large numbers of skilled and unskilled construction workers from the concentration camps. It was estimated that between 8,000 and 12,000 men would be required to construct the factory, and with the *Reichsführer*'s new plans to increase the pool of prisoners at Auschwitz to 30,000, they had more than enough. By expanding Auschwitz Himmler not only provided IG Farben with adequate amounts of slave labour, but he could commit 10,000 inmates to his planned agricultural estate as well.

The *Reichsführer*'s audacious plan of turning Auschwitz into a huge agricultural experimental centre was still very much a fundamental part in his overall vision. He also made it known he had no intention of giving up the plans for the gravel and sand pit enterprises either. He tried his best to assure his officials that the enterprises would be good for the region, and it could not be made possible without expanding and developing Auschwitz. It was for this reason, he said, IG Farben had to be given the highest priority. A site had already been chosen for a factory about two miles away. It would be built to produce synthetic rubber, called Buna, and inmates from Auschwitz were to help construct it. Other construction workers from Germany would be brought in and accommodated in vacant homes in Auschwitz town. The town itself would be redeveloped and schools and hospitals built purely for the German workers. Himmler also announced that he intended to move some of the arms industry into the area as well.

Initially, the proposals seemed grandiose to the point of being unfeasible. Only months earlier Höss's staff had been pillaging local towns and villages for building materials in order to construct a relatively small and unknown camp in south western Poland. Now he was supposed to construct what Himmler was calling '*the largest concentration camp in the Reich*'. '*You will*', he said, '*just have to make improvements as you go*'. Himmler repeated this once again, telling him that it was his problem. '*Draining marshes and providing water supplies*', he added, '*are a question of technology, which is a matter to be solved by the experts, but are not reasons for rejection … Epidemics will occur and must be ruthlessly fought against. But the camp categorically cannot be closed to new arrivals. My orders for police roundups must be continued. I do not acknowledge the difficulties in Auschwitz.*'

A week after the *Reichsführer*'s visit, on 7 March Höss, accompanied by the soil expert Professor Zunker who was in charge of investigating the water and ponds in the Auschwitz area and *SS Sturmbannführer* Heinrich Vogel who headed Main Office for Administration and Economics Office III D in the HAVW, toured the area around Auschwitz again to deduce how they were going to construct thousands of acres of future farmland for Himmler's agricultural vision. For a number of hours they toured the region and suggested ways to hydrologically improve the Sola and Vistula to prevent flooding. They recommended various ways of improving the area, from reconstructing massive lakes, to cleaning existing drainage systems, to laying nearly four million drainage pipes in 3,000 acres of farmland.

The whole agricultural enterprise was truly on a grand scale, but with Auschwitz in its early stage of development the project was constantly curtailed by other more pressing plans. In spite of the problems, Himmler nonetheless made it known that he would press ahead with the agricultural work and use the expansion of Auschwitz and the satellite camp to achieve his ambition of forging a new fertile land in the East.

During the remaining weeks of March there was increased planning of Auschwitz, with Höss and staff trying to construe the potential effectiveness of the future plans of the region. One particular plan was recognizing the importance of Himmler's vision for IG Farben and its usefulness in the development and expansion of Auschwitz. At a meeting held on 27 March, chaired by Höss, with his Auschwitz officials and company representatives of IG Farben, they spoke at length about the company's involvement and the advantages that it would bring by working together. During their conversation the IG Farben engineers were interested to know how many prisoners could be supplied from Auschwitz, but Höss was unable to give them a positive answer. There were many difficulties, he said, that prevented him from housing more inmates. Although he agreed about a prosperous business relationship with IG Farben, he added that there were immense problems with the lack of raw materials, which as a result were causing accommodation problems at the camp. He had not hidden the fact either of trying to solve the problem himself by travelling all over the countryside thieving what material he could muster along the way. In order to overcome these immense problems, he argued that if IG Farben agreed to help supply adequate materials and resources for the extension of Auschwitz, then this would overcome the housing problems and thus benefit both the camp and the Buna factory.

Concluding their meeting it was agreed that the commandant could provide at least 1,000 prisoners immediately and this number would increase accordingly on the anticipated expansion of Auschwitz and the building of the satellite complex. The inmates would be used both for construction of the factory and to work in the plant following its completion. The IG Farben officials reiterated again that they would seriously consider supplying additional building materials to ensure the rapid housing of more inmates at Auschwitz so that the camp could reach its maximum capacity of 30,000. The success of the deal, and indeed the future role of Auschwitz, now depended on how fast this massive chemical conglomerate could work in the favour of Höss.

In early April, construction work finally began on the new Buna factory. Without delay gangs of prison workers from Auschwitz were sent to the village of Monowitz on foot every morning to commence their shift building the new IG Farben plant. Already plans were being drawn up and approved to construct additional quarters for the inmates and to build a bridge over the Sola to connect the camp and factory. A narrow gauge railway line too was considered so that the inmates could be quickly transported to the plant.

The construction of this new enterprise was of giant proportions, and assistance from Auschwitz's slave labour population ensured its rapid creation. Almost as soon as the building work commenced the relationship between the SS and IG Farben thrived, with both parties enthusiastically planning to develop a new dominion befitting the SS. In fact, the Auschwitz camp too had been incorporated into this new master plan with architects designing a general plan for its expansion.

With plans for Auschwitz being quickly expanded, on 13 June Höss travelled to Berlin to meet Himmler and to be introduced to the new chief of Office II of the SS Main Office Household and Buildings, Hans Kammler. Kammler was an old *Freikorps* comrade and Nazi member, and had been a qualified architect for some years. Together they discussed at length the expansion of Auschwitz, with Kammler revealing drawings of the general new plan of the site. A letter confirmed their discussions a few days later which referred to the construction projects for the '2nd and 3rd year of war economy'. Kammler outlined that construction measures were ordered locally by *SS Gruppenführer* Pohl which would include the following:

Completion of utility buildings
30 new accommodations for detainees
Housing for Kommandantur staff
Housing for one guard battalion
Completing existing temporary officers' club and officers' housing
Five watchtowers
Road constructions and gardens
Sewage system
Water supply
Electrical installations internal and external
Gate building for Birkenau
Extension camp wall and wire
Delousing unit
Laundry building
Admission building
New construction planning office with garages
Military offices building
Sentry building area
Motor pool area
Various buildings
Work camp for civilian workers

Kammler then writes that the construction project at Auschwitz could no longer be registered for the second year of the war economy, but the camp would receive 18,000 detainees by 31 December 1941. He agreed to the start or the continuation of the following items:

Adding upper storeys to 14 existing accommodations for detainees
Thirty new accommodations for detainees
Delousing unit
Laundry unit
Housing for military staff/barracks
Completing temporary officers' club with accommodation/dorms
Sewage system
Water supply
Roads
Completion of utility buildings
New construction planning office with garages
Motor pool area
Work camp for civilian workers

As previously agreed with the *Reichsführer*, the camp would accommodate 30,000 inmates. There would be the immediate construction of: thirty new two-storey barracks, which were to be extended towards the station; housing for the commandant's staff and for officers; a delousing facility; a laundry, a storehouse for prisoners' belongings; and even a large roll call area flanked by an entrance pavilion. Among other things there were plans for a camp for civilian employees and construction workers. New streets would be built with an extensive new drainage and sewer system including a drinking water installation. There were also plans for an SS private railway station, an SS settlement and – one of Himmler's largest ideas – the massive agricultural project, which included the building of new villages, farmsteads and the construction of an agricultural estate with barns and giant greenhouses.

During the meeting Himmler spoke for considerable time about the expansion project and made a number of important references to the design of the camp itself. One particular part of the camp that was mentioned was an area behind the camp prison near to the hospital and close to a newly designed crematorium. Architects had chosen this area with its own execution yard in the centre. It was proposed that both the camp authorities and the Gestapo would use this area in a similar manner to the way executions were conducted at Block.11, but with a difference. According to the plan the condemned would be taken straight to this execution yard, stripped naked, executed and their corpses carried immediately into the crematorium to be incinerated. The idea seemed perfect, but even Himmler wanted the plans changed, outlining that it would be more practical and efficient to run the new and old crematoria side-by-side, and close to the back gate of the camp. In this way he was sure that Auschwitz could handle larger groups of victims. He made it known that permanent crematoria, incinerating sites, and execution grounds of various designs were being installed elsewhere at a number of concentration camps. Therefore, he felt it was very important to discuss with the commandant the execution facilities at Auschwitz and the possibilities to make them even more sophisticated. He went on to tell Höss that the killings would be undertaken with the least amount of disorder and disturbance. According to the '14f13' programme guidelines, all those regarded to be chronically sick, mentally ill, and invalid inmates who were Jewish were now automatically to be selected for immediate removal from camp life.

Himmler did not have to tell his faithful subordinate how to undertake these so-called 'removals', for he knew the commandant and his camp officials were quite capable of improvising. Already camp conditions had deteriorated and a great many of the inmates were looking increasingly emaciated, and the prison hospital was filling up daily with the sick. Many were regarded as so unwell that the concentration camp authorities were becoming progressively more insistent on removing those unfit for work and having them executed. As a result, executions at the camp had increased immeasurably by the summer of 1941. Although many of the victims had been brought in by the local Gestapo and hurriedly marched through the main gates down to Block 11 and killed, Höss too was beginning to receive more orders to execute. Quite regularly a telprinter messages would arrive from the Security Police or from the Reich Security Head Office, stating which prisoners should be shot or hanged. Every four to six weeks the Kattowitz military court would visit the camp and the accused prisoners, most of which were already inmates, were brought before a tribunal, and in many cases were sentenced to death. The extent of the executions had in fact increased to such high numbers that the Gestapo had decided it would be more efficient to bring the condemned straight to the crematorium, where they were ordered to undress in the mortuary before being shot. Their naked corpses were then incinerated in the room next door and the ashes disposed with the rest of the day's killings.

Since September 1940 the Auschwitz crematorium had been working at a steady pace, burning the bodies of prisoners that died of illness or were killed or executed. Within weeks of it going into operation it was estimated that two bodies were being burnt every twenty minutes, and this number had soon doubled. By 1941 the crematorium had in fact reached its maximum capacity of eighteen bodies per hour. In direct response to the dramatic increase of deaths in the camp, Höss was prompted to authorise the expansion of the crematorium and approach the SS New Construction Office with an urgent request for a second double-muffle incinerator. The second incinerator was fitted at a reduced cost owing to the fact that it was attached to the ventilator of the first. With the new second double-muffle incinerator the rate of cremation doubled, but still more and more people were found to liquidate. In the summer heat the stench was foul and Grabner requested that the camp's architect, Schlachter, install a more sophisticated ventilation system so it could not only extract the bad odours, but also provide a fresh supply of air from outside the building.

The Auschwitz authorities were well aware of why it was most important to equip and expand the camp with a facility to murder, for the destruction of Bolshevism was about to begin in earnest.

During the morning of 22 June news arrived at Auschwitz that a massive assemblage of more than three million German troops had attacked the Soviet Union and were victoriously forging ahead. Within days of the invasion special action squads were already ruthlessly murdering Russian Jews, Communist politicians and political commissars. Although Auschwitz remained a camp primarily for Polish prisoners, there were growing reports that the SS were actually weeding out commissars that were found hiding in German army PoW camps.

The first of these Soviet prisoners were transported to Auschwitz in July. Several hundreds of them were marched through the main gate and from the moment they arrived they were treated much worse than the Polish inmates. They were hated at Auschwitz. Many of them were beaten and tortured, whilst some were shot in the gravel pits or were condemned to the cellars of Block 11. Here they were locked in the dark cold cells and left to starve to death.

As a result of these increased deaths at Auschwitz the crematorium was once again working to full capacity. Executions were now so frequent that the SS personnel began discussing a more effective method of killing than just starving, shooting and hanging the victims, or having them murdered by lethal injection. An effective method was essential to guarantee the rapid effectiveness of cleansing the camp of '*undesirables*', and those unfit for work.

Höss already knew, as did his closest associates, of the euthanasia programme. In fact, the 14f13 programme had already reached Auschwitz, with effective results. Inmates had been removed from the camp and transported to special killing centres in Germany, which were vans converted into mobile gas chambers but were purposely built to look like shower rooms. The sick, chronically ill or physically disabled were sent to the compartment of a converted van, the airtight doors were then slammed shut, and the victims inside were asphyxiated by bottled carbon monoxide. Both Höss and his deputy, Fritzsch, thought the idea of asphyxiation was probably the most effective means of homicide. It was thus proposed that they considered it further as to best implement such a killing process at Auschwitz.

As Höss and Fritzsch considered ways of killing by asphyxiation, in late August *SS Obersturmbannführer* Adolf Eichmann of the RSHA (*Reichssicherheitshauptamt*) or Reich Security Office in Berlin arrived at Auschwitz to meet with the commandant. Eichmann was a Jewish emigration specialist who had been given the task of facilitating and managing the logistics of mass deportations of Jews to ghettos and concentration camps in Nazi-occupied Eastern Europe. He had been sent specifically to Auschwitz to discuss new deportation plans and to look at the camp's facilities.

By the summer of 1941 Auschwitz had changed, with the camp constantly evolving. The two-storey block brick barracks, though, remained generally unaltered, and new blocks that were constructed duplicated the existing buildings. This also included the arrangement of the buildings constructed in the roll-call square, which was situated in the centre of the camp, and was still being planned during this time. Plans were also being put together for the camp fence. The original barbed wire fence initially surrounded the first three prisoner blocks, with wooden posts erected. However, these were not electrified. The design of the camp fence was drawn by Haftling 538 (construction technician Leon Sawka), but was not submitted until 29 October 1941. This fence plan was designed to be electrified and attached to reinforced concrete posts, complete with insulators attached to the barbed wire with high voltage.

Plans were also put together for a further thirty new prisoner blocks, and according to a building order submitted on 27 June 1941, these were planned during the financial year commencing on 1 October 1941. Further alterations were also made to the camp, with the introduction of even more buildings to be added which initially increased to thirty-six blocks and later to fifty buildings.

The urgency to expand the Auschwitz camp was associated with the need for the labour required to construct the IG Farben factories, the surrounding sub-camps, and plans for the main new satellite camp at Birkenau.

During Eichmann's visit to Auschwitz he was under no illusion of the importance of its expansion. However, Eichmann had not come to Auschwitz just to see the progress of its construction; he had been sent by the *Reichsführer* to discuss new matters relating to effective methods of killing at Auschwitz, and how best to deal with the Jewish question. He had been well informed on the expansion of Auschwitz, including the plans for the new satellite camp, which was soon slated to be constructed. During their conversation Eichmann made it clear that the *Reichsführer* wanted the Jewish question solved once and for all, and it was the SS that were to implement that order. Preparations for the mass deportation

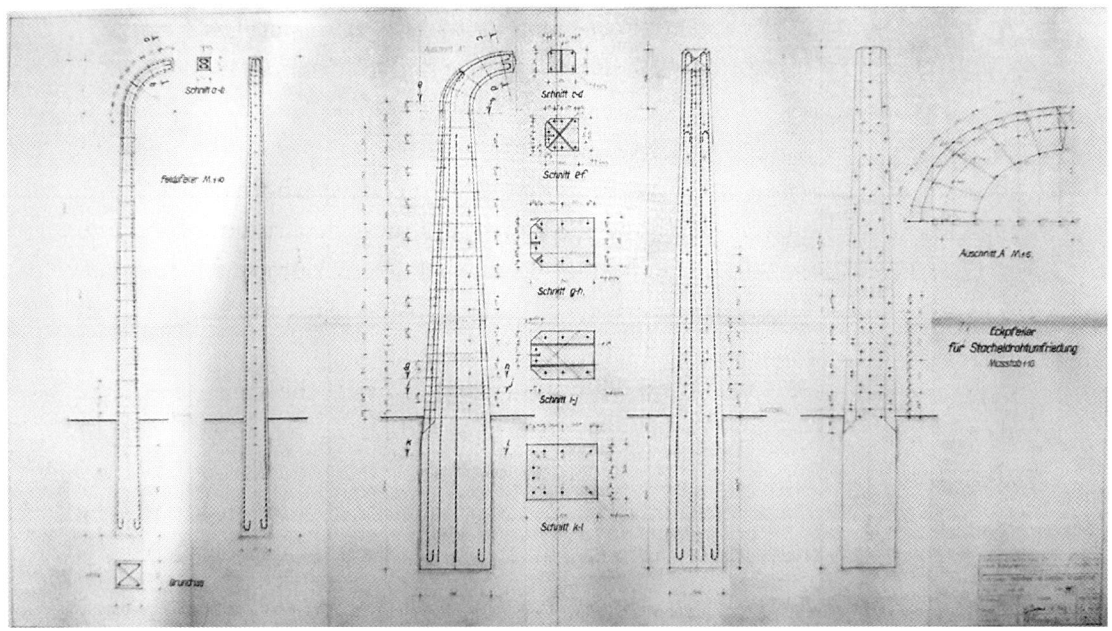

This drawing shows two types of fence post. On the left is the normal *Feldfeiler* (field pillar) and to the right is the *Eckpfeiler* (corner pilar). All the posts were installed by the concrete workers Kommando units. (*Auschwitz State Museum Archives*)

Four photographs taken by the author during a visit to Auschwitz I in February 2007 showing what was known as the *Feldfeiler* (field pillar). (*HITM courtesy of Auschwitz/Birkenau State Archive*)

of Jews were now going to take place, and with the excellent railway network to Auschwitz coupled with the expansion programme of the camp, it was considered the most viable location to transport Jews. He made it quite clear that Himmler also envisaged Auschwitz as the main hub of a huge semi-industrial complex. Here the transports would arrive on a large scale, selected Jews would be sent to work at one of the many sub-camps being built nearby, and then, when they were no longer required or deemed unfit for work, they could be transported the few miles back to the camp and exterminated.

The plan was grandiose, but logistically not viable, as there was still more planning involved in the operation. For the time being, it was agreed that the Jews would have to remain in the Ghettos until the camp was prepared and ready for them. In the meantime, Eichmann would have to wait. Another important question on Eichmann's list was the design of an improved killing facility at the camp which would be capable of exterminating larger numbers of inmates. Since early summer Höss had been aware of growing plans to systematically murder prisoners at Auschwitz. Initially, the condemned had just been the sick and disabled; now Eichmann announced that Himmler had decided about a grander plan of producing a factory-like killing installation that was capable of removing anyone that was deemed a threat to the *Reich* or unfit for slave labour. Those that were regarded subhuman, for instance Russian PoWs, were certainly on the *Reichsführer*'s agenda for liquidation, and it was suggested that it would be practical to use the Russian PoWs in a killing experiment.

It had been proposed during a conversation with Eichmann that the carbon monoxide chambers used in the mobile gas chamber vans were far too expensive, so Höss proposed using hydro cyanide. The commandant told his guest that he was in the process of constructing a delousing installation at Auschwitz and could perhaps use a lethal substance made up of hydro cyanide.

On 3 September, in total secrecy, an experiment on Russian PoWs was carried out in Block 11 with the chemicals used for delousing. It was the first mass execution using crystallized prussic acid, which was sold in tins marked under the name Zyklon B. In fact, during this period of the camp's evolution, Zyklon B had been used just for disinfecting the clothes of new arrivals. Their clothes were sanitized in specially-adapted chambers termed *Gaskammer* (gas chambers). This was the first attempt by the SS to reduce the threat of typhus in the camp by adapting disinfection chambers in Block 1, on the first floor of Block 3, and in Block 26. It was for this reason that the SS decided to experiment using Zyklon B.

The first gassing experiment on Russian PoWs was successful. However, it took two days to air out the building and transport the corpses to the already overflowing crematorium. It was agreed that the basement was not ideal and it was imperative that they find an alternative method of dropping the Zyklon B into a gas chamber. It was agreed that the camp's crematorium could be used. It not only had a flat roof, but could easily be adapted with various openings in order to allow the Zyklon B crystals to be poured through. The new powerful ventilation system that had just been fitted in the morgue would be more than capable of dealing with the poisonous gas.

Almost immediately Fritzsch's men began transforming the crematorium into a gas chamber. On the flat roof the three portholes through the morgue roof were constructed and attached with wooden lids. It was through these portholes that the Zyklon B crystals would be poured.

J. A. TOPF & SÖHNE
24 September 1941

To
Reichsführer SS
and Chief of German Police
and Waffen-SS Bauleitung
Auschwitz. Upper Silesia

Subject
Topf cremation furnace

Your ref Our Ref D IV
Prf [Prüfer}

Further to the conversation between the representative of your director of construction, *SS-Oberscharführer* Urbanczek and our chief engineer, Mr Prüfer, we enclose herewith three copies of the operating instructions for the Topf cremation furnaces and the Topf forced-draught installation. We would ask you to post a copy of each set of instructions under glass cover in the furnace room, to ensure that the furnaces are operated correctly.
We greet you with

Heil Hitler!

J A TOPF & SONS

Auschwitz SS Construction Management
Received 26 September 1941

Enclosures: 3 operating instructions for cremation furnaces
3 operating instructions for forced draught installation

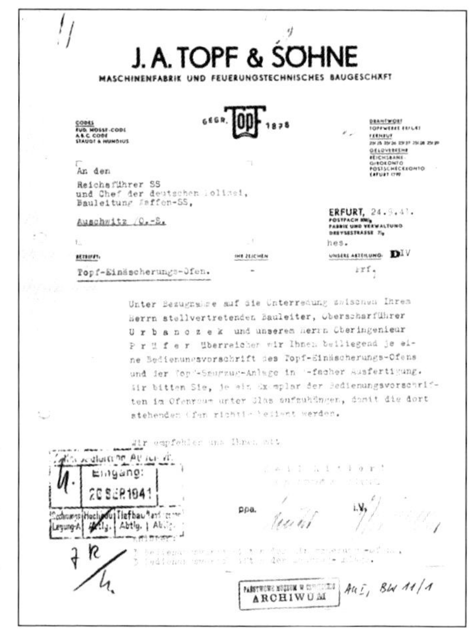

J. A. TOPF & SÖHNE
MASCHINENFABRIK UND FEUERUNGSTECHNISCHES BAUGESCHÄFT

GEGR. TOPF 1878

An den
Reichsführer SS
und Chef der deutschen Polizei,
Bauleitung Waffen-SS,

Auschwitz /O.-S.

ERFURT, 24.9.41.

Betrifft: Topf-Einäscherungs-Ofen.
Unsere Abteilung: D IV
Prf.

Unter Bezugnahme auf die Unterredung zwischen Ihrem Herrn stellvertretenden Bauleiter, Oberscharführer U r b a n c z e k und unserem Herrn Oberingenieur P r ü f e r überreichen wir Ihnen beiliegend je eine Bedienungsvorschrift des Topf-Einäscherungs-Ofens und der Topf-Saugzug-Anlage in 3-facher Ausfertigung. Wir bitten Sie, je ein Exemplar der Bedienungsvorschriften im Ofenraum unter Glas aufzuhängen, damit die dort stehenden Öfen richtig bedient werden.

Eingang: 26 SEP 1941

ppa. i.V.

ARCHIWUM

(*Auschwitz-Birkenau Archive Museum*)

Once the crematorium had been prepared for a mass killing experiment on 16 September, 900 Russian soldiers were chosen to be gassed. Prior to the gassing an area around the crematorium was sealed off and it was forbidden to look at the roof of the crematorium, which was visible from the windows of the SS hospital on the first floor. The crematorium forecourt too was closed off to all prisoners working in the camp, for it was being utilised as an undressing area for the victims. From the edge of this forecourt Höss watched with Fritzsch the whole procedure take place. First the victims were ordered to undress and then they were herded naked into the morgue. '*The entire transport fit exactly in the room*', wrote Höss, '*The doors were closed and the gas poured in through the openings in the roof. How long the process lasted, I don't know, but for quite some time sounds could be heard. As the gas was thrown in some of them yelled 'Gas!' and a tremendous screaming and shoving started toward both doors, but the doors were able to withstand all the force*'. After the gassing

Operating Instructions for Coke-Fired Topf Double-Muffle Incineration Furnace

Before charging the two hearths with coke, the two furnace dampers and the main rotary damper in the chimney must be open.

The fire can now be lit and maintained, being sure to open both secondary openings to the right and left of the cinder removal doors (of the coke furnace).

Once the cremation chamber (muffle) has been brought to a good red heat (approximately 800°C), the corpses can be introduced one after the other in the cremation chambers.

Now the pulsed air blower situated to the side of the furnace should be switched on and run for about 20 minutes, ensuring that the two cremation chambers do not receive too much or too little fresh air.

Regulation of the fresh air is by means of a rotary valve in the air duct. In addition, the air intakes, to the right and left of the chamber doors, should be half open.

As soon as the remains of the corpses have fallen from the chamotte grid to the ash collection channel below, they should be pulled forward towards the ash removal door, using the scraper.

Here they can be left for a further 20 minutes to be fully consumed, then the ashes should be placed in the container and set aside to cool.

In the meantime, further corpses can be introduced one after the other into the chambers.

The two coke furnaces must be fed with fuel from time to time.

Every evening, the furnace fire bars must be cleaned of clinker and the cinders removed.

In addition, care must be taken that at the end of operations, as <u>soon as the furnace, having burnt everything, is empty and no coals remain</u>, that all the air valves, doors and dampers are closed, so that the furnace does not cool.

After each incineration, the temperature rises in the furnace. For this reason, care must be taken that the internal temperature does not rise above 1100°C (white heat).

This increase in temperature can be avoided by introducing additional fresh air.

<u>Betriebsvorschrift des</u>

<u>koksbeheizten Topf-Doppelmuffel-Einäscherungsofen</u>

Vor Beschickung der beiden Koksgeneratoren mit Koks müssen die beiden Rauchkanalschieber am Ofen geöffnet werden, desgl. auch der Hauptrauchkanalschieber bzw. die Drehklappe am Schornstein.

Nunmehr kann in den beiden Generatoren Feuer angefacht und unterhalten werden, hierbei beachten, dass die Sekundärverschlüsse rechts und links der Ascheentnahmetüren (Koksgenerator) geöffnet sind.

Nachdem die Einäscherungskammer gut rotwarm (ca 800°C) ist können die Leichen hintereinander in die beiden Kammern eingefahren werden.

Jetzt ist es zweckmässig das seitwärts am Ofen stehende Druckluftgebläse anzustellen und ca 20 Minuten laufen zu lassen. Hierbei ist zu beobachten, ob zuviel oder zu wenig Frischluft in die beiden Kammern eintritt.

Die Regulierung der Frischluft erfolgt durch die Drehklappe die sich in der Luftrohrleitung befindet. Weiterhin müssen die rechts und links der Einführtüren angeordneten Lufteintritte, halb geöffnet werden.

Sobald die Leichenteile vom Schamotterost nach der darunter liegende Ascheschräge gefallen sind, müssen diese mittels der Kratze nach vorn zur Ascheentnahmetür gezogen werden. Hier können diese Teile noch 20 Minuten zum Nachverbrennen lagern. Dann wird die Asche in den Aschebehälter gezogen und zur Abkühlung beiseite gestellt.

Zwischendurch werden neue Leichen in die Kammern nach einander eingeführt.

Die beiden Koksgeneratoren müssen von Zeit zu Zeit mit Brennstoff beschickt werden.

Jeden Abend muss der Generatorrost von den Koksschlacken befreit und die Asche herausgenommen werden.

Zu beachten ist ferner, das nach Betriebsschluss, <u>sobald der Generator leer gebrannt ist und Glutteile nicht mehr vorhanden sind</u>, alle Luftschieber und Türen desgl. auch die Rauchkanalschieber am Ofen geschlossen sein müssen um den Ofen nicht auszukühlen.

Nach jeder Einäscherung steigt die Temperatur im Ofen. Daher bitte beachten, dass die Innentemperatur nicht über 1100°C kommt (Weissglut).

Diese Temperatursteigerung kann durch Lufteinblasen verhindert werden.

Operating Instruction for the Topf Force Draught Installation

If the furnace does not draw properly, the forced draught installation incorporated in the chimney must be brought into service.

Here, care must be taken to first switch on the motor and only afterwards close the rotary damper in the chimney. The cold water supply from the tank should also be opened immediately.

At the end of the incineration, the rotary damper in the chimney must be opened <u>first</u> and then the motor and the water supply shut off.

In addition, care must be taken to ensure that there is always enough water in the tank.

Another Topf & Sons drawing was submitted on 26 September showing Crematorium I.

(*Auschwitz-Birkenau Archive Museum*)

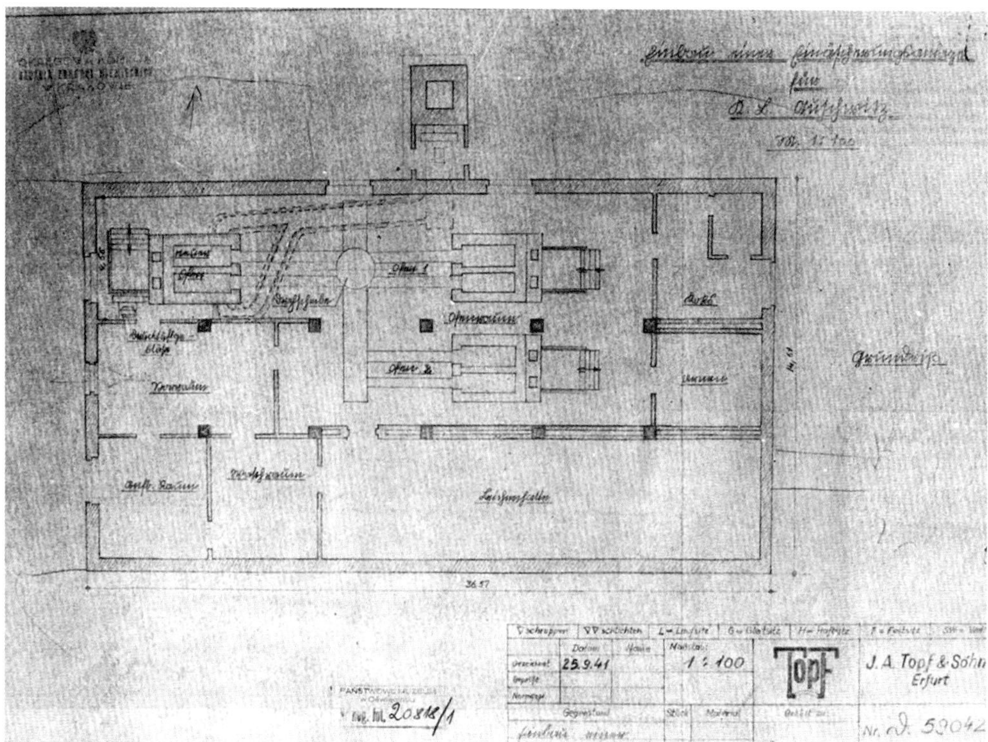

Topf & Sons Drawing 59042, 25 September 1941

Scale 1:100

Entwurf für das Krematorium (design for the crematorium) South elevation Bauleitung drawing 938, scale 1:100. Drawn on 15 January 1942 by SS Sergeant Ulmer, checked on 28 January by SS Second Lieutenant Dejaco and approved on the same day by Captain Bischoff.

(*Auschwitz-Birkenau State Museum*)

the fans were turned on and the doors opened. *'I really did not waste any thoughts about the killing of the Russian PoWs … it was ordered and I had to carry it out …'*. The gassing had been a complete success, and in front of his officers Höss appeared relieved. No longer would they have to look into the eyes of their victims as they murdered them. Now they could transport their victims straight into a specially adapted gas chamber and have them killed altogether, sparing, as Höss called it, a bloodbath.

This new procedure appealed greatly to the commandant and staff. They had found by simple innovation that the new arrivals could quite easily be led into the crematorium not knowing they were going to be killed, simply disinfected by taking a shower. It had proven very easy to get the inmates into the gas chamber by deception rather than using varying degrees of force. By using gas as a method of execution they saw its implementation as being less stressful for the guards that were assigned to these new murderous duties. Höss expected more shipments of

2nd April 1942
Correspondence register no 5999/42/de/Qu.

Subject: Ventilation and air extraction installation for the crematorium to be built in

Auschwitz Concentration Camp

Ref: Your letter of 12.3.42 from your department D - Schm
Encl: Four drawings

To Messrs Topf & Söhne
Erfurt

Please find attached a set of modified drawings for the crematorium to be built in Auschwitz Concentration Camp.

These drawings show the desired positions for the ventilation intake and outlet ducts. We would ask you, in any development or change in your project as shown on drawing D 59 366, to adapt as far as possible to the duct positions shown on our drawings.

The intake and outlet ducting above the roof is to be in the form of brick chimneys.

We would ask you to finish this work as soon as possible, in view of the urgency of the construction project.

Head of the of Auschwitz Waffen-SS and
Police Central Construction Management

[initialled by Bischoff]

SS-Hautptsturmführer (Specialist)

2. April 1942

Bftgb.-No. 5999 /42/De/Qu. **Einschreiben**

Betr.: Be- und Entlüftungsanlage für das zu errichtende Krematorium im K.L. Auschwitz
Bezg.: Ihr Schreiben vom 12.3.42, Ihrer Abteilung D - Schm.
Anlg.: 4 Pläne

An die
Firma Topf u. Söhne
Erfurt

In der Anlage erhalten Sie einen Satz geänderte Pläne, über das zu errichtende Krematorium im K.L. Auschwitz.

In den Plänen ist die gewünschte Führung der Be- und Entlüftungskanäle eingezeichnet. Es wird gebeten, sich bei Ausarbeitung bezw. Abänderung Ihres Projekts lt. Zeichnung D 59 366 nach Möglichkeit der in unseren Plänen eingezeichneten Kanalführung anzupassen.

Die Führung der Be- u. Entlüftung über Dach soll in Form gemauerter Kamine erfolgen.

Um baldige Erledigung wird wegen der Dringlichkeit des Bauvorhabens gebeten.

Der Leiter der Zentral-Bauleitung
der Waffen-SS und Polizei Auschwitz

(*Auschwitz-Birkenau State Museum*)

PoWs to be killed in this manner, but he was concerned, not by the gassing process, but because of the problems of the storage and incineration of the corpses. Once the gassing had been completed the dead were laid out in the laying room, washing room and morgue, where they were stored while awaiting cremation. The majority of them were in fact stored in the morgue, but with so many corpses, other rooms had to be used. The delay between being killed and incinerated could take three or even four days. There were now 900 corpses piled high awaiting incineration, and the burning procedure could take around twenty-five hours to complete. Between 16 and 20 September the crematorium was overflowing with the dead and working well over its full capacity.

Four days later, on 24 September 1941, Topf & Sons sent a letter enclosing three copies of the operating instructions for the Topf cremation furnaces and the Topf forced-draught installation for the camp crematoria.

After it was decided to transfer this crematorium from the Auschwitz main camp to Birkenau, this drawing was copied and included in Bauleitung drawing 936 dated 15 January 1942 showing the four fronts of the future Crematorium II at Birkenau.

Although the improved killing facility at Auschwitz had more or less been achieved with the use of Zyklon B crystals, Höss had become increasingly concerned at the number of Russian PoWs that would be sent to the camp and pass through the crematorium. During this period of time, on the Eastern Front, the Germans had already captured an estimated three million Soviet prisoners. Some 100,000 of them were transferred from the Army to the SS in September, and many were earmarked for Auschwitz. According to a report, Himmler had ordered SS Hans Kammler, head of the Central SS Building Office, to inform the commandant of Auschwitz that the long-awaited giant PoW camp at Auschwitz would be constructed next to the parent camp. Its construction was to house many of the new Soviet PoWs and the environment in which they were to be placed would ensure that large numbers of them would perish.

SS men who appear to be in the *Bauleitung* office in 1941. As early as late February 1941 a map of the proposed Birkenau site had been sketched in preparation for *SS-Reichsführer* Heinrich Himmler's tour of the area. The final drawing was drawn on 1 March 1941, the day Himmler visited Auschwitz. A few days later, following Himmler's tour, a letter was sent to the construction projects for the '2nd and 3rd year of war economy'. Chief of Office II of the SS Main Office Household and Buildings, Hans Kammler, outlined that construction measures were ordered by *SS Gruppenführer* Pohl which would comprise of new proposals and complete with a list of new buildings to be constructed at Birkenau. (*Yad Vashem*)

Two photographs showing *Kommandos* constructing the new Auschwitz administration building. (*Yad Vashem Archive*)

Expansion works at Auschwitz I during 1941. A steam shovel can be seen digging out earth in preparation for foundations to be laid. In early 1941 there had been extensive plans to expand the camp with twenty new prisoner block houses which were later called the 'Camp Expansion' or '*Lagerweiterung*'. It was not until the summer of that year that detailed work on this project commenced. (*Yad Vashem Archive*)

Three photographs showing construction work in 1941 of the *Lagerweiterung*. During this period plans were drawn up by the *Bauleitung* to extend the camp with the construction of a new hospital, warehouses and workshops together with additional blockhouses encompassing eventually some fifty buildings. (*Yad Vashem Archive*)

A labourer can be seen on top of a building with a winch during the construction work in 1941 of the *Lagerweiterung*. In total a complex of twenty buildings were constructed in an area adjacent to Auschwitz I as part of plans for expanding the camp. In the course of the planning phase of this new complex, many technical drawings of the construction site and the buildings to be built on them were drawn by the different offices and companies involved in the project. (*Yad Vashem Archive*)

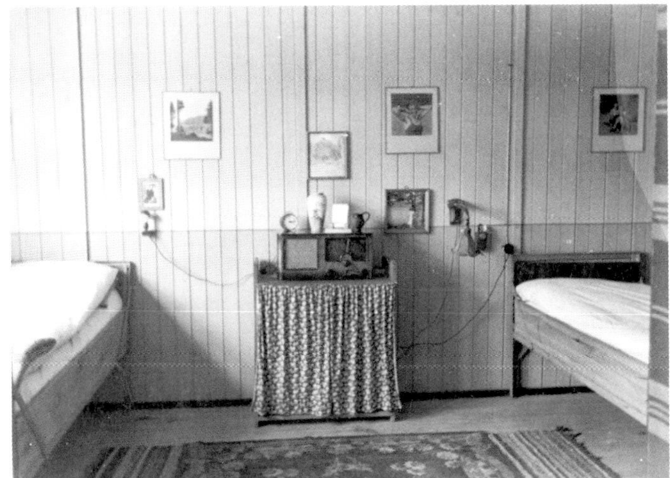

Three photographs showing Waffen-SS wooden barracks at Auschwitz. (*Yad Vasham*)

At Birkenau digging drainage ditches in late 1941 to the south of where Crematorium II will be constructed. (*Yad Vasham*)

Chapter III

Blueprint to Murder – Birkenau 1941–1943

Surprisingly, commandant Hoss had received the construction plans of the extension of Auschwitz with some relief. Though he had been initially unenthusiastic about the proposals due to the lack of materials, he had become increasingly drawn to the idea, purely on the basis that it would reduce the overcrowding of the main camp.

The site chosen for the extension of Auschwitz was near the Polish village of Brzezinka, where Höss had visited with Himmler in March 1941. This marshy tract of land surrounded by birch woods was situated nearly two miles west of the main camp. Although there had never been any concrete plans to construct a massive PoW camp on the land, as a precaution the houses of the small village of Brzezinka were cleared by the SS in July 1941 and all its inhabitants relocated elsewhere. The Germans renamed the area Birkenau.

On 1 October 1941, the task of designing Birkenau was left in the hands of *SS-Hauptsturmführer* Karl Bischoff, the newly-appointed chief of the Auschwitz construction office, and the thirty-three-year-old architect *SS-Rottenführer* Fritz Ertl. Supporting this office was the 'Blueprint Office', which was headed by *SS-Hauptscharführer* Wichmann. He was responsible for preparing the construction plans, which were drawn up by SS officers who were qualified in architecture or engineering. There were also a number of prisoners who had technical training. Herta Soswinski, a prisoner who worked as a clerk at the *Bauleitung* recalled: *'The task of the Bauleitung* [Building Authority] *was the overall planning of all the construction works within Auschwitz, including living quarters, medical facilities, crematoria, gas chambers … The Bauleitung was not only responsible for the planning, but also for the labour itself, the allocation of materials and supervision. The SS men who worked on the plans, were also active at the building sites, when necessary'.*

The *Bauleitung* had been told to design the camp like a large-scale urbanized project that would involve thousands of prisoners and private companies who would assist in its construction. Even by Third Reich standards, the project was not cheap. The total budget for the construction was to be 8.9 million *Reichsmarks*. The projected number of prisoners to be housed in the camp was 97,000. It was planned that Birkenau would be divided into a two-part camp, with the smaller part of only 17,000 inmates located in a quarantine camp. The accommodation was to be very overcrowded and initial plans for one barrack block was to contain 550 inmates. This amount was soon altered to a final figure of 744.

In the quarantine camp it was planned that there were going to be two delousing stations, two kitchens, thirty barracks each accommodating 744 men, five toilet barracks, and five washrooms. In the main part of the installation, the camp was to be divided into twelve camps, each with twelve barracks, one kitchen, one toilet barracks, and one washroom. All inmates were to be housed in 174 barracks, each barrack subdivided into sixty-two bays, and each bay having a three bunk-bed system.

The size of the construction was to be on a scale that not even Höss could have ever envisaged. The whole area covered over eighty hectares. On a couple of occasions, the commandant visited the location on his own in order to try and formulate an impression on the sheer size of the area of land on which the new

Location map of the Auschwitz Prisoner of War Camp
This is the earliest map of Birkenau layout still known as the *Kriegsgefangenenlager* or prisoner of war camp. It was drawn on 7 October 1941 by Fritz Ertl and approved by Bischoff. Scale: 1:2000, 895x695mm. Even at this early stage of planning it clearly shows the railway ramp between the quarantine camp and the main camp. The drawing shows no main gate garrison or crematoria. (*Yad Vashem Museum*)

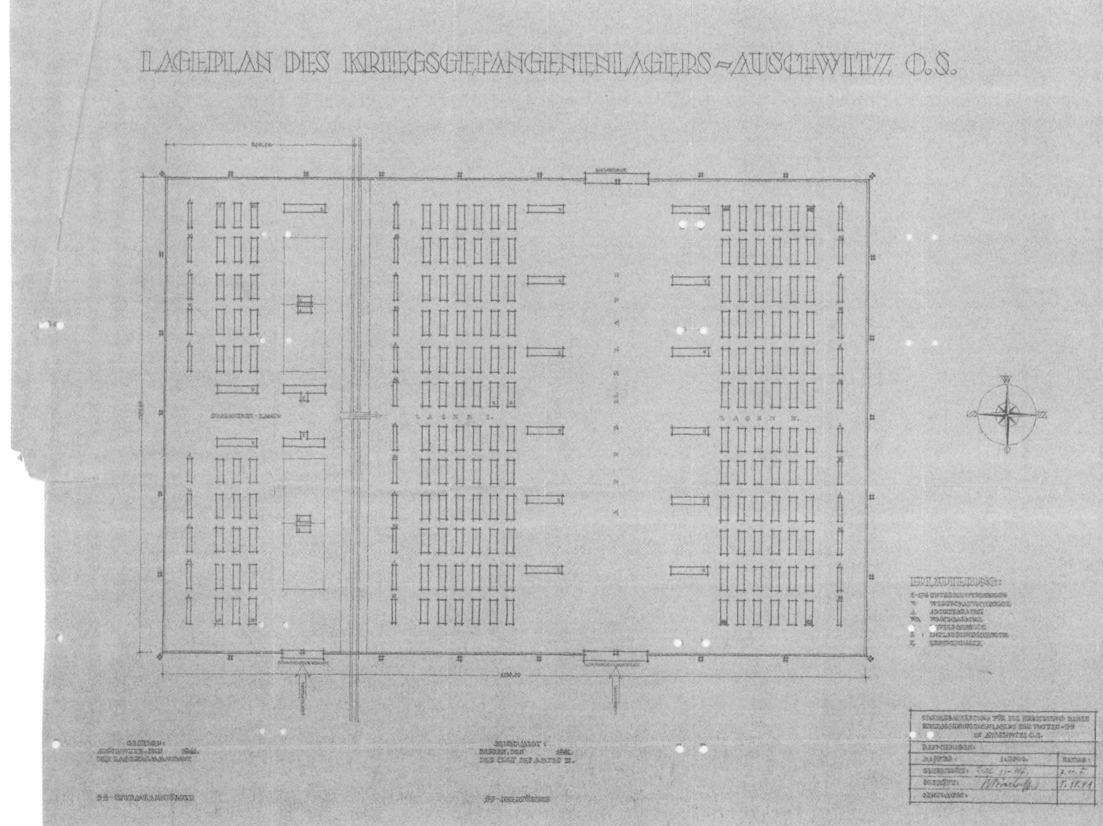

satellite camp would be built. Following the example of the main camp, Höss had been entrusted with selecting inmates to build the Birkenau site. With so many Russian PoWs in captivity, he was ordered to use the vast pool of prisoners offered from the German Army.

The first plans that were drawn for the new Birkenau site were undertaken on 7 October 1941 by Fritz Ertl, and approved by Bischoff on the following day. The camp was divided in three sections comprising of a Quarantine Camp (later B.I) which consisted of a '*Leichenhalle/Corpse hall*' and two internment camps (Camps I and II, slighter larger than the B.II area). Initially, there were no plans for a railway with the main station at Auschwitz.

A week later, on 14 October 1941, another plan was produced which was modified slightly to show the barracks for the SS guards to the east and a double track railway running from the station and terminating between Camp I and the Quarantine Camp.

Site map of the Auschwitz Prisoner of War Camp

Below is the second modified drawing of Birkenau dated 14 October 1941 by Haftling 471 (student Alfred Przybylski). On the drawing the quarantine *kommandantur* has been removed and at the bottom of the drawing an outline of the SS garrison has been drawn-in. The camp has now been divided into II and III sectors. (*Yad Vashem Museum*)

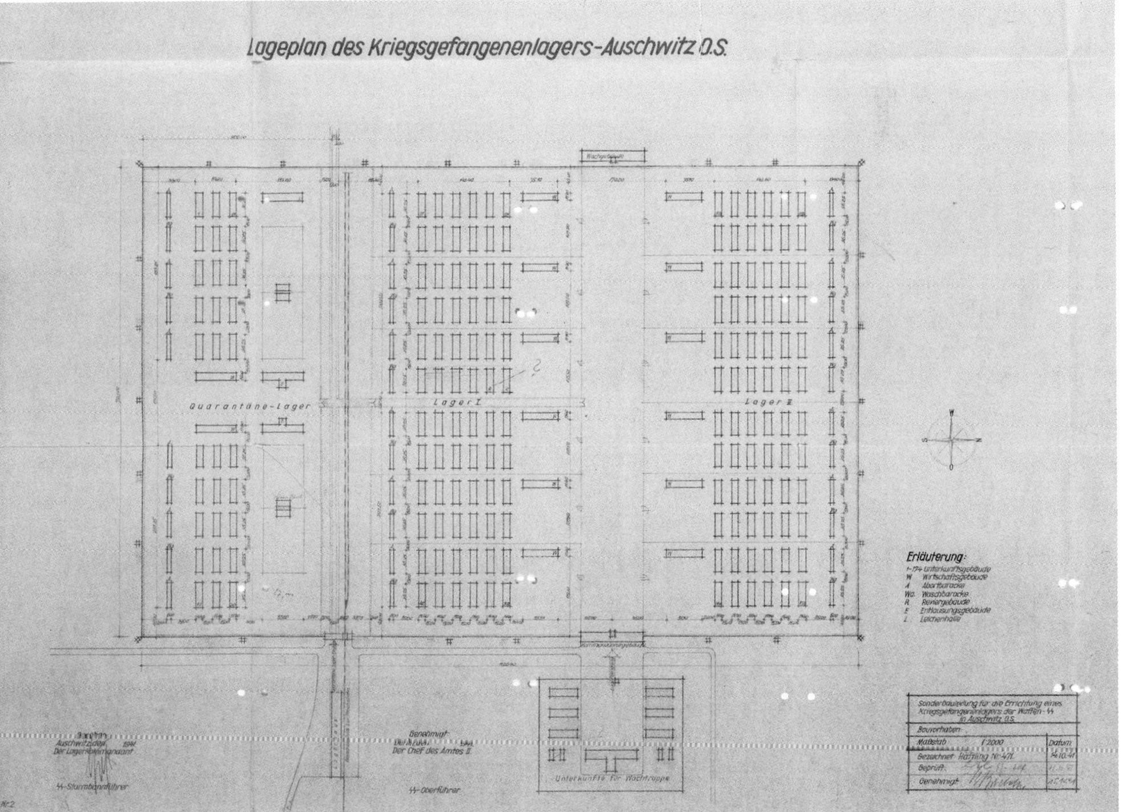

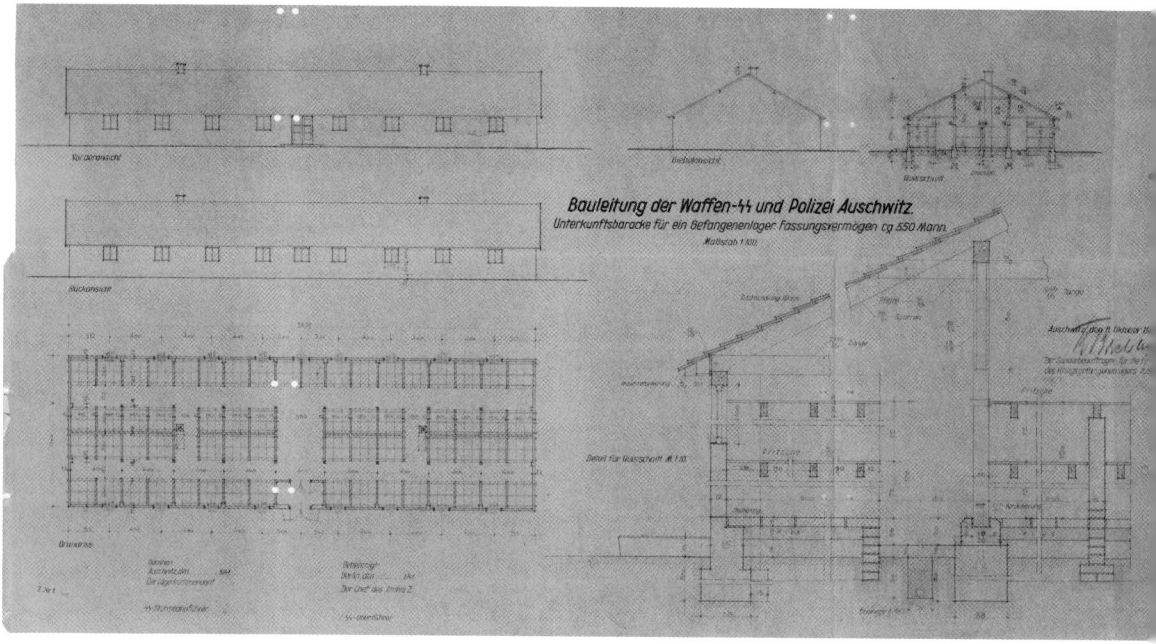

Construction Management of the Waffen-SS and Auschwitz Police

Here is a plan of the brick barracks that were constructed in Birkenau. Thirty of these buildings were constructed in the first part of the camp, fifteen in sector BIa and fifteen in sector BIb. The drawing planned to accomodate 550 PoWs. This estimate was then crossed-out and corrected to house 744 prisoners with 62 bunks. The bunks were a permanent structure and built in three tiers. The base was brick, and the other two wooden. The barracks did not have proper foundations and were supported by a thin layer of concrete, which could become wet and cold. (*Yad Vashem Museum*)

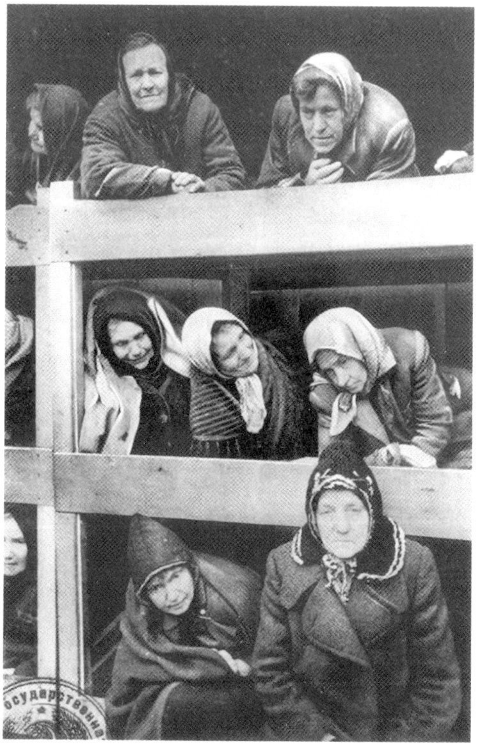

A Russian photograph showing former women prisoners on the wooden bunks that served as beds in Birkenau.

Two photographs taken in sequence by the author during a visit to Auschwitz-Birkenau in August 2024 showing the three-tier bunk system in one of the brick buildings in B1a Women's Camp. (*HITM courtesy of Auschwitz-Birkenau State Museum*)

In early October, a transportation order was authorized for a new Russian labour force. In total 10,000 Russian prisoners from Lamsdorf were to be marched to Auschwitz. The journey to the camp was one of complete horror. When they arrived at Auschwitz, hundreds had already perished. Many of them had died of thirst or exhaustion on the fatal journey. Those that were fit enough to be rounded up and marched off to Auschwitz were led to one side by SS guards, whilst those too weak to be moved were simply shot where they lay. The corpses were then dragged away by Polish prisoners and thrown into a pile for disposal. Those PoWs that survived were herded into an area selected for labour. Most of them were half dead, and infested with lice. Those that were lice ridden were stripped of their clothes and ordered to take a cold disinfecting bath before entering the camp.

Almost as soon as the Russian PoWs arrived in Auschwitz they were ordered to work. Those that were too weak were killed and disposed of in the crematorium, whilst the remaining prisoners were dragged from their barracks and marched the forty-minutes to the Birkenau construction site. The first job was to dismantle the existing village and then start building the camp. The Russians had not been given any tools with which to demolish the houses. Instead they were required to pull down the buildings with their bare hands and build the barracks in a similar method. The physical condition of the men was appalling, but they were still forced to work. All day long they laboured in terrible freezing temperatures. First they had to level the ground, then drainage ditches had to be dug, and then finally the various brick barracks and prefabricated wooden horse stables had to be constructed. The speed of the work was of utmost importance, and within fourteen days the quarantine camp had been completed.

On 30 October 1941, Bischoff drew up a first cost estimate for the Auschwitz camp (*SS Unterkunft und Konzentrationslager Auschwitz*). The total cost was estimated at a total of 7,057,400 RM. The document mentions the following items (BW = *Bauwerk* or construction office, building):

BW 12, 20A, 20B, 20D, 20E, 20F, 20G, 20L, 20M, 20N, 20O, 20Q, 20R:
Accommodation for detainees

BW 62:
Kitchen barrack for detainees

BW 300A-F:
Housing and utility barracks of camp for civilian workers

BW 300E:
1 utility barrack

BW 300F:
1 washing and toilet barrack

BW 172:
Utility barrack for guard unit

BW 100-107 and 112-132:
Accommodation for detainees

BW 9A:
Sanitary installations in the Auschwitz concentration camp (water and sewage installation, sewers)

BW 9B:
Drainage ducts

BW 21:
Roads

The same day, Bischoff made a report plan for what was initially called the 'new construction of the Waffen-SS PoW camp at Auschwitz'.

"O/S" (= Upper Silesia), which contained the following *Bauwerke*:

1. BW 3: Prisoner housing barracks 1-174
2. BW 4: Utility barracks 1-14
3. BW 5a: Delousing barrack 1
4. BW 5b: Delousing barrack 2
5. BW 6: Washing barracks 1-16
6. BW 7: Toilet barracks 1-18
7. BW 8: Corpse barrack
8. BW 9: Quarantine camp, entrance building
9. BW 10: Kommandantur building
10. BW 11: Guard building
11. BW 12: Area, fenced in, with open toilets
12. BW 13: Watchtowers, wood
13. BW 14: Barrack camp for guard unit
14. BW 15: Warehouse
15. BW 16: Access road and parking area
16. BW 17: Road consolidation within camp
17. BW 18: Sewage system with treatment plant
18. BW 19: Water supply plant
19. BW 20: Power plant
20. BW 21: Electrical power line from Birkenau

21. BW 22: Telephone system
22. BW 23: Alarm system
23. BW 24: Enclosure
24. BW 25: Wiremesh fencing within camp
25. BW 26: Transformer station
26. BW 27: Siding from Auschwitz station

Throughout the building project at Birkenau, Höss was constantly updated with its progress by the *Bauleitung*. Regularly he was seen visiting the construction site, either by motor vehicle or on horseback. On numerous occasions he could be seen wandering around the building site discussing details of the construction programme with site managers and subordinates. He soon discovered, which came as no surprise, that the labour force had not been supplied with adequate building materials. Consequently, the barracks had to be built from brick, as there were dwindling supplies of wood. Most of the building material during October and November was taken from the demolition of the hamlet of Birkenau, but this did not meet the requirements of Bischoff. The mortality rate too was also considered a problem as Höss and Bischoff hoped to complete the camp in the shortest possible time. By the end of 1 October, 255 Soviet prisoners had died. News of the high death rate concerned the SS headquarters in Berlin, as the prisoners were an asset.

However, the death rate continued to rise. Many inmates were dying of starvation, illness, injuries, and being subjected to more or less unrestrained killing. Höss recalled that Soviet prisoners died more rapidly than he ever expected. According to him the situation became much worse during the muddy period of the winter of 1941 and many began to die as a result. With the increased fatality rate the crematorium in Auschwitz was once again approaching its maximum incineration capacity. The crematorium was not built for an inmate population of 10,000, and with the influx of Russian prisoners, it could not possibly service the PoWs as well. Bischoff immediately summoned the Topf engineer Kurt Prufer, who had supplied the main incineration to Auschwitz. He arrived in the camp on Tuesday, 21 October to go over plans, suggesting that the crematorium combine three muffles in a single furnace. In their view it was deemed impractical to waste money building a crematorium on the new Birkenau site, as the camp promised to be only a temporary solution until the war in Russia was won. Therefore, it was agreed that a new crematorium could perhaps be built in the main camp near the administration building and alongside the existing crematorium.

Bischoff had a meeting with Kurt Prüfer, Chief Engineer of the '*Krematoriumbau*' department of the firm Topf & Söhne of Erfurt, concerning the construction of a new crematorium behind the existing one. It was proposed that the new building

Five photographs taken in sequence by the author during a visit to Auschwitz-Birkenau in August 2024 showing the *Feldfeiler* (field pillar) that was erected along the perimeter of B11a Men's Quarantine Camp. These posts were installed almost four metres tall and they were electrified with high voltage barbed wire. (*HITM courtesy of Auschwitz/Birkenau State Archive*)

would have a furnace room with five 3 muffle furnaces, two *'Leichenkeller'* (basement morgues) and a dissecting room, and all these rooms would have to be well ventilated with adequate air extraction systems. The components for the furnaces were to be delivered within three months.

A photo taken by the author during a visit to Auschwitz-Birkenau in August 2024 showing an *Eckpfeiler* (corner pillar) that was erected along the perimeter of B11a Men's Quarantine Camp near the main entrance. (*HITM courtesy of Auschwitz/Birkenau State Archive*)

Over the ensuing weeks, construction of the Birkenau site continued. Many of the Soviet workers laboured for hours in terrible freezing conditions. An outbreak of dysentery had caused numerous problems, and because they were unable to leave their place of work they often soiled their own ragged clothes. Caked in thick mud and faeces the Russian inmates were forced to work, many of them too weak to show any sign of human dignity. At the end of November snow began to fall and the arctic temperatures dramatically increased the number of fatalities. The conditions had become so dreadful that the prisoners were actually dying on site. Concerned that it may soon jeopardize the construction programme, Höss sent an urgent report to Berlin informing them of the disastrous situation. In direct response to the commandant's report Bischoff immediately informed Berlin, making it clear that in spite of the increased death rate among the Soviet prisoners, much work had been achieved at Birkenau. In fact, according to reports Bischoff had confirmed that in just over one month 140,000 cubic feet of earth had been excavated, 1,600 concrete foundations laid, 600 concrete posts erected for the fence with 100,000 feet of barbed wire, and 86,000 cubic feet of brickwork had been constructed, using more than one million bricks. Constructing the actual barracks, however, was still a slow process. Much of the construction of the barracks was to be built from wood. A German company had already designed the standard army horse stable barrack, and this would be produced and dispatched to Auschwitz in kit form, where it could easily be erected and dismantled. It was argued that these prefabricated wooden huts could be assembled very rapidly with a gang of just thirty unskilled men led by one carpenter. In total 253 of these huts were assigned to Birkenau.

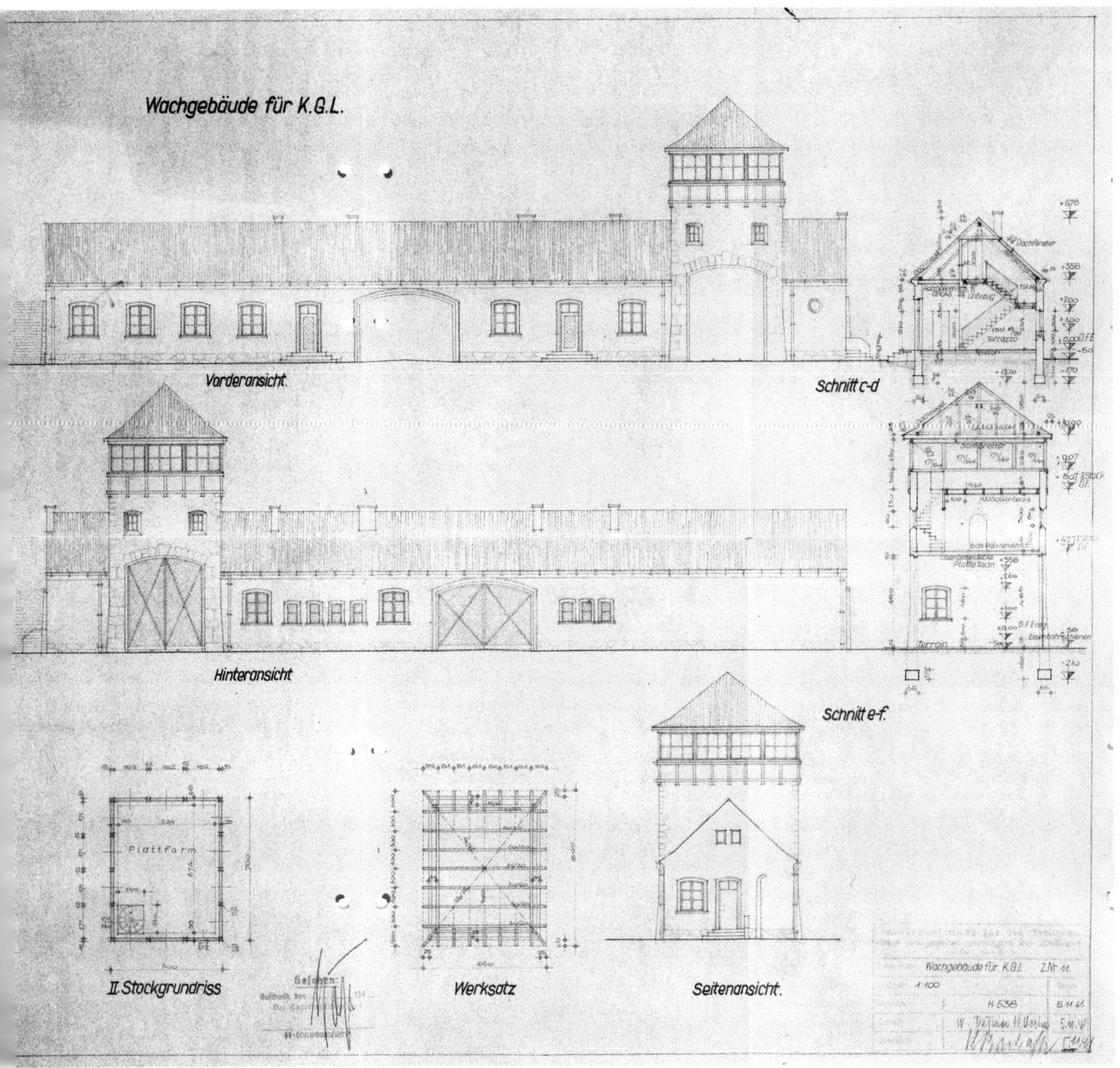

Wachgebäude für KGL (Guardhouse for PoW Camp)
In early November 1941 plans were drawn-up for the main brick gate at Birkenau. This is a drawing showing the façade, cross-section and plan view of the gate building. It was drawn by Haftling 538 (construction technician Leon Sawka) and reviewed by Dejaco and approved by Bischoff on 5 November 1941. (*Yad Vashem Museum*)

By the end of 1941 Auschwitz slowly transformed from a quiet backwater quarantine camp in south western Poland, into one of the largest concentration camp systems of the *Reich*. In little over a year Auschwitz had developed into a dual-function camp, with many of the inmates that were sent there now living and working. Höss's innovative skills had produced an institution of brutality where it frequently killed others. With an effective killing facility mastered, more and more prisoners could be given passage through the now-infamous gates of '*Arbeit Macht Frei*'. In fact, during 1941 there had been a number of meetings and

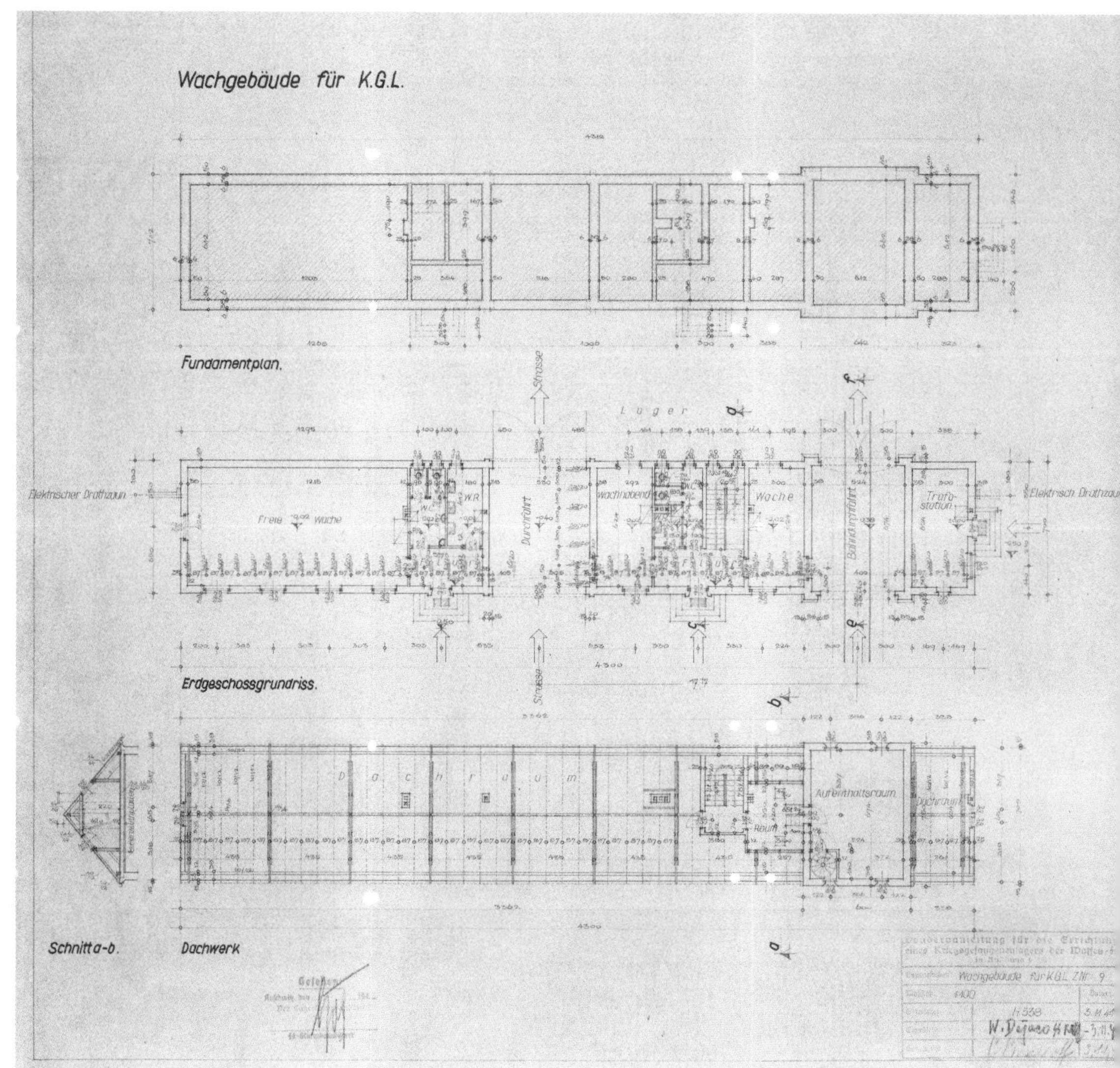

Another drawing by Haftling 538 (construction technician Leon Sawka) and reviewed by Dejaco and approved by Bischoff on 5 November 1941. It shows the façade, cross section and plan view of the Birkenau gate building entrance. (*Yad Vashem Museum*)

discussions regarding expanding and developing Auschwitz I. There were plans to dismantle the camp kitchen and rebuild it from scratch with a new and extensive roll-call square. A plan was also drawn-up for prisoners to be put into the original SS quarters, camp canteen, adminstistration and *Kommandantur* buildings. The entire administrative section of buildings was to be moved to a massive complex of buildings to the west of the camp. The camp extension was to be built northwards and comprise a new hospital, camp jail, warehouses and workshops. Beyond this new row of buildings, a new crematorium was to be constructed. There were even two farms, much to the behest of Himmler, planned to be built south west of the camp towards the town of Rajsko. There were designs and plans for the residential

Prisoners are seen under the supervision of *Kapos* working the main gate of Birkenau in late 1941 or early 1942. (*Yad Vasham*)

A photograph taken by the author in August 2024 showing inside the main entrance of Auschwitz-Birkenau. It shows a relative comparison of now and then. (*HITM courtesy of Auschwitz-Birkenau State Archive*)

A photograph showing a narrow gauge rail-line used for construction purposes such as transporting materials into the camp for building. (*Yad Vasham*)

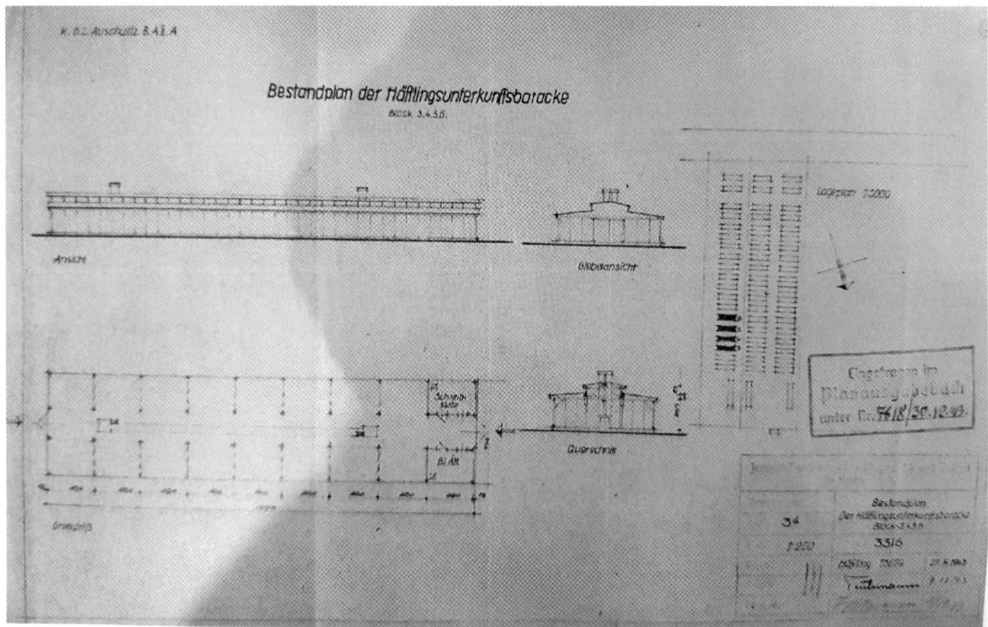

A plan of the horse stable barracks or *Pferdestallbaracke*, which was the most common structure built at Birkenau during its operation. The size of these barracks measured 40.76 x 9.56m. The barracks had no windows, only skylights in the roof. (*Auschwitz-Birkenau State Archive*)

A photograph showing the barracks with their skylights in the roof. This image was taken in the summer of 1944 and shows new arrivals in the camp. After being processed for labour they have been disinfected and issued underclothing. (*Auschwitz-Birkenau State Museum/Yad Vashem*)

New arrivals await to be taken to another section of the camp during the summer of 1944. Behind the fence wooden barracks can clearly be seen. (*Auschwitz-Birkenau State Museum*)

Two photographs taken by the author in August 2024 along the perimeter fence of BIIa Men's Qurantine camp at Auschwitz-Birkenau. It shows the *Pferdestallbaracke* or horse stable barracks. As can clearly be identified, the barracks had no windows only skylights in the roof. (*HITM courtesy of Auschwitz-Birkenau State Archive*)

quarters for the SS personnel to be built north-east of the camp towards the railway station, suggesting that SS families and individual SS personnel were to be located nearer to the town of Auschwitz.

Over the coming weeks and months there were further plans and designs drafted on the shape of camp. There was even a plan for a temporary kindergarten for the children of SS personnel to be constructed on the road running along the Sola River. With this in mind, architects were given the task of drawing plans for a SS zone. These were to comprise SS barracks and a large residential area north-east of the camp. The SS barracks were to be constructed near to the camp, and the houses in which the personnel would live with their families would be built slightly further away. The houses would comprise gardens for married officers and non-commissioned officers. There would be a specially designed neighbourhood, which would comprise various shops and other facilities. There would be a square with fountains; a beautiful well tended garden; and a sports area with a football pitch for recreation activities just for SS personnel and their families. There were further modifications and ideas which included constructing SS barracks complete with camp administration, SS hospital, rest and recreation centre and military facilities, including a shooting range. Many of these structures were planned to be built to the south, adjacent to the new Birkenau camp, and there would be many hundreds of SS men billeted in these barracks that would serve the Auschwitz complex. Both brick and wooden structures would eventually be built and expanded in the direction of the main town of Auschwitz.

Many of these plans were not just an idea; Himmler himself wanted the whole area transformed. The region was termed the camp's zone of interest, and encompassed a section covering some 30 square miles between the Sola and Vistula Rivers. The area encompassed forests, ponds, waterways, fields, roads and railway tracks, including facilities for SS personnel to live. There were also to be shops, factories, fishpond systems, and drainage ditches. New roads were to be built, which included various electrical and water supply networks. All of this served the planned expansion of the camp. Although the plan was ambitious, the SS were serious about its construction. In fact, in a number of villages in the camp's 'zone of interest' the Polish inhabitants had been evicted from their homes and their houses either dismantled by *Kommandos* of prisoners for the sole purpose of scavenging for building materials for the construction of the camp or were adapted as new homes for the SS. All these projects required specialist surveys to be undertaken, so a special survey *Kommando* team was formed.

The survey team was set to work and they were fully aware of the immense problems in the plans for such an extensive area. The biggest challenge was the prescence of water and boggy terrain, which in some areas were measured to be twenty centimetres deep. In order to overcome this problem a massive network of drainage ditches and irrigation ponds was required. Already the company *Messtruppe Landwirtschaft*, which was independent of the *Bauleitung*, had worked along with the private company based in the town of Bydgoszcz called *Lotzki* surveying and drainage office. They had been entrusted to deal with the continually problematic water management issues in the Auschwitz area, which included the new Birkenau site. Over the coming weeks and months, the company with its *Kommando* teams was set to work on the drainage system throughout the whole complex, including Birkenau. There were special penal companies put together to dig the main drainage system and, a result of working under such terrible conditions, there was a high mortality rate.

The whole drainage system was planned on a massive scale with a considerable amount of investment made in order to make the area viable for living and working for the SS. There was also some assistance from a number of private firms, all coming forward for financial reward.

From 1941 until late 1942 various waterworks were designed using mechanical filters to supply water to some 150,000 people. However, due to lack of funding and materials, untreated running water in the area was drawn from five wells situated between the main Auschwitz railway line and the camp's warehouses.

The expansion programme for the Auschwitz area was an immense undertaking, not only due to topography issues, but also to limited funds and materials available for drainage, water supply and construction of the many buildings that were being proposed. One of the major concerns by the end of 1941 was the eagerness for Berlin to send more prisoners to Auschwitz, where logistical problems were already manifesting. However, although commandant Höss had been increasingly troubled throughout the year concerning the mounting numbers of prisoners entering the camp, the construction of Birkenau was in fact his saving grace. Here Soviet PoWs could be sent direct and used as slave labour. Once the war on the Eastern Front had been won, the Russians could be disposed of, and the temporary camp of Birkenau could be converted into a huge farming facility.

However, by the end of the year the German Army had still not won their war on the Eastern Front during one of the worst winters in living history. As a result of the military set-back, Germany was thus compelled to mobilize all its resources to continue the war effort and this would include greater demands on German industry, especially in armaments. The armaments industry had become seriously undermanned and Russian PoWs had become a supply far too valuable to waste on places like Auschwitz. All prisoners were now going to be assigned to the armaments industry, and this included Russian PoWs. Himmler's dream of amassing a huge Soviet labour force for his farming enterprise and vast construction programme for the new town of Auschwitz had been postponed until the war was won. As for the building of the 'Birkenau PoW' camp, this proceeded as planned, regardless of the change of policy. In Berlin they had a number of practical problems to work out. If

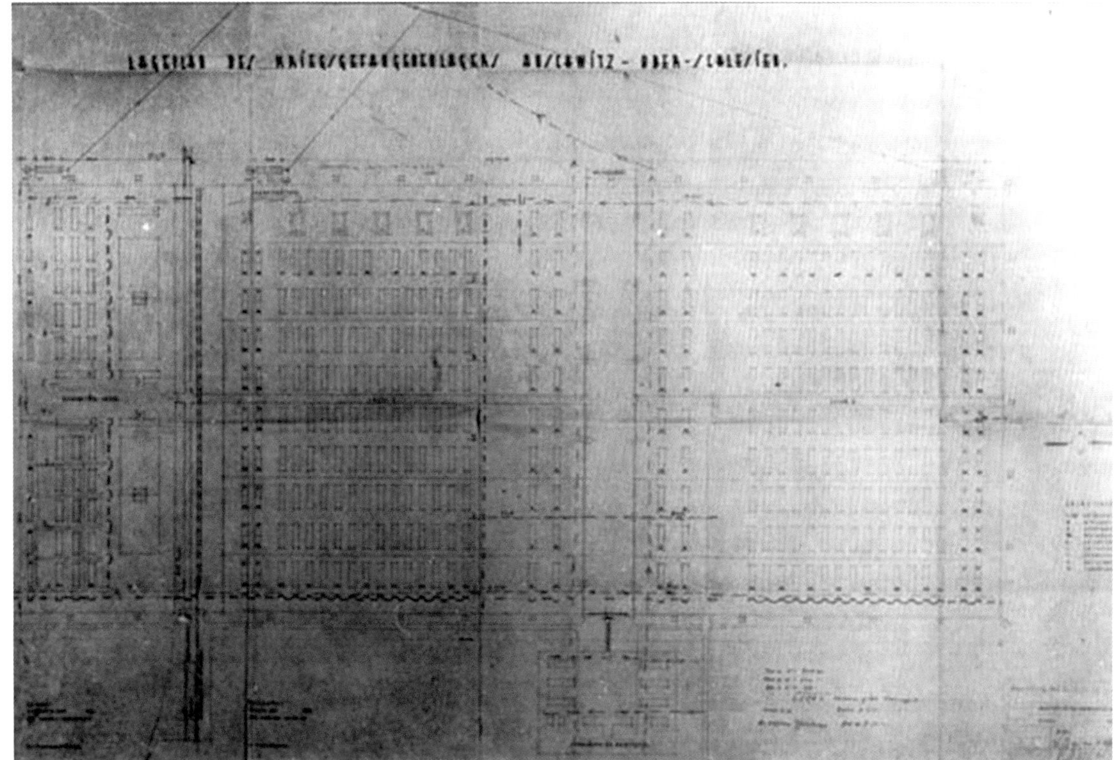

LAGEPLAN DES KRIEGSGEFANGENENLAGERS AUSCHWITZ OBER SCHLESIEN
(Site map of Auschwitz PoW Camp, Upper Silesia)

Sonderbauleitung für die Errichtung eines Kriegsgefangenenlager der Waffen-SS in Auschwitz OS (Special Construction Management for the erection of a Waffen-SS prisoner of war camp in Auschwitz, Upper Silesia)

Map was drawn by SS W. Uhlmer on 5 January 1942. It was checked by SS Second Lieutenant Walter Dejaco on the same day. Approved by SS Captain Bischoff the following day.
(*Auschwitz-Birkenau State Museum*)

they could no longer fill Birkenau with Soviet prisoners, then it could be used for the shipment of another even greater issue in the General Government and across Europe – the Jews.

Already, there had been growing reports of the escalating policies against the Jews in the East, especially by those of the *Einsatzgruppen* (Operational Groups). Through the Soviet heartlands there was a blood bath against the Jewish population with widespread murders and executions.

However, in spite of the mass killings, the method of shooting was not regarded as practical as this was not only time consuming, but would have diverse effects on the troops, and most importantly would lower morale. Since the summer of 1941

Himmler had been making preparations for the mass deportation of Jews to the East. During the first cold weeks of January 1942, Berlin confirmed that Himmler had authorised Glücks by telegram that he was to receive over 150,000 Jews in the concentration camps. However, it was not specified at first how many Jews would be dispatched to Auschwitz.

In fact, the first Jews destined for Auschwitz came from a small transport that arrived on 15 February 1942, and were from the Upper Silesian town of Beuthen. The majority of them were elderly, and because they had already been deemed unfit for work they were immediately led to the camp's crematorium, and killed.

However, it was noted at Auschwitz that the increased killing in the crematorium was not an ideal situation. Over the next several days the problem continued to manifest itself regarding the question of an adequate crematorium. It was suggested that if they were going to open Birkenau with a large influx of Jews, then Auschwitz would need to improve its cremation facility. Building another crematorium had already been proposed in the base camp alongside the existing one.

However, against potential plans to build another crematorium in the main camp, it was agreed that if Birkenau was to follow the same crooked path to murder – as Auschwitz had done with the Soviet PoWs – it was unquestionably easier installing a crematorium at Birkenau. Commandant Höss chaired a meeting with his staff concerning the dilemma. If new policies towards the Jews meant they were now being shipped to the concentration camps, then they would need sufficient tools to dispose of those unfit for work.

On Thursday, 27 February Höss, SS architect Bischoff and Kammler, head of the Central SS Building Office, held a meeting to discuss the construction programme for the third year of the war economy. The meeting was to encompass the complete Auschwitz site. A list was drawn up which was to be approved by *SS-Gruppenführer* Oswald Pohl. The list was as follows:

I. Agricultural constructions
   1. 30 to 35 horse stable barracks for the temporary housing of animals, etc
   2. 2 permanent cow-sheds for a total of 400 head of cattle
   3. 3 field barns and 4 temporary farm barns
   4. Temporary greenhouse of 3000m^2
   5. 4 storage buildings for potatoes
   6. Completion of Raisko building as a laboratory

II. Erection of temporary buildings for Deutsche Wirtschaftsbetriebe
   1. Construction of a temporary bridge across the Sola River toward detainee entrance, making use of temporary road overpass of road administration, to be dismantled

2. Adding upper storeys to 6 permanent detainee buildings
3. Completion of 5 permanent detainee buildings and new construction of 15 detainee buildings to be used initially as follows:
   5 housing buildings as workshops
   5 housing buildings for storage
   5 housing buildings for the guard units
   The distance between the permanent buildings will be 14m edge to edge.
4. Laundry building
5. Entrance building, detainees
6. Water supply system
7. Sewage system
8. Bio-gas utilization system
9. Finishing utility barrack, Kommandantur
10. Crematorium in the PoW camp
11. 4 officers' housing barracks
12. Construction office barrack
13. Roads as required

An artist's impression of the 'little red house' prior to its operation as a killing facility. This may not be a precise detail of the farmhouse for there are a number of variations of the way it appeared. According to reports the windows of the 'little red house or cottage' were not bricked-up but equipped with 'special shutters' which were used for ventilation purposes when opened. This also included the old door being replaced with a gas-tight door. According to Rudolf Höss he was the initiator of the installation, comprising a converted farmhouse and two undressing huts. The killing capacity was estimated at 800 persons. (*Renato Dalmaso*)

14. Completion of existing houses and completion of one house for the commander of the agricultural units at Auschwitz.

In late February 1942 Höss announced that he had personally visited Birkenau to find the perfect killing installation. Scouring the far north western corner of the camp he had found an abandoned small brick farm cottage with a tiled roof. He decided that the cottage, known as Bunker I and nicknamed 'the little red house' because of the colour of its walls, should be converted as quickly as possible into a killing facility. As part of the conversion, Höss wanted its windows and doors bricked up, edges sealed with felt in order to ensure it was air tight, and the interior gutted to form two rooms. The doors to both rooms were to have a sign attached over the entrance, '*Zur Desinfektion*' ('To Disinfection'). To anyone looking from outside the building it looked like an innocent little cottage.

Having such an isolated murder site as the 'red house', those unfit for work could be taken away with ease and gassed in secrecy, and their death agonies would not disturb the local surroundings. As far as Höss was concerned, plans for this new killing facility at Bunker I was primarily to be used along similar lines to that of the main camp, but on a grander scale.

Bunker I was completed within a few weeks and on 20 March was made operational for the first time. The RSHA *Reichssicherheitshauptamt* or Reich Security Main Office in Berlin then communicated that a group of Jews unfit for work from Upper Silesia had been chosen locally for what the SS authorities were now calling 'special treatment'. Under the cover of darkness, the Jews were transported directly to Birkenau. Despite the panic among some of the elderly Jews that arrived, the first gassing operation in Birkenau had been a complete success. Most of the Jews had calmly filed into the 'The Little Red House' with no trouble caused to the normal operation of camp life.

SS-Unterscharführer Richard Böck who served as a driver at Auschwitz from 1941 until the camp was evacuated was later to write about this new bunker:

> *'One day, it was in the winter of 1942/43, H[öblinger] asked me if I would like to go along to see a gassing action. He would pass me off as his assistant in the ambulance, because otherwise it was strictly prohibited to be present there. So we went to the motor pool, took the ambulance, and went directly to Birkenau. We did not touch the Birkenau camp on that route. I cannot even say that I saw any part of the camp at that time. The train stood in the open country somewhere between Auschwitz and Birkenau, and the detainees were just being unloaded. It was about 21:00 hours* [9 p.m.]. *Broad steps had been placed at the back of the trucks for the people to climb up. All vehicles were chock-full and could not have accepted any more. On the trucks,*

the people were standing. I did not see that a selection was done by an SS doctor or any other SS member. These [people] *were all loaded* [on the trucks] *and taken to a former farmstead about 1.5km away from the unloading area. I can no longer indicate the place precisely, because it was dark. Anyway, I did not see the Birkenau crematoria and I think that they were not yet in operation at the time. In any case, H. and I went to that place with the Sanka, following the trucks. When we arrived, the people had already been unloaded and had to undress in several barracks near that old farmstead. When they came out from the barracks, naked, they were told that they should go into the building that had a sign 'Disinfection.' This building was the former farmstead that had been transformed at that time into a gassing room. As far as I can remember, it* [the inside] *was well laid out in concrete all around and had gates on both sides that were made of wood, I believe. H. had previously told me that the incoming transports were being gassed in this room. Besides, those gassing actions were something every one of us knew about. I remember that this transport consisted of Dutch Jews – men, women and children – who were all well dressed and looked like wealthy people. I have to correct something here. The modified farmstead had only one gate, consisting of two leaves. The 'Disinfection' sign was not attached to the building either but stood a few metres away from it, like a signpost. They had set up this sign to make the people believe they would be disinfected here. Once the total transport had entered that building – some 1,000 persons, I think – the gate was closed. Then an SS man, a Rottenführer I think, came to our Sanka and took out a gas can. With this can he went to a ladder which stood on the right side of the building, seen from the door. I noticed that he was wearing a gas-mask when he went up. When he had reached the end of the ladder he opened a circular trap made of steel plate and poured the contents of the can against the wall when he hit it while pouring. At the same time, I could see brown dust coming out of the opening. Whether that was gas, I cannot say. When he had closed the little trap, indescribable screams came from that room. I simply cannot describe how these people screamed. That went on for 8–10 minutes and then everything was quiet. A little later, the gate was opened by detainees and one could still see a bluish mist floating above a pile of corpses. The corpses were so strongly interlaced that it was impossible to say to whom the individual limbs and body parts belonged. This allows one to understand how indescribably horrible the agony of these persons must have been. I was surprised, though, to see that the detainees who had to move the corpses out entered the room without gas masks even though this blue mist, which I thought to be gas, floated above the corpses. The corpses were loaded onto farm carts* [rack-carts] *and pushed away by detainees. Where the corpses went, I could not see. I did not see a crematorium either.* […] *I remember well that the Sanka was marked with a 'Red Cross' sign on the sides. That vehicle, though, was never used as an ambulance, but only for this purpose, for camouflage.'*

Though Bunker I at Birkenau had solved the problem of how to kill in relative secret, the only concern now was how to dispose of the evidence. Without the advantages of a crematorium on site, the only short-term solution was to have the corpses buried in a nearby pit.

On 26 March 1942, the first trainloads of prisoners assigned to Birkenau, comprising 999 able-bodied Slovakian female Jews, were unloaded from ramps just outside the Auschwitz station. However, because Birkenau was still under construction, the women were reluctantly sent to the main camp, where they were herded into ten specially-adapted walled-off barracks. The following day they were ordered to have their heads shaved and were told to wear old Russian uniforms. Housing the Slovakian Jews in the main camp was an administrative nightmare. There had been no proper preparation for their arrival, which consequently led to numerous problems. Living conditions there too had already deteriorated to such a point that there were growing concerns of a typhus epidemic.

In Birkenau conditions were considerably worse than in the main camp. Birkenau had been officially in operation since early March, with the remaining Soviet PoWs, a group of German criminals, and 1,200 sick prisoners incarcerated in the area designated for the women, officially known as BIa. It was here that the Slovak transport was soon to be moved. In March Birkenau was like a quagmire. There was hardly any water and washing facilities, and the weak and starving prisoners were living in utter filth and degradation. But despite the abysmal conditions the SS looked upon Birkenau as their only solution to the already overflowing Auschwitz I. Those considered unfit for work would be sent to Bunker I, and given 'special treatment'.

Although Birkenau appeared to be the answer for a vast slave labour pool, there were newer harsher policies against the Jews. As a result of these policies from Berlin other camps in Poland were now under construction near the villages of Belzec, Sobibor and Treblinka, which were to include their own crematoria as well. It appeared all Jews would be sent to these camps. The future for these hapless people looked bleaker than ever before.

In early June Höss was ordered to Berlin where he met Himmler at the SS headquarters. It was here that he was told that there was a new change in policy and as commandant of Auschwitz he had been given a new role in the implementation of the genocidal solution of what was known as the 'Jewish problem'. Himmler told him that the *Führer* had ordered that the Jewish question be solved once and for all and that the SS were to implement that order. He went on to outline that the existing extermination centres in the East were not in a position to carry out the huge actions which are anticipated. He had therefore earmarked Auschwitz for this purpose, both because of its good position as regards to communications and because the area can easily be isolated and camouflaged. He was informed that the killing facility at Birkenau or Bunker I was to continue to function similar to that of the crematorium in the main camp. Those convicted by the Gestapo court in Kattowitz would also be sent to Birkenau and gassed in Bunker I.

Throughout the spring and summer Bunker I, together with Crematorium I in the main camp, simultaneously continued to operate, killing convicted criminals and those unfit for work. During early June Bunker I was being used to kill an ever growing number of people, but in spite of the increased numbers going to their death it was still deemed inefficient. In order to facilitate and overcome the growing problems with transports arriving at the camp, Höss held a meeting with *SS-Sturmbannführer* Karl Bischoff and other members of the Auschwitz Construction Office to discuss plans to convert a second cottage, known as the 'Little White House', into what the SS called a 'bathing facility for special actions'.

By the end of June this quiet and unobtrusive looking house, known as Bunker II, went into operation. The interior of the cottage comprised of four narrow rooms that were constructed as gas chambers. With better ventilation and a killing capacity of around 1,200 people at any one time, Höss was sure that Birkenau would run efficiently as never before. As the last finishing touches were made to Bunker II more shipments of Jews were destined for Auschwitz.

On 4 July the first transport of 1,000 Jews arrived outside Birkenau and was submitted for selection. Höss was there witnessing the spectacle with *SS-Sturmbannführer Lagerführer* Hans Aumeier and his new adjutant *SS-Hauptsturmführer* Robert Karl Ludwig Mulka. The transports were unloaded at a side-line at Birkenau. Aumeier wrote: '*Upon arrival of the transport, the prisoners were divided by male and female. Those children up to the age of 14 stayed with their mother in the women's camp, and those over 14-years-old with their fathers in the men's camp* ...'. In total, 108 able-bodied women and 264-able bodied men were chosen for work, whilst the remaining 638 people were herded off under the cover of darkness to barracks where the victims undressed and then went naked to the gas-chambers.

All through the procedure the victims were told calmly that they were to bathe and be deloused. Once crammed inside the gas chamber and the doors shut, *SS-Unterscharführer* Moll, dressed in a special white protective suit with gasmask, threw the saturated Zyklon B pellets through a little vent, and then waited twenty-five minutes until all the screams of those fighting for their lives fell silent. During the gassing procedure SS surgeons, on duty in the camp, regularly waited nearby with an SS hospital orderly with an oxygen apparatus to revive SS men, in case any of them succumbed to the poisonous fumes. Once they were certain that all inside were dead, the doors and the windows were then opened to ventilate the rooms. The tangled corpses were later removed by the *Sonderkommando* for disposal.

In fact, the saturated Zyklon B pellets were so poisonous that Höss sent out a special order on 12 August 1942:

Auschwitz Concentration Camp Commandant's Office — Auschwitz 12 August 1942

Special Order

A case of indisposition with slight symptoms of poisoning by hydrocyanic gas which occurred today makes it necessary to warn all those participating in the gassings and all other SS members that in particular on opening rooms used for gassing SS not wearing masks must wait at least five hours and keep at a distance of at least 15 metres from the chamber. In addition, particular attention should be paid to the wind direction.

The gas being used at present contains less odorous warning agent and is therefore especially dangerous.

The SS garrison doctor declines all responsibility for any accident that should occur in the case where these directives have not been complied with by SS members.

Signed: Höß

SS Lieutenant Colonel and Commandant

For files

SS Captain and Adjutant

Distribution:

7 to SS T Stuba	1 each to:
7 Administration	SS Hosp, HWL, DAW, Radio station
3 Store	Telegraph station
2 Construction Management	Telephone exchange
2 Political Section	SS Canteen
1 9th SS T Stuba	Transport Section
1 Agriculture	KL Labor Office
1 Stables	Women's KL Labour Office
1 Protective Detention Camp	Detachment VI
1 Women's KL (concentration camp)	External Service Station of the WI
1 Legal Officer	Office
1 Personnel Division	Zeppelin Special Kommando
1 Waffen-SS House	

Konzentrationslager Auschwitz — Auschwitz, den 12. August 1942
Kommandantur

Sonderbefehl.

Ein heute mit leichten Vergiftungserscheinungen durch Blausäure aufgetretener Krankheitsfall gibt Veranlassung, allen an Vergasungen Beteiligten und allen übrigen SS-Angehörigen bekanntzugeben, daß insbesondere beim Öffnen der vergasten Räume von SS-Angehörigen ohne Maske wenigstens 5 Stunden hindurch ein Abstand von 15 Metern von der Kammer gewahrt werden muß. Hierbei ist besonders auf die Windrichtung zu achten.

Das jetzt verwendete Gas enthält weniger beigesetzte Geruchstoffe und ist daher besonders gefährlich.

Der SS-Standortarzt Auschwitz lehnt die Verantwortung für eintretende Unglücksfälle in den Fällen ab, bei denen von SS-Angehörigen diese Richtlinien nicht eingehalten werden.

gez.: Höß
SS-Obersturmbannführer und Kommandant.

F.d.R.:
SS-Hauptsturmführer und Adjutant.

Verteiler:

7 Stück an SS-T-Stuba.	je 1 Stück an:
7 " " Verwaltung	SS-Revier, HWL, DAW, Funkst.
3 " " Ablage	Fernschreibstelle
2 " " Bauleitung	Telefonvermittlung
2 " " Polit. Abt.	SS-Kantinengemeinschaft
1 " " 9./SS-T-Stuba.	Fahrbereitschaft
1 " " Landwirtschaft	Arbeitseinsatz KL
1 " " Reitstall	Arbeitseinsatz FKL
1 " " Schutzhaftlager	Abteilung VI
1 " " FKL.	Außendienststelle des
1 " " Gerichtsoffizier	Amtes W.I.
1 " " Personalabteilung	Sonderkommando Zeppelin.
1 " " Haus der Waffen-SS	

(422)

(*Auschwitz-Birkenau State Museum*)

On Friday, 17 July Himmler, Fritz Bracht, and Higher SS and Police Leader Ernst-Heinrich Schmauser and other personnel made a visit to Auschwitz via the airport at Kattowitz. It was on this day that the *Reichsführer* visited the main camp and the women's camp, and then the following day he inspected Monowitz. Below is the itinerary for his two-day meeting, as noted in his diary:

Friday, 17 July 1942
1200 trip, Friedrichsruh airport, Lötzen
1245 take off Lötzen
RFSS, Prof. Wüst, Kersten, Grothmann, Kiermeier
1512 landing, Kattowitz
Pick up Gauleiter Bracht, O'Gruf. Schmauser and Stubaf
Höß Trip to Auschwitz, Tea in the Commandant's quarters
Talk with Stubaf. Caesar and O'Stubaf. Vogel
Stubaf. Höß
Inspection of the agricultural operations
Inspection of the prisoners' camp and of the FKL
Dining in the Commandant's quarters
Auschwitz-Kattowitz trip to the residence of Gauleiter Bracht
Evening with Gauleiter Bracht
Sunday evening July 18, 1942
0900 breakfast with Gauleiter Bracht and wife
Trip to Auschwitz, Talk with O. Graf. Schmauser
Stubaf. Caesar
The Commandant of the FKL
Inspection of the factory grounds of the Buna
Auschwitz-Kattowitz trip
1300 flight, Kattowitz-Krakow-Lublin
1515 landing, Lublin Pick up O. Gruf. Krüger and Brigf. Globocnik. Tea with Globocnik
Talk with Staf. Schellenberg
Trip to the Jastrow fruit concern 2100 talk at Globocnik's with SS O'Gruf. Krüger, SS O'Gruf. Pohl, SS Brigf. Globocnik, SS O'Stuf. Stier

Commandant Höss wrote in his diary later about the *Reichsführer*'s visit:

'The next meeting was in the summer of 1942, when Himmler visited Auschwitz for the second and last time. The inspection lasted two days and Himmler looked at everything very thoroughly. Also present at this inspection were District Leader

Bracht, SS General Schmauser, Dr. Kammler, and others. The first thing after their arrival was a meeting in the officers' club. With the help of maps and diagrams, I had to show the present condition of the camp. After that we went to the construction headquarters, where Kammler, using maps, blueprints, and models explained the planned or already progressing construction. He did not, however, keep quiet about the difficulties that existed which hindered the construction. He also pointed out those projects which were impossible not only to start, but to finish. Himmler listened with great interest, asked about some of the technical details, and agreed with the overall planning. Himmler did not utter a single word about Kammler's repeated references to the many difficulties. Afterwards there was a trip through the whole area of concern: first the farms and soil enrichment projects, the dam-building site, the laboratories and plant cultivation in Raisko, the cattle-raising farms and the orchards. Then we visited Birkenau, the Russian camp, the Gypsy camp, and a Jewish camp. Standing at the entrance, he asked for a situation report on the layout of the swamp reclamation and the water projects. He also wanted a report on the intended expansion projects. He watched the prisoners at work, inspected the housing, the kitchens, and the sick bays. I constantly pointed out the shortcomings and the bad conditions. I am positive he noticed them. He saw the emaciated victims of epidemics. The doctors explained things without mincing words. He saw the overcrowded sick bays, and the child mortality in the Gypsy camp and he also witnessed the terrible childhood disease called noma (a gangrenous mouth disease in children weakened by disease and malnutrition). Himmler also saw the overcrowded barracks, the primitive and totally inadequate toilet and wash facilities. He was told about the high rate of illness and the death rate by the doctors and their causes. He had everything explained to him in the greatest detail. He saw everything in stark reality. Yet he said absolutely nothing. He really gave me a tongue lashing in Birkenau, when I went on and on about the terrible conditions. He screamed, "I don't want to hear anymore about any existing difficulties! For an SS officer there are no difficulties. His task is always to immediately overcome any difficulty by himself! As to how? That's your headache, not mine!" Kammler and Bischoff got the same answers. After inspecting Birkenau, Himmler witnessed the complete extermination process of a transport of Jews which had just arrived. He also looked on for a while during a selection of those who would work and those who would die without any complaint on his part. Himmler made no comment about the extermination process. He just looked on in total silence. I noticed that he very quietly watched the officers, the NCOs and me several times during the process. The inspection continued to the Buna Works, where he inspected the plant as thoroughly as he had done with the prisoner workers and how they did their jobs. He saw and heard about their state of health. Kammler was told in no uncertain terms, "You complain about problems, but just look at what the IG Farben plant has accomplished in one year in spite of having the same problems as you!" Yet he said nothing about the fact that IG Farben had thousands of experts and approximately thirty thousand prisoners available at that time. When Himmler asked about the work quotas and the performance of the prisoners, the spokesmen for IG Farben gave evasive answers. Then he told me that no matter what, I had to increase the prisoners' output of work! Again it was up to me to find a way to accomplish this. He said this in spite of being told by the district leader and by IG Farben that soon the food rations for all prisoners were to be considerably decreased; even though he saw for himself the general conditions of the prisoners. From the Buna Works we went to the sewer gas installations. There was no programme at all because the materials were not available. This was one of the sorest points at Auschwitz and was everyone's main concern. The almost untreated sewage from the main camp was draining directly into the Sola River. Because of the continuing epidemics raging in the camp, the surrounding civilian population was constantly exposed to the danger of epidemic infections. The district leader quite clearly described these conditions and begged Weise to remedy this situation. Himmler answered that Kammler would work on the matter with all his energy. Himmler was much more interested in the next part of the inspection, the natural rubber plantations Koc-Sagys. He was always more interested in hearing positive reports rather than negative ones. The SS officer who was able to give only positive reports and was clever enough to show even the negative things in a positive light was both lucky and enviable. On the evening of the first day of the inspection tour, all the guests and camp officers of Auschwitz were present at a dinner. Himmler asked all of them to introduce themselves before dinner; to those he was interested in, he asked about their families and the various' duties they performed. During the dinner he questioned me more closely about some of the officers who caught his special attention. I took this opportunity and explained my needs concerning staffing. I stressed in detail the large number of officers who were unable to run a concentration camp and their poor leadership qualities concerning the guard troops; I also asked him to replace many of them and increase the number of guard troops. "You will be surprised," he answered, "to see how you will have to deal with impossible leadership types. I need every officer, NCO, and soldier that I can use on the front lines. For these reasons it is impossible to increase your guard units. Just get more guard dogs. Invent every possible technical way to save on manpower to guard the prisoners. My deputy of the dog squad will soon acquaint you with the modern, up-to-date deployment of guard dogs to illustrate how the number of guards can be reduced. The number of escapes from Auschwitz is unusually high and has never before happened to such a degree in a concentration camp. Every means," he repeated, "every means that you wish to use is perfectly all right with me to prevent escapes or attempts! The epidemic of escapes at Auschwitz must be stopped!" After dinner the district leader invited Himmler, Schmauser, Kammler, Caesar, and me to his house near Katowice. Himmler was also supposed to stay there because on the following day he had to settle some important questions concerning the local population and resettlement with the district leader. Even though he had been in a very bad mood during the day and had hardly talked with civility to any of us, during the evening he was just the opposite in our small circle; He was in a very good mood that evening, charming and very talkative, especially with the two ladies, the wife of the district leader and my wife. He discussed every topic that came up in conversation; the raising of children, new houses, paintings, and books. He told about his experiences with the Waffen-SS divisions at the front lines and about his front line inspection tours with Hitler. He carefully avoided mentioning, even with a single word, anything that he had seen during the day or any matters concerning official business. Any attempt by the district leader to bring business into the conversation was ignored by Himmler. We broke up quite late. Himmler, who usually drank very little alcohol, that evening had a few glasses of red wine and smoked, which was another thing he didn't usually do. Everyone was captivated by his lively stories and cheerfulness. I had never seen him like that before. On the second day Schmauser and I picked him up at the district leader's house, and the inspection continued. He looked at the original camp, the kitchen, and the women's camp. At that time the women were located in the first row of barracks, numbers 1 to 11, then next to the SS Headquarters building. Then he inspected the stables, the workshops, Canada, and the DAW (German armaments factories), the butcher shop, the bakery, the construction units, and the planning board for the troops. He examined everything thoroughly and saw the prisoners, asked about their reasons for being there, and wanted an accurate count. He did not allow us to lead him around. Instead he demanded to see the things he wanted to see. He saw the overcrowding in the women's camp, the inadequate toilet facilities, and the lack of water. He demanded to see the inventory of clothing from the quartermaster, and saw that everywhere there was a lack of everything. He asked about the food rations and extra rations given for strenuous labour down to the smallest detail. In the women's camp he wanted to observe the corporal punishment of a woman who was a professional criminal and a prostitute. She had been repeatedly stealing whatever she could lay her hands on. He was mainly interested in the results corporal punishment had on her. He personally reserved the decision about corporal punishment for women. Some of the women who were introduced to him and who had been imprisoned for a minor infraction he pardoned. They were allowed to leave the camp. He discussed the fanatical beliefs of the Jehovah's Witnesses with some of the female members. After the inspection we went to my office for a final discussion. There, with Schmauser present, he told me in essence the following. "I have looked at Auschwitz thoroughly. I have seen everything as it is: all the deplorable conditions and difficulties to the fullest, and have heard about these from all of you. I cannot change a thing about it. You will have to see how you can cope with it. We are in the middle of a war and accordingly have to learn to think in terms of that war. Under no circumstances can the police actions of the roundups and the transports of the enemy be stopped – least of all because of the demonstrated lack of housing which you have shown me. Eichmann's programme will continue and will be accelerated every month from now on. See to it that you move ahead with the completion of Birkenau. The Gypsies are to be exterminated. With the same relentlessness you will exterminate those Jews who are unable to work. In the near future the work camps near the industrial factories will take the first of the large numbers of able-bodied Jews; then you will have room to breathe again here. Also, in Auschwitz you will complete the war production facilities. Prepare yourself for this. Kammler will do his very best to fully support you concerning the construction programme. The agricultural experiments will be pushed ahead intensively, as I have the greatest need for the results. I saw your work and your accomplishments. I am satisfied with them and I thank you. I hereby promote you to lieutenant colonel!" This is how Himmler finished

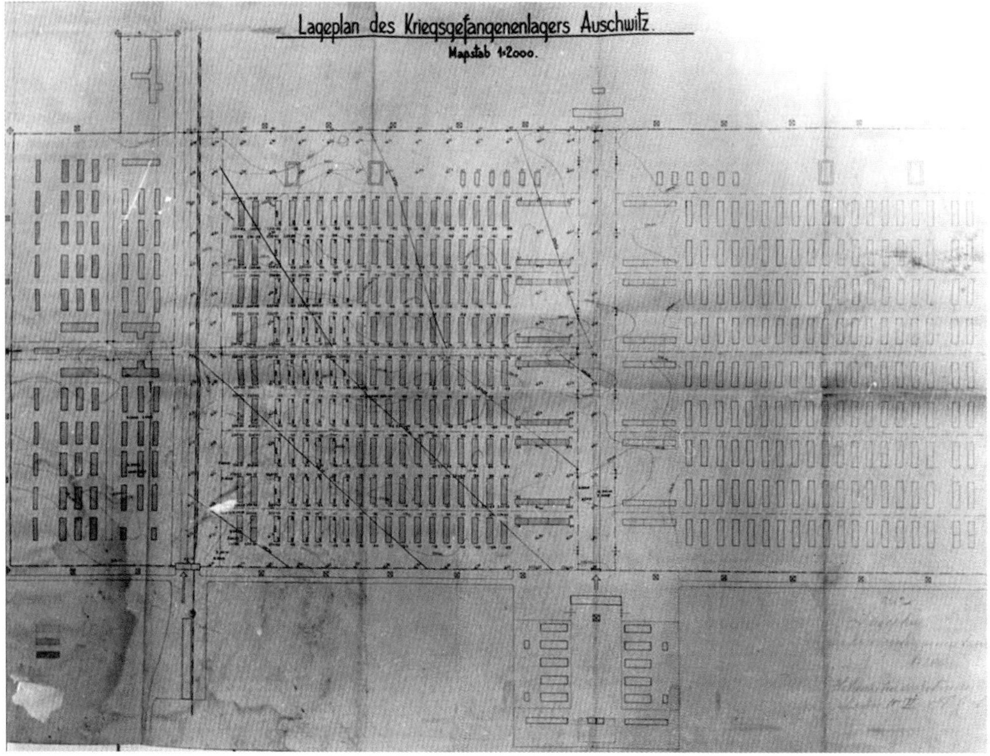

This map of the Birkenau camp was probably drawn on 6 June 1942.
Bauleitung drawing with no identification block.
Lagesplan des Kriegsgefangenenlagers (Situation plan of PoW camp).
Maßstab (Scale) 1:200 [should be 2000].
Hohenkoten des Gelandes im Abschnitt II GKL (Ground level contours in construction stage II of PoW camp). (*Auschwitz-Birkenau State Museum*)

his important inspection of Auschwitz. He saw everything and understood all the consequences. I wonder if his 'I am unable to help you' statement was intentional? After our meeting and discussion in my office, he made an inspection of my home and its furnishings. He was very enthusiastic about it and talked at length with my wife and the children. He was excited and in high spirits. I drove him to the airport; we exchanged brief goodbyes, and he flew back to Berlin'.

By the time Himmler arrived in July the Birkenau site had been completely transformed, with many of the drainage ditches dug and lots of the barracks assembled. But the camp still resembled a building site. The first sector, known as BI, intended for 20,000 inmates, had already been completed. Located next to this area, which was still under construction, was sectors II and III. These sectors would soon be capable of holding more than 60,000 prisoners. The whole site was built on a truly grand scale, and although Himmler said nothing as he toured the site on 17 July, Höss noted that the *Reichsführer* appeared impressed. He showed particular interest in the drainage and sewage works that were under construction by gangs of emaciated inmates. As Himmler made his way through the site he witnessed first-hand the terrible overcrowding of the barracks, and the primitive existence in which the prisoners lived. For some time he watched the prisoners at work, inspected the kitchens and saw the sick bays. Here in the overcrowded sick bays, where conditions were dreadful, the camp doctor openly explained to Himmler the deteriorating situation among many of the able-bodied inmates. Sickness among them was spiralling out of control. It was clear that the camp was in a catastrophic condition. Whether it had been bad planning, poor design or just incompetence, the sewage and washing facilities needed to be rectified rapidly before disease wiped out all those fit for hard labour.

After inspecting the Birkenau camp, according to Höss, their attention was turned to the other reason Himmler had visited, to see firsthand the complete process of 'special treatment'. Since early summer the *Reichsführer* had taken direct personal control over the RSHA and was determined to demonstrate his competence and ability in his new role as the architect of genocide. For the first time in his murderous career, he watched the complete procedure of extermination. From the main entrance of Birkenau Höss led the company to the railway spur, which was adjacent to the main line. Here the *Reichsführer* watched with interest as a new Jewish transport from the Netherlands were being selected. Those fit enough for work would live; those unfit would be loaded onto waiting trucks and transported to the Birkenau gas chamber for 'special treatment'. They finally completed the inspection by watching the killing procedure at Bunker II. Afterwards, Himmler and the delegation departed from the camp, saying very little to each other.

During the early evening all guest and camp officers of Auschwitz were present at a formal dinner in the presence of their *Reichsführer*. The following morning Himmler inspected more of the main camp, but this time did not want to be led around and demanded to inspect only areas that he wanted to see. After the tour of the camp, Himmler made it clear to Höss that although he understood the difficult circumstances of overcrowding and other problems in the camp, he would have to live with it. He told him that he had already authorised a major expansion of the camp at Birkenau and this would ensure Eichmann would be able to intensify his deportation programme of Jews. He added that Gypsies too would also be shipped to Birkenau, and all those unfit for labour would be exterminated along with the Jews. He tried to reassure his commandant that the work camps near the industrial factories would soon take large numbers of able-bodied Jews, and this would allow him room to breathe again. He also told Höss that he was to complete the war production facilities at Auschwitz. Kammler would do his very best to fully support him concerning the construction programme.

Soon afterwards both men, accompanied by their entourage, set out for Monowitz. Touring the massive IG Farben site, the *Reichsführer* appeared once more thoroughly impressed. From the Buna works they proceeded to tour a wastewater treatment plant.

Already tons of untreated sewage flowed into the Vistula and Sola rivers from Birkenau. Himmler had seen firsthand the terrible sanitary problems at the camp and was increasingly concerned that illness and disease would spread throughout the Auschwitz zone of interest. During the tour he proposed that a sewage plant needed to be built at Birkenau. Himmler also made it known that Höss must reduce the pollution problems. The 107,000 corpses that had been buried in Birkenau that were decomposing were polluting the ground water. These corpses, he added, had to be dug up and burned on specially constructed grills. June and July had been particularly hot months and during the first week of July the buried corpses had started to putrefy. Rotting bodies were rising to the surface and there was a terrible stench across the camp. Plagues of rats too were seen gnawing at the corpses and there was evidence of the first cases of typhus fever in the communal camp of the civilian workers deployed in Birkenau.

In order to reduce the problem a giant improvised makeshift cremation pit was soon erected. A massive hole was dug and wooden beams acting as a grill were placed across at ground level. At once a number of special units consisting of 1,400 prisoners were ordered to disinter the bodies with their bare hands. A huge fire was built with wood and petrol and the corpses were simply thrown on to the enormous pyre of burning rags, flesh and bone.

The already terrible state of affairs was made worse by the typhus epidemic, which by the second week of July had spread to the prisoners of Birkenau. A report in early July outlined that sanitary conditions were rapidly worsening, the mortality rate among able-bodied prisoners was rising, the Jewish transports were arriving so frequently that there was concern that hygienic and sanitary conditions in the camp would worsen to catastrophic levels. To make matters even worse, the crematorium in the main camp had not been functioning properly since early June because its chimney was worn-out. At the beginning of July the crematorium went out of service so that the chimney could be removed and relined.

In spite the mounting problems that commandant Höss and his staff faced during July 1942, the *Bauleitung* continued improvising plans for existing buildings and designing new structures as well. In fact, following Himmler's visit on 24 July plans were drawn for new apartments in the *Haus der Waffen-SS*, which was situated opposite the Auschwitz railway station. The plans were at the behest of Höss himself following his uncomfortable tour of Birkenau and the terrible conditions he witnessed. The drawings were for an apartment which would be built for his boss. It would include a room for his adjutant and a couple of additional rooms for the *Obergruppenführers* which might be staying with Himmler on his future visits to the area. Furthermore, the drawings also included ornate furniture too, specially designed for the apartment.

Whilst plans were being put together for Himmler's new apartment, another building which had already been planned and approved was being completed

Solahütte (SS-Hütte Soletal, or SS Hütte Porabka), which was a little-known resort for SS personnel and administration of the Auschwitz/Birkenau/Buna concentration camp complex. It was built by camp prisoners in 1940, 1941 and 1942. (*USHMM*)

Another image showing the *Solahütte* retreat. Originally, some twenty prisoners were selected for the construction of the building, but later this number was increased to around forty. Eight SS men were assigned from Auschwitz, headed by *Kommandoführer SS-Oberscharführer* Franz Hössler. (*USHMM*)

some thirty miles away. It was a sanatorium and recreation building for the SS. This wooden-structured building was called *Solahütte* and was built on a hillside overlooking the Porabka Lake. Construction on the building had commenced in 1941. It was primarily built for visiting SS personnel wanting to relax and play following a day's murdering at the camp. It would also be used for SS men and women recuperating from typhus.

Prisoners that were employed constructing *Solahütte* were housed in the basement of a house located on the slope below the construction site. Artur Rablin, a former prisoner, testified: '*There were about fifty prisoners working there with me – all of them Polish – and we all lived in a basement situated under some villa*'. SS personnel lived on the ground floor and upper floor of the building. The site was heavily guarded.

Below is a list of the initial group of prisoners sent from Auschwitz to assist in the construction of the retreat:

Stefan Krawczuk	Jan Lupa Nr. 63
Konstanty Krawczuk	Franciszek Kmak
Bogdan Sawczuk	Tadeusz Orłowski
Zbigniew Zasadzki	Roman Pociecha
Paweł Gacki	(?) Gabryś
Ludwik Kubacki	(?) Galas (Kapo)
Józef Podeszwa	(?) Winand
Marian Mykała	Władysław Gut, zam. Sanok

Source: Setkiewicz, Piotr, *Voices of Memory 13: The SS Garrison in KL Auschwitz*, published by International Center for Education About Auschwitz and the Holocaust. Auschwitz-Birkenau State Museum, 2018, p.174.

According to accounts of former prisoners, the construction of the *Solahütte* was completed in 1942. By this period, the first group of prisoners was returned to the Auschwitz main camp, and another group of prisoners were sent in order to complete the interior of the building.

The *SS Hütte* Porombka was officially opened on 21 April 1941. Commandant Höss announced the opening of the SS rest and recreation centre in an order to SS staff which read:

'Special Commandant Order

Auschwitz, April 17, 1941
Re: Leave for the Soletal (Sola Valley) SS rest and recreation centre
The Soletal centre will open on Monday, 21 April 1941

The head chef will be SS-Sturmmann Setzer from the 1st guard company and as cook SS-Mann Herms from the SS kitchen, seconded to the centre on Friday, April 18, 1941. Both of these SS men will be in contact with SS-Oberscharführer Blaufuß,

At *Solahütte SS-Obersturmführer* Karl Höcker and some women belonging to the *SS-Helferinnen* (women volunteers who worked in the administrative offices of the concentration camps, mainly as typists, telephone, telegraph clerks, and secretaries) relax on lounge chairs on a deck in *Solahütte*, probably at the end of July 1944. The original caption reads 'On the terrace of the lodge'. The SS retreat was visited not only by low-ranking SS men, but also commanders of the individual camps of the Auschwitz complex and their senior officers. (*USHMM*)

SS officers together with women and a baby relax on lounge chairs on a deck in *Solahütte*. (*USHMM*)

A group of SS officers stand in front of a building at *Solahütte*. Pictured facing the camera, second from the left, is *SS-Obersturmführer* Karl Höcker. Next to him is *SS-Obersturmführer* Max Sell, between 1943 and 1945 first *Arbeitseinsatzführer* in Auschwitz and afterwards in Mittelbau-Dora. (*USHMM*)

who will be responsible for supplying the Soletal men. The SS canteen will open as a sales point at the centre. The average capacity will be about 30 persons. By Friday of every week, the guard battalion shall report the number of designated SS men. They will depart at 04.00 hrs from the SS quarters in Auschwitz and return on Saturday afternoon. For every group of SS men the battalion shall designate a non-commissioned officer responsible for the training conducted in Soletal and for keeping the centre in proper order; he will also be responsible for any damage. On weekends the centre shall be at the disposal of the SS men from the commandant staff. Those who wish to spend the weekend there are to report by 14.00 hrs every Friday to SS-Unterscharführer Woldförster at the commandant's office secretarial pool. They will leave from Auschwitz at 14.00 hrs on Saturday and return in the early hours of Monday morning. Telephone communication with Auschwitz will be by way of the camp for Volksdeutsche from Bukowina in Soletal.'

Source: Setkiewicz, Piotr, *Voices of Memory 13: The SS Garrison in KL Auschwitz*, published by International Center for Education About Auschwitz and the Holocaust. Auschwitz-Birkenau State Museum, 2018, p.174.

A group of SS officers standing in front of a building in *Solahütte*, the SS retreat outside of Auschwitz. Among those pictured are Franz Hoessler (front) and Karl Solahütte (third from the right). Also pictured on the far right is *SS-Obersturmführer* Max Sell. At the back centre is Hermann Baltasar Buch. From 1943 until September 1944 Buch was in charge of the crematory IV in Birkenau. (*USHMM*)

A photograph of SS officers at *Solahütte* enjoying a moment of camaraderie as they sing to the accompaniment of an accordion. Note the men in the front row who are not singing. They include: Karl Hocker, Otto Moll (head of the gas chambers at Birkenau), Rudolf Höss, Richard Baer, Josef Kramer (standing slightly behind Hossler and partially obscured), Franz Hossler, Josef Mengele, Anton Thumann, and Walter Schmidetzki. Konrad Wiegand, head of the *Fahrbereitschaft* (car and truck pool) is also present. (*USHMM*)

The *Solahütte* was often regarded as a treat for the SS personnel that were given leave there. These gatherings were known as *Kameradenschaft*, or social meetings where the SS could recuperate, relax and build a bond of camaraderie. These vacations could vary from a day's stay to a week. It was not just low-ranking SS personnel that would visit; it was also senior officers and members of the *SS Helferinnen* too that would travel by car or bus from Auschwitz. In fact, there were many high ranking officers from Auschwitz that visited the retreat including Otto Ambros, a manager of the German IG Farben chemical firm, which exploited Auschwitz prisoners as slave labourers.

Visiting the retreat meant that the SS and their guests could escape from the everyday, criminal operations that they themselves had instigated or played a part in. Many of them were well aware of the significant tasks ahead. The evolution of Auschwitz in 1941 meant that most personnel that visited the retreat, especially those of high ranking status, bore the pressures of Himmler's ever demanding needs and requirements to turn the Auschwitz complex into a vast labour pool and murder factory.

During late July 1942 a number of important meetings were held to discuss and further Himmler's new master plan for the transformation of Auschwitz-Birkenau. In their discussions they decided how best to enlarge camp Birkenau to a capacity of 200,000 inmates. During the meeting it was outlined that the Birkenau killing facility was totally inadequate and nothing more than a short-term solution to the 'mast plan' of the camp. For this reason, Bischoff had drawn up a plan of the Birkenau site to include two crematoria, numbered II and III. The crematorium at the main camp was renamed Crematorium I. Another crematorium, known as Crematorium IV was sketched in next to Bunker I, and Crematorium V sketched next to Bunker II. It was estimated that each crematorium had an incineration capacity of 576 corpses a day. From inception both Crematoria IV and V were to operate as killing centres. They would have their own gas chambers, morgue, and a furnace hall. The other crematoria would also be transformed to operate as killing machines. Birkenau, it seemed was finally evolving and developing into a major factory of death.

However, in the meantime as further plans were drawn-up for the new crematoria, Bunkers I and II continued gassing many more Jews. From all over Europe, including Slovakia, France, Belgium and the Netherlands, Jewish men, women and children were herded into Birkenau like cattle and sent to their death. Yet in the midst of this horror Auschwitz was still playing only a minor part in the slaughter of the Jews. The major killings were already established in the forests of Poland – Belzec, Sobibor and Treblinka. But the final transformation of Auschwitz came on 26 September. Höss received instructions from Pohl that all possessions belonging to the majority of prisoners entering Auschwitz were to be confiscated for good, labelled and stored. Initially, all possessions had been stored in Block 26 in the main camp, but there was so much looted property that the Auschwitz authorities were forced to erect six barracks near to the main camp. From these special storage facilities all foreign currency, valuables, gold and other precious metals were authorised to be transported to SS headquarters in Berlin. Usable clothing, shoes, bed linen, blankets, fabrics, and household utensils were to be directed to the Ethnic German Liaison Office and distributed for the use of German settlers. As for unusable clothing and other pieces of material, these were instructed to be sent directly to the Reich Ministry of Economy and used for the war effort. It was confirmed that the transportation of all these goods was being planned, and with the number of Jews destined for Auschwitz the yield would be enormous.

However, the biggest problem that summer was still corpse disposal and the sanitary conditions. In order to accelerate the cremations, Höss accompanied by *SS-Untersturmführer* Franz Hössler and the head of the blueprint office *SS-*

Obersturmführer Walter Dejaco visited the Linzmannstadt Ghetto to see for themselves the open air cremation ditches run by *SS-Standartenführer* Blobel. When Höss returned he ordered the acceleration of the exhumations and cremation of the corpses. Initially they had been burning the dead and using the body fat to help keep the pyres alight. But now they had decided to douse them with crude oil, but later this was replaced by methanol.

The cremations, however, did not prevent typhus spreading across the camp. On 23 July there had been a total lock-down of the installation, but the spread of disease was still killing people. In August alone 14,300 inmates died from the epidemic. The guards too were not immune from the outbreak and a number of them were struck by the disease. So virile was the infection that even the wife of *SS-Obersturmbannführer* Joachim Caesar contracted typhus and died. Caesar himself also came down with the disease and was off duty for nearly two weeks. It had also spread into the town of Auschwitz as well. With the epidemic ravaging Birkenau and surrounding areas, including cases in the main camp, there was an eagerness to get the construction of the crematoria completed as quickly as possible. In fact, construction of the crematoria had already begun in earnest with several hundred workers allocated to building them.

Despite the massive pool of labour, the Auschwitz construction office knew they would be unable to carry out the building project on their own. Although the inmates were capable of building wooden barracks, residential buildings and digging drainage systems, they required civil engineering firms for the actual construction. In total, eleven construction companies were involved in the building of all the crematoria. The civilian firm Huta from Kattowitz was already working on the shell of Crematorium II, and then on Wednesday, 23 September began work on Crematorium IV. A total of about 80 men worked on the site, 60 or so were prisoners, of which 20 worked for the Auschwitz contractor Koehler on building the chimneys. In total between 100 and 150 persons, of whom the majority were prisoners, were employed on the individual work sites. In order to ensure all the firms worked well together a *Sonderführer* would manage the works in progress and see that the job was completed efficiently and as quickly as possible. For the ensuing weeks and months to come he oversaw firms like Karl Falck from Gleiwitz and the Triton Company from Kattowitz that handled the drainage work of Crematoria III, IV, and V. The Klug Company from Gleiwitz which helped Topf and Sons build the furnaces of Crematoria IV and V. Huta who were contracted to complete the floor and walls of the two underground morgues of Crematorium II, whilst the Vedag Company from Breslau were paid to waterproof the cellars of Crematoria II and III.

Overleaf are drawings of the future Crematorium IV.

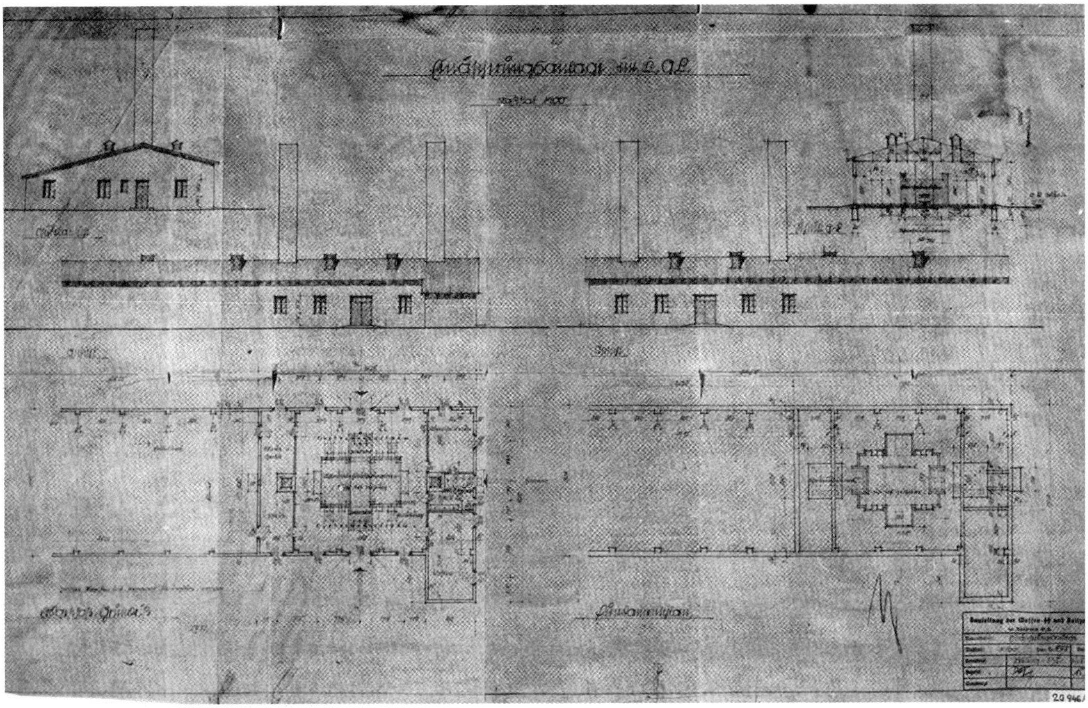

This first drawing by the *Bauleitung* was drawn by prisoner 538 on 14 August 1942. It was checked by SS Dejaco and approved by SS Bischoff on 15 September 1942. (*Auschwitz-Birkenau State Museum*)

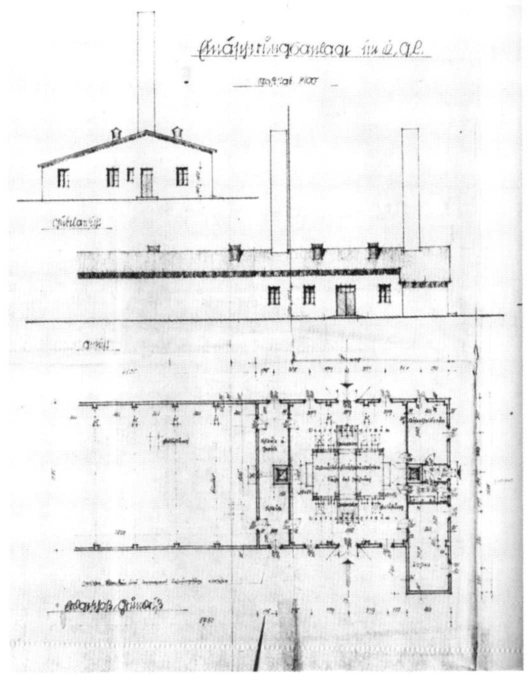

(*October Revolution Central State Archives*)

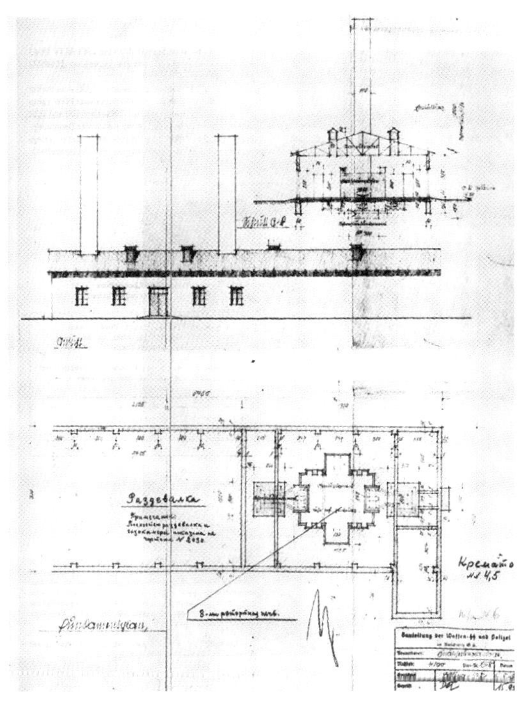

(*October Revolution Central State Archives*)

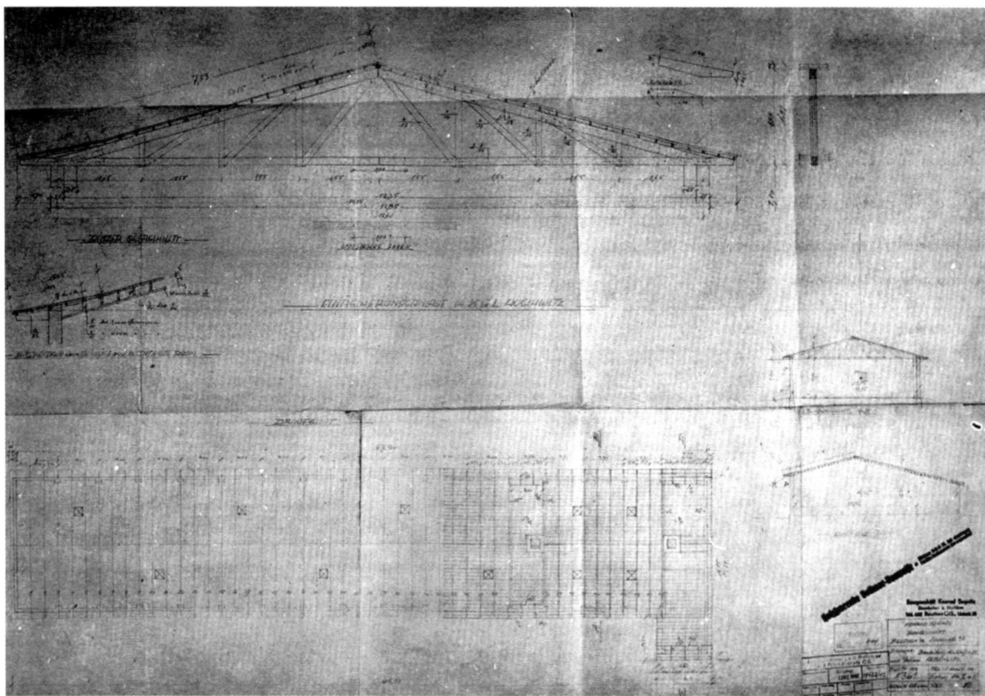

Konrad Segnitz drawing 1361, dated 14 October 1942. The drawing shows a cross section through the truss of the roof, including supporting plates and the roof over air lock and rest room. (*Auschwitz-Birkenau State Museum*)

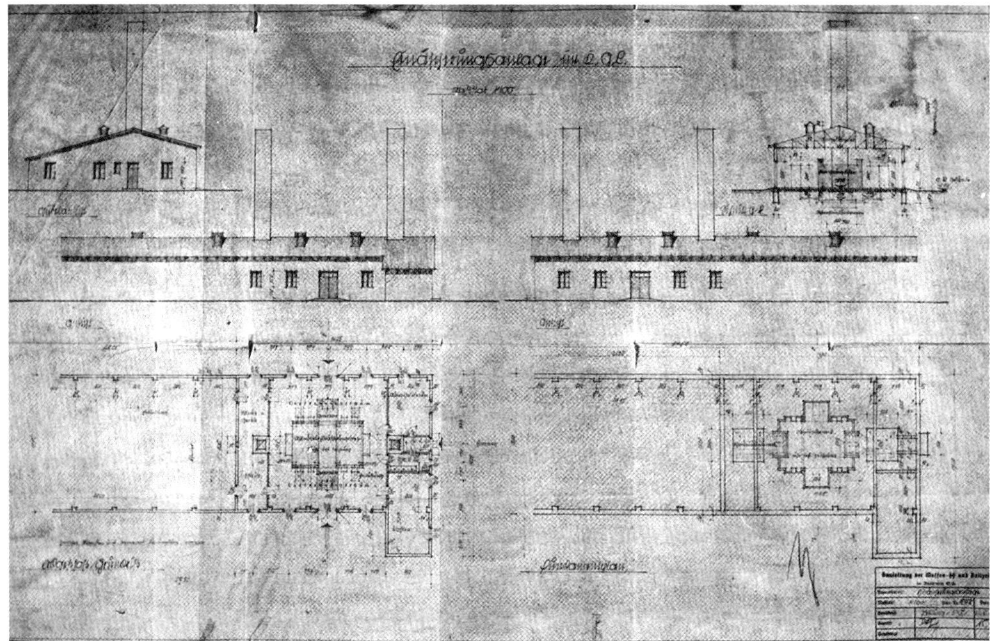

An interesting drawing showing facades (north, south and east and one on the top includes a plan view of one level) of Crematorium IV dated 14 August 1942 by Haftling 538 (construction technician Leon Sawka), and reviewed on 15 September 1942 by Walter Dejaco and then approved by Karl Bischoff. (*Auschwitz-Birkenau Archives*)

Whilst the building of the crematoriums continued laboriously at Birkenau, on 23 September Pohl arrived on a special visit to see firsthand the progress made at Auschwitz and to inspect the SS factories that he himself had initiated. After a discussion about the building projects in the construction headquarters they toured the local area, including a visit to the local armaments works. Pohl's inspections were very thorough and his officials then proceeded to Birkenau. Here they inspected the camp, which by this stage was ravaged by disease, and then watched a gassing procedure at Bunker II. In the evening, along with other senior personnel, they had dinner in the officers' mess, which was remembered as a real feast. There was baked pike, open sandwiches, real ground coffee and excellent beer. Afterwards Pohl made a speech and told his audience of the special task ahead, an assignment, he said, which was not to be spoken about. To the SS personnel listening to Pohl's speech it was obvious he was referring to the so-called 'Final Solution' of the Jewish question.

During this period plans were still being discussed and drawn-up for the construction of the crematoria in Birkenau. On 13 October a letter was sent regarding an award of the contract for construction work at Auschwitz.

13 October 1942

Correspondence register no. 16093 /42/Ja/Mh

Subject: Award of contract for construction work in the construction work in the Waffen-SS prisoner of war camp at Auschwitz, Upper Silesia

Reference: None
Enclosures: 14

SS Economic and Administrative Head Office
Head of Office C/III
Berlin Lichterfelde West
Unter den Eichen 126 135

Enclosed please find the following estimates, with request for authorization to conclude contract:

1) Estimate of 27/1/42, tender of Huta, Civil Engineers, Kattowitz, Friedrichstraße 19, with 9 annexes, for a total of RM 227 321.59

2) Estimate of Messrs Lenz & Co. Industrial Builders, Kattowitz, Grundmannstraße 23. i.e.:

Estimate no 1 of 31/12/41 amounting to	RM	145	543.70
with a supplement of 7/7/42 of	RM		406.40
Estimate no 2 of 7/7/42 amounting to	RM	53	854.98

3) Estimate of 13/7/42 for the construction of the new crematorium according to the tender by Huta, Civil Engineers, Kattowitz, Friedrichstraße 19 amounting to

RM 133 756.65

PTO

Another letter noted the urgency for work to commence due to the situation caused by what it refers to as 'special treatment'.

> 'Because of the extreme urgency, the above mentioned work has already been allocated to the firms, subject to approval by the competent service. The contracts will be concluded on receipt of this authorization.
>
> Regarding 1) and 2)
> As regards the PoW camp construction work, it was necessary to start at once in October 1941 on special contract. The construction order was given by Zl. II B So 8/3/Se/Lo of 1/11/41.
>
> In view of the urgency of the work, the normal call for tenders procedure was not followed, because in any case Huta, Civil Engineers. and Lenz & Co. Industrial Builders, both of Kattowitz, were the only firms we were able to find who would be able start immediately, and who, at the same time had available the vast amount of equipment necessary, such as portable packs, excavators, cement mixers and other machinery.
>
> The orders for the work were given verbally, to Huta on 4 and 6/10/41 and to Lenz on 8/10/41, with the instruction to commence construction work immediately. Both firms declared that they could not make a firm estimate at the beginning of the job because they did not know the conditions of work within the camp, and in particular the capabilities of the prisoners to be employed.
>
> The estimates subsequently submitted have been checked and found to be in accordance with local usage.
>
> Regarding 3)
> As regards the construction of the new crematorium building, it was necessary to start immediately in July 1942 because of the situation caused by the special

actions. The firms Huta, Civil Engineers, Kattowitz Friedrichstraße 19, and Lenz & Co, Industrial Builders, Kattowitz, Grundmannstraße 23, were invited to tender, as they were already working in the PoW camp.'

According to their letter of 15/7/42, Messrs Lenz & Co declined to tender because of a shortage of labour. For this reason, Huta was asked to commence work immediately on the basis of their tender of 13/7/42.

'The Central Construction Management requests your approval and the return of the enclosed original estimates with a view to concluding the contracts.

Head of the Waffen-SS and Police
Construction Management Auschwitz

[signed] Bischoff
SS Captain

Copy to:
Waffen-SS Construction Inspectorate
For the Eastern Reich
Posen

The summer of 1942 saw the inception of the construction of crematoria at Birkenau. In fact, contracts for the building work for Crematoria II and III were awarded on 29 July, with the first drawing for the future Crematorium IV created on 14 August. The contract for the construction of the four chimneys for Crematorium IV was awarded to Messrs Robert Koehler on 20 August. It was agreed that the incineration capacity of the camp was to be increased to 52 muffles.

Plans for Crematorium IV measured 67m x 12m, and comprised of a cremation area, which included a furnace room, a separating airlock, and a morgue. In total there were three different phases to the plans for this crematorium. The second phase of the plans, was submitted later that year. The drawing of the roof produced by Messrs Konrad Segnitz showed a complete cremation installation with its furnaces and morgue and these areas were ventilated by six chimneys. Further modifications included the creation of two gas chambers which were designed to be used alternately. There was no undressing room at this stage of the planning and it was proposed a nearby undressing hut would be erected in order to facilitate with the gassing process. Inside the gas chambers there were plans for 4 gas-tight doors and 6 openings for pouring in the Zyklon-B. These would be fitted with gas-tight shutters.

An acceptance tender form dated 29 July was sent by the Auschwitz Waffen-SS and Police Central Construction Management to Huta, which was a structural and civil engineering firm, regarding the construction of works for a new crematorium. The letter outlined the following:

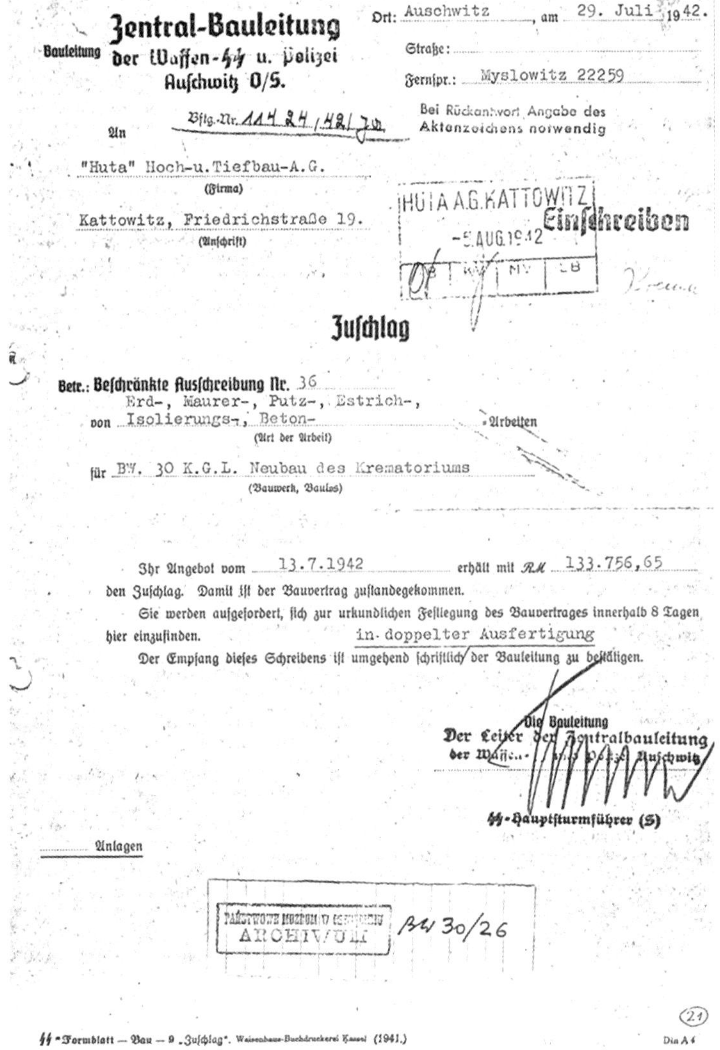

Zentral-Bauleitung der Waffen-SS u. Polizei Auschwitz O/S.

Ort: Auschwitz, am 29. Juli 1942.
Straße:
Fernspr.: Myslowitz 22259

Bftg.-Nr. 14424/42/Jo

Bei Rückantwort Angabe des Aktenzeichens notwendig

An "Huta" Hoch-u.Tiefbau-A.G. (Firma)
Kattowitz, Friedrichstraße 19. (Anschrift)

HUTA A.G. KATTOWITZ
-5. AUG. 1942

Einschreiben

Zuschlag

Betr.: Beschränkte Ausschreibung Nr. 36
von Erd-, Maurer-, Putz-, Estrich-, Isolierungs-, Beton- Arbeiten (Art der Arbeit)
für BW. 30 K.G.L. Neubau des Krematoriums (Bauwerk, Baulos)

Ihr Angebot vom 13.7.1942 erhält mit RM 133.756,65 den Zuschlag. Damit ist der Bauvertrag zustandegekommen.
Sie werden aufgefordert, sich zur urkundlichen Festlegung des Bauvertrages innerhalb 8 Tagen hier einzufinden. in doppelter Ausfertigung
Der Empfang dieses Schreibens ist umgehend schriftlich der Bauleitung zu bestätigen.

Die Bauleitung
Der Leiter der Zentralbauleitung der Waffen-SS u. Polizei Auschwitz
SS-Hauptsturmführer (S)

Anlagen

ARCHIWUM
BW 30/26

21

SS-Formblatt — Bau — 9 „Zuschlag". Waisenhaus-Buchdruckerei Kassel (1941.) Din A 4

Acceptance of tender form, dated 29 July 1942, and sent by the Auschwitz Waffen-SS and Police Central Construction Management to Huta, a structural and civil engineering firm, concerning the site preparation, bricklaying, facing, flooring, insulation and concreting work for the new crematorium building BW [worksite] 30 at Birkenau, in accordance with the estimate of 13 July 1942 amounting to 133,756.65 RM. The acceptance was signed by the Head of the *Bauleitung*, Karl Bischoff, and was received by Huta on 5 August 1942. Two buildings were in fact constructed, the second being the future Crematorium III, worksite 30a. No acceptance of tender has been found for it. (*Auschwitz-Birkenau State Museum*)

Waffen-SS and Police
Central Construction Management
Auschwitz

Auschwitz 3 September 1942
When replying
quote Reference number

Correspondence register no. 12771/42/Str/Qu

Subject: Damp-proofing work in the Crematorium of the PoW camp
Reference: Inspection of the worksite by SS Captain (S) Bischoff on 3/9/42
Enclosure/

Huta, Hoch- und Tiefbau-
Aktiengesellschaft
Kattowitz

The two excavations for the above building were completed about 10 days ago, so that the damp-proofing work absolutely must begin immediately.

After several conversations on this subject with your foreman Herr Stephan, the start of this work has been fixed for Monday, 7/9/42. The Bauleitung expects this date to be respected without fail, for the lateness of the season allows of no further delay.

Head of the Waffen-SS and Police
Construction Management Auschwitz

[signed] Bischoff
SS Captain (S)

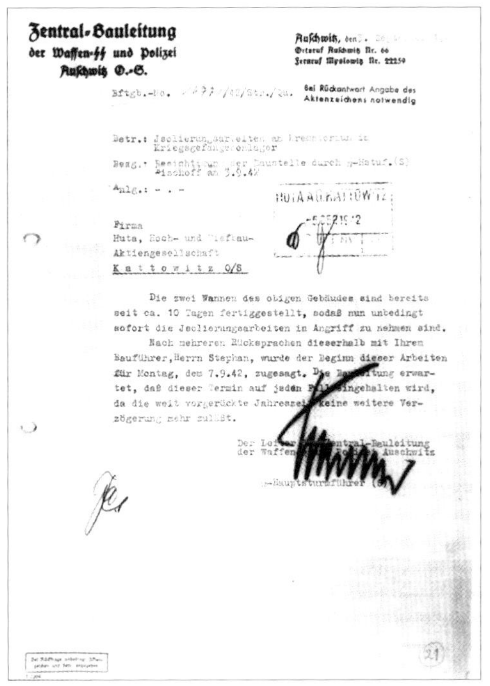

Zentral-Bauleitung
der Waffen-SS und Polizei
Auschwitz O.-S.

Auschwitz, den 3. [illegible]
Ortsruf Auschwitz Nr. 66
Fernruf Myslowitz Nr. 22259

Bftgb.-No. [illegible]/42/Str./Qu.

Bei Rückantwort Angabe des Aktenzeichens notwendig

Betr.: Jsolierungsarbeiten am Krematorium im Kriegsgefangenenlager
Bezg.: Besichtigung der Baustelle durch SS-Hstuf.(S) Bischoff am 3.9.42
Anlg.: - . -

HUTA AG KATTOWITZ

Firma
Huta, Hoch- und Tiefbau-
Aktiengesellschaft
K a t t o w i t z O/S

Die zwei Wannen des obigen Gebäudes sind bereits seit ca. 10 Tagen fertiggestellt, sodaß nun unbedingt sofort die Jsolierungsarbeiten in Angriff zu nehmen sind.

Nach mehreren Rücksprachen dieserhalb mit Ihrem Bauführer, Herrn Stephan, wurde der Beginn dieser Arbeiten für Montag, den 7.9.42, zugesagt. Die Bauleitung erwartet, daß dieser Termin auf jeden Fall eingehalten wird, da die weit vorgerückte Jahreszeit keine weitere Verzögerung mehr zuläßt.

Der Leiter der Zentral-Bauleitung
der Waffen-SS und Polizei Auschwitz

SS-Hauptsturmführer (S)

(*Auschwitz-Birkenau State Museum*)

In early October 1942 work began on Crematorium II, although no exact date exists regarding when work got underway. There was indication of works on 9 October from the fitters Martin Holick and Willi Koch, but there is proof that senior SS and civilian officials visited the site on 20 August and it's likely the foundations and basement construction began probably at the end of the month. Huta, for instance, requested to carry out the damp proofing work on the basements as early as 12 August. Vedag was the company that undertook the damp proofing and gave a guarantee of two years.

On 7 September Vedag agreed to Huta's request to carry out the work required, whilst outlining they needed the specific materials to undertake the job. Huta informed Vedag that they needed felt and bitumen, but warned that the initial quotation of two layers of bitumen was not enough. They now required three layers.

On 22 September a drawing was submitted and approved by Bischoff. The digging of the drainage ditches was to coincide with the construction of the crematoria.

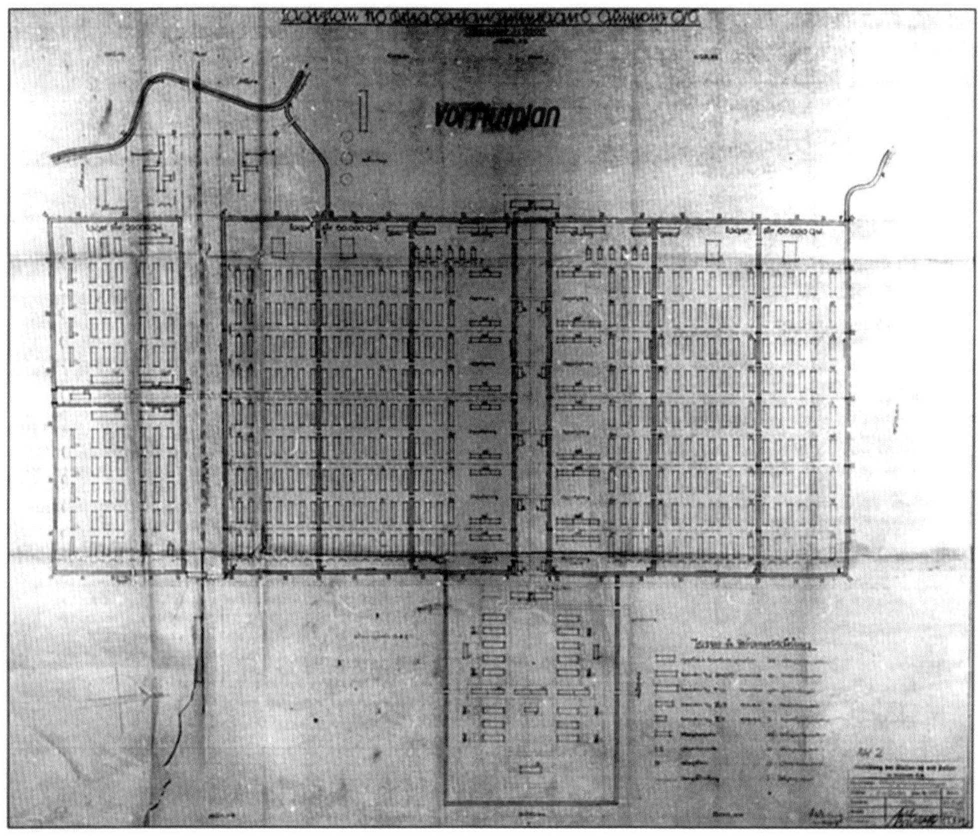

(*Auschwitz-Birkenau State Museum*)

Plan of Auschwitz PoW Camp, Upper Silesia

Plan of drainage ditches

Scale 1:2000

Drawing 1697

Drawn 22/9/42 by prisoner 15592

Checked by SS Second Lieutenant Ertl and approved by SS Captain Bischoff.

The first construction stage was to contain 20,000 prisoners, the second 60,000 and the third 60,000.

At the same time the drainage ditches were being discussed and planned, between 26 and 29 October Bischoff compiled a cost estimate of the complete Birkenau project, outlining it for 'carrying out special treatment'. The list of works included:

27 washing and toilet barracks
12 infirmary barracks
10 block leader barracks

182 housing and storage barracks
3 washing barracks
6 toilet barracks
3 utility barracks
11 uniform store and administration barracks
Substation
Electric lighting
Emergency power plant
Alarm and telephone installation
2 *Kommandantur* and washing barracks
Sewage system
Water supply installation
Railroad siding
Cooking kettles and stoves
Troop housing barracks
Troop delousing unit
Delousing unit
Warehouse 1
Watch-towers and barbed wire for fence
4 crematoria
4 morgues
Workshop hall, 3 camp barracks and 1 housing barrack for supervisors
Disinfestation plant II, 2 washing and 2 toilet barracks for civilians
Workers camp II
Disinfestation plant I and 4 housing barracks for civilian workers
Utility barracks
Bakery

'Vorhaben: Kriegsgefangenenlager Auschwitz (Durchführung der Sonderbehandlung)', VHA, Fond OT 31(2)/8.

A photograph taken by the author during a visit to Birkenau in August 2024. It shows one of the drainage ditches that was dug in BIa Women's camp between the fence perimeter and the service road towards the main camp gate. (*HITM courtesy of Auschwitz-Birkenau State Archive*)

On the same day as the inspection report on Crematorium II, another report was sent. This report followed a visit by Bischoff, Kirschneck and Prüfer, accompanied by other *Bauleitung* SS and representatives of all the civilian firms working on the work sites 30, 30a, 30b, and 30c. It reported:

Copy
29 January 1943
Correspondence register no. 22250/43/Bi/L

Subject: Crematorium II. State of construction
Reference: SS WVHA telegram 2648 of 28/1/43
Enclosure: 1 Inspection Report

Head of Amtsgruppen C
SS Lieutenant General and Waffen-SS Major General
Dr Ing [Engineer] Kammler
Berlin Lichterfelde West
Unter den Eichen 126-135

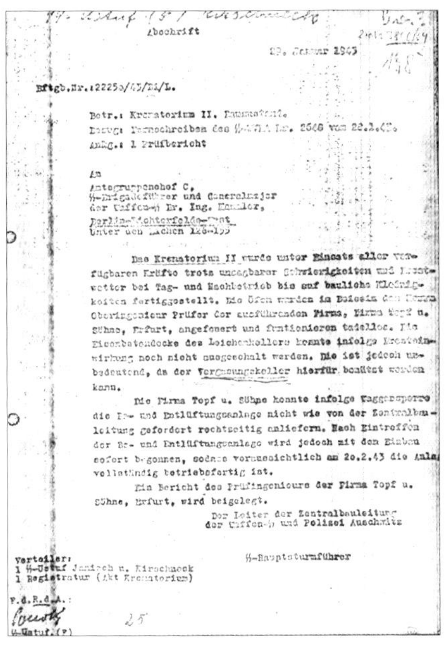
Abschrift

29. [illegible] 1943

Bftgb.Nr.:22250/43/Bi/L.

Betr.: Krematorium II. [illegible]
[illegible] Fernschreiben des [illegible] Nr. 2648 vom 28.1.43.
Anlg.: 1 Prüfbericht

An
Amtsgruppenchef C,
[illegible]-Brigadeführer und Generalmajor
der Waffen-[illegible] Dr. Ing. [illegible],
Berlin-Lichterfelde-[illegible]
Unter den Eichen 126-135

Das Krematorium II wurde unter Einsatz aller verfügbaren Kräfte trotz [illegible] Schwierigkeiten und [illegible]wetter bei Tag- und Nachtbetrieb bis auf bauliche Kleinigkeiten fertiggestellt. Die Öfen wurden im Beisein des Herrn Oberingenieur Prüfer der ausführenden Firma, Firma Topf u. Söhne, Erfurt, angefeuert und funktionieren tadellos. Die Eisenbetondecke des Leichenkellers konnte infolge [illegible]einwirkung noch nicht ausgeschalt werden. Die ist jedoch unbedeutend, da der Vergasungskeller hierfür benützt werden kann.

Die Firma Topf u. Söhne konnte infolge Waggonsperre die Be- und Entlüftungsanlage nicht wie von der Zentralbauleitung gefordert rechtzeitig anliefern. Nach Eintreffen der Be- und Entlüftungsanlage wird jedoch mit dem Einbau sofort begonnen, sodass voraussichtlich am 20.2.43 die Anlage vollständig betriebsfertig ist.

Ein Bericht des Prüfingenieurs der Firma Topf u. Söhne, Erfurt, wird beigelegt.

Der Leiter der Zentralbauleitung
der Waffen-[illegible] und Polizei Auschwitz

[illegible]-Hauptsturmführer

Verteiler:
1 [illegible]-Ustuf Janisch u. Kirschneck
1 Registratur (Akt Krematorium)

F.d.R.d.A.:
[signature]
[illegible]-Ustuf.(F)

25

Crematorium II has been completed but for minor details, thanks to employing all available forces, despite enormous difficulties and freezing weather, using day and night shifts. The furnaces have been lit in the presence of Herr Chief Engineer Prüfer of the firm responsible for their construction, Topf & Sons of Erfurt, and they function perfectly. Because of the frost, it has not yet been possible to remove the formwork from the ceiling of the corpse cellar. This is of no consequence, however, as the gassing cellar can be used to this end [i.e, as a morgue].

Because the wagons are blocked, Messrs Topf & Sons have not been able to deliver on time the ventilation and air extraction installations as requested by the Bauleitung. These will be fitted as soon as they arrive, so that it is probable that the installation will be entirety ready for service on 20th February 1943.

Please find enclosed a report by the inspecting engineer of Topf & Sons, Erfurt.

Head of the Auschwitz Waffen-SS and Police
Central Construction Management

[signed] Bischoff
SS Captain

Distribution:
1 SS Second Lieutenants Janisch and Kirschneck
1 Registration F

or Archives
(signed) Pollok
SS Second Lieutenant (S)

(*Auschwitz-Birkenau Museum*)

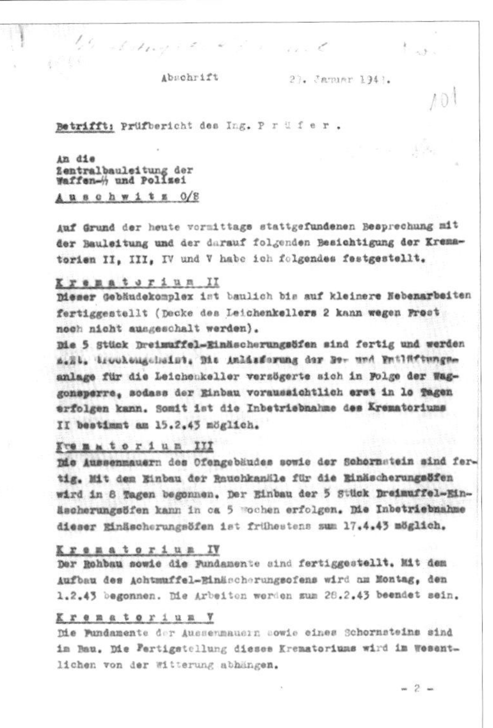

Abschrift 29. Januar 1943.

/101

Betrifft: Prüfbericht des Ing. P r ü f e r .

An die
Zentralbauleitung der
Waffen-SS und Polizei
A u s c h w i t z O/S

Auf Grund der heute vormittags stattgefundenen Besprechung mit der Bauleitung und der darauf folgenden Besichtigung der Krematorien II, III, IV und V habe ich folgendes festgestellt.

K r e m a t o r i u m II
Dieser Gebäudekomplex ist baulich bis auf kleinere Nebenarbeiten fertiggestellt (Decke des Leichenkellers 2 kann wegen Frost noch nicht ausgeschalt werden).
Die 5 Stück Dreimuffel-Einäscherungsöfen sind fertig und werden z.Zt. trockengeheizt. Die Anlieferung der Be- und Entlüftungsanlage für die Leichenkeller verzögerte sich in Folge der Waggonsperre, sodass der Einbau voraussichtlich erst in 10 Tagen erfolgen kann. Somit ist die Inbetriebnahme des Krematoriums II bestimmt am 15.2.43 möglich.

K r e m a t o r i u m III
Die Aussenmauern des Ofengebäudes sowie der Schornstein sind fertig. Mit dem Einbau der Rauchkanäle für die Einäscherungsöfen wird in 8 Tagen begonnen. Der Einbau der 5 Stück Dreimuffel-Einäscherungsöfen kann in ca 5 Wochen erfolgen. Die Inbetriebnahme dieser Einäscherungsöfen ist frühestens zum 17.4.43 möglich.

K r e m a t o r i u m IV
Der Rohbau sowie die Fundamente sind fertiggestellt. Mit dem Aufbau des Achtmuffel-Einäscherungsofens wird am Montag, den 1.2.43 begonnen. Die Arbeiten werden zum 28.2.43 beendet sein.

K r e m a t o r i u m V
Die Fundamente der Aussenmauern sowie eines Schornsteins sind im Bau. Die Fertigstellung dieses Krematoriums wird im Wesentlichen von der Witterung abhängen.

– 2 –

Copy
29 January 1943
Subject: Inspection report by engineer Prüfer

To Waffen-SS and Police Central Construction Management

Auschwitz Upper Silesia

As a result of this morning's conversation with the Bauleitung and the subsequent visit to Crematoria II, III, IV and V, I have established the following:

Crematorium II
This complex is completed, from the standpoint of construction, but for secondary details (the form work cannot yet be removed from corpse cellar 2 because of the frost).

The 5 three muffle incineration furnaces are completed and are at present being warmed through to dry them. Delivery of the ventilation and air extraction systems for the corpse cellars has been delayed by the blockage of wagons, so that it will probably not be possible to install them for another 10 days. It will therefore certainly be possible to bring Crematorium II into service on 15/2/43.

Crematorium III
The external walls of the furnace building [actually room) and the chimney are completed. In 8 days installation of the incineration furnace flues will begin. Installation of the 5 three-muffle incineration furnaces can be done in about 5 weeks. It will be possible to bring these incineration furnaces into service at the earliest on 17/4/43.

Crematorium IV
The shell and the foundations are completed. Construction of the eight muffle incineration furnace will begin on Monday, 1/2/43. Work will be completed for the 28/2/43

Crematorium V
The foundations of the external walls and of one chimney are under construction. Completion of this crematorium will depend mainly on weather conditions.

(*Auschwitz-Birkenau Museum*)

On Monday, 1 February, a team of bricklayers, civilians and prisoners, working for Messrs Robert Koehler, finally completed the chimneys of Crematoria III. The following day Bischoff sent Prüfer a report to Höss, to inform him of progress on all four crematoria.

There was still slow progress with the construction of Crematoria IV and V. Walls on both crematoria were built in mid-December 1942, following order for bricks placed on 9 December. Order 9680 authorised 70,000 bricks for Crematorium IV

The inspection of the above mentioned crematoria and their internal installations has shown that despite the great amount of construction work involved and the difficulties due to weather conditions and the supply of materials, work has progressed rapidly.

Signed for J A Topf & Sons
Chief Engineer Prüfer

For Archives
[signed] Pollok
SS Second Lieutenant (S)

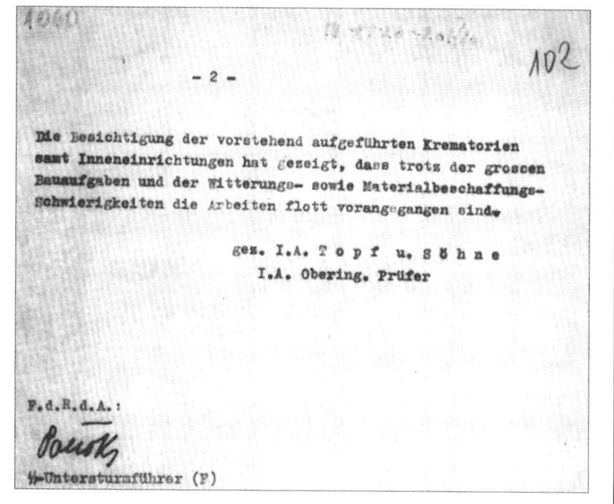

4060

102

- 2 -

Die Besichtigung der vorstehend aufgeführten Krematorien samt Inneneinrichtungen hat gezeigt, dass trotz der grossen Bauaufgaben und der Witterungs- sowie Materialbeschaffungs-Schwierigkeiten die Arbeiten flott vorangegangen sind.

gez. I.A. T o p f u. S ö h n e
I.A. Obering. Prüfer

F.d.R.d.A.:
Pollok
SS-Untersturmführer (F)

(*Auschwitz-Birkenau State Museum*)

and Order 9682 was made for an additional 100,000 bricks. For Crematorium V Order 9681 was made for 120,000 bricks. A total of 290,000 bricks were ordered for the construction.

For the building of these two sites there were no less than nine civilian firms in Upper Silesia participating in their construction. Each company was given a specific role and job in the construction process. The shells were constructed by Huta of Kattowitz and Riedel & Sons of Bielitz. The roof was designed by Konrad Segnitz of Beuthen and built by Industrie-Bau AC of Bielitz. The chimneys were built by Robert Koehler of Myslowitz. The 8-muffle furnaces were constructed by Josef Kluge of Alt Gleiwitz under the supervisor of the manufacturers, Topf & Sons of Erfurt. The external sewers and drains were installed by Karl Falck of Gleiwitz and 'Triton' of Kattowitz. The initial estimate of costs for Crematorium IV was 247,000 RM, but following a correction by the *Bauteilung* or the Inspectorate for Silesia they were able to reduce the cost to 203,000 RM. The largest saving was on the shell of the building. Work on Crematorium IV had begun on 23 September 1942 and the building was formally handed over by the *Bauleitung* to the Camp Administration on 22 March 1943. However, there were minor works and alterations carried out between 24 April and 8 May 1943.

The firms involved in the construction were paid well for their efforts. Messrs Topf & Sons received 22,000 RM for the 8-muffle furnace and an air extraction system costing some 8,000 RM, whilst Koehler was paid 60,000 RM for the two chimneys. No other costs were found regarding the paying of the other firms.

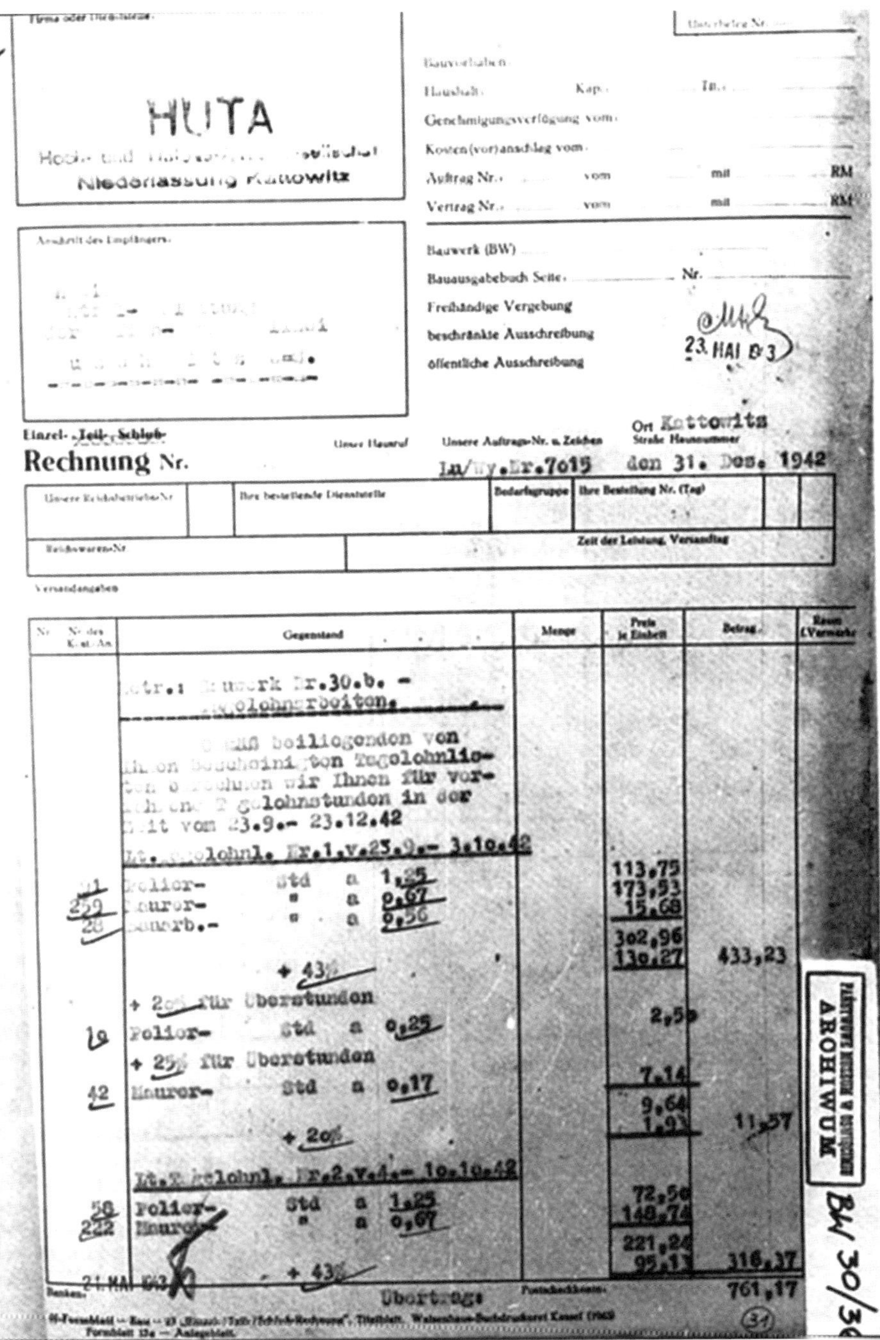

Firma oder Dienststelle:

HUTA
Hoch- und [illegible] gesellschaft
Niederlassung Kattowitz

Bauvorhaben:
Haushalt: Kap.: Tit.:
Genehmigungsverfügung vom:
Kosten(vor)anschlag vom:
Auftrag Nr.: vom mit RM
Vertrag Nr.: vom mit RM

Anschrift des Empfängers:
[illegible]

Bauwerk (BW)
Bauausgabebuch Seite: Nr.
Freihändige Vergebung
beschränkte Ausschreibung
öffentliche Ausschreibung

23. MAI 43

Einzel- ~~Teil-~~ ~~Schluß-~~
Rechnung Nr.
Unser Hausruf
Unsere Auftrags-Nr. u. Zeichen: Ia/[illegible].Nr.7015
Ort Kattowitz
Straße Hausnummer
den 31. Dez. 1942

Unsere Reichsbetriebs-Nr. | Ihre bestellende Dienststelle | Bedarfsgruppe | Ihre Bestellung Nr. (Tag)
Reichswaren-Nr. | Zeit der Leistung, Versandtag
Versandangaben

Nr.	Nr. des Kost.-An.	Gegenstand	Menge	Preis je Einheit	Betrag	Raum f. Vermerke
		Betr.: [illegible] Nr.30.b. - [illegible]lohnarbeiten.				
		[illegible] beiliegenden von [illegible] Tagelohnlis- [illegible] wir Ihnen für vor- [illegible] Tagelohnstunden in der [illegible] vom 23.9.- 23.12.42				
		Lt. [illegible]lohnl. Nr.1,v.23.9.- 3.10.42				
	91	Polier- Std a 1,25		113,75		
	259	Maurer- " a 0,67		173,53		
	28	[illegible]arb.- " a 0,56		15,68		
				302,96		
		+ 43%		130,27	433,23	
		+ 20% für Überstunden				
	19	Polier- Std a 0,25		2,5[illegible]		
		+ 25% für Überstunden				
	42	Maurer- Std a 0,17		7,14		
				9,64		
		+ 20%		1,93	11,57	
		Lt. T[illegible]lohnl. Nr.2,v.4.- 10.10.42				
	58	Polier- Std a 1,25		72,50		
	222	Maurer- " a 0,67		148,74		
				221,24		
		+ 43%		95,13	316,37	
		Übertrag:			761,17	

21. MAI 1943

Banken: Postscheckkonto:

PAŃSTWOWE MUZEUM W OŚWIĘCIMIU ARCHIWUM

BW 30/3[illegible]

(31)

(*Auschwitz-Birkenau Museum*)

Below is an invoice dated 31 December 1942 sent to the Auschwitz *Bauleitung* by the Kattowitz branch of Huta, regarding the hours of work to be paid for foremen, bricklayers and labourers employed at worksite 30b, Crematorium IV, for the period 23 September to 23 December 1942.

Tagesbericht

Baustelle: Enteisungsanlage 4

Arbeiter- und Stundenzahl — Verarbeitete Baustoffe

	Arbeiterzahl	Arb.-Stunden
[...]iere	2	19½
[...]urer	23	218½
[...]merleute	2	19
[...]eiter	58	552
[...]chinist		
[...]iede		
[illegible]	1	10
	86	819

Tagesleistungen

Position	Art und Menge der geleisteten Arbeiten
1.	Weitere Wänden und Decken [illegible]
2.	Die Fenster, Entlüftungen u. Türstöcken einsetzen samt Schrägen herstellen.
3.	Zementestrich legen, [illegible] d. Fußboden, sowie Aufschüttung anfahren planieren und stampfen in beiden Kammern.
4.	Den Giebelmauer gleich mit d. Lattung aufmauern Dachplatten [illegible]
5.	4 Maurer bei Ofenbau Kremat. 3.
6.	1 " Kanhrame [illegible] fertig stellen in Kremat. 3
7.	Ordnungsdienst Unterkunft

Bemerkungen:

W. RIEDEL & SOHN Eisenbeton- und Hochbau BIELITZ

(*Auschwitz-Birkenau Museum*)

The timesheet was completed by a Riedel & Son foreman who listed the works undertaken by himself and his team of labourers on Crematorium IV dated Wednesday, 3 March 1943. Riedel & Son worked on the site BW 30b from 23 January until 18–20 March 1943.

In fact, Topf & Sons only gave a two month guarantee on the furnaces as the company knew that the SS would overload them and burn them to full capacity, causing constant technical issues.

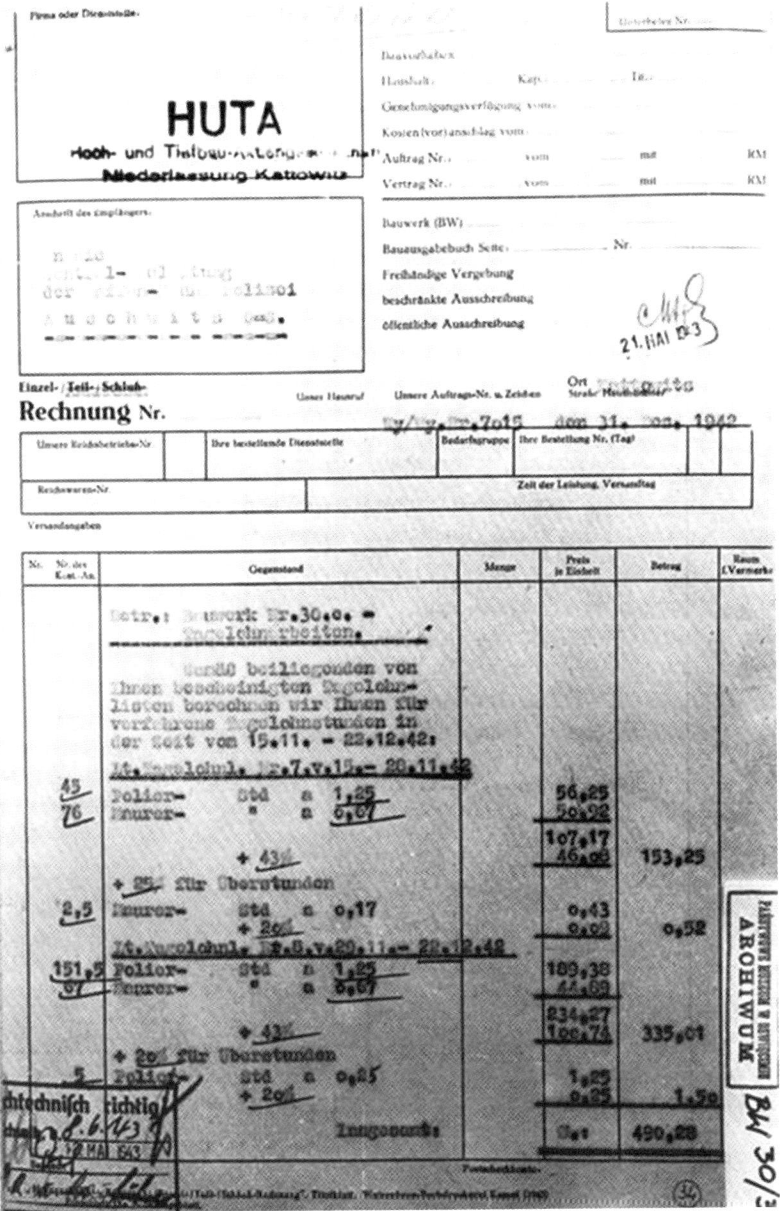

Firma oder Dienststelle:

HUTA

Hoch- und Tiefbau-[illegible]

Niederlassung Kattowitz

Bauvorhaben

Haushalt: Kap: Tit.:

Genehmigungsverfügung vom:

Kosten(vor)anschlag vom:

Auftrag Nr.: vom mit RM

Vertrag Nr.: vom mit RM

Anschrift des Empfängers:

[illegible] Polizei

Auschwitz [illegible]

Bauwerk (BW):

Bauausgabebuch Seite: Nr.

Freihändige Vergebung

beschränkte Ausschreibung

öffentliche Ausschreibung

21. MAI 1943

Einzel- / Teil- / Schluß-

Rechnung Nr.

Unsere Auftrags-Nr. u. Zeichen: [illegible] 7015

Ort: Kattowitz den 31. [illegible] 1942

Nr.	Nr. des Kont.-An.	Gegenstand	Menge	Preis je Einheit	Betrag	Raum (Vermerke)
		Betr.: Bauwerk Nr. 30.c. – [illegible]lohnarbeiten.				
		Gemäß beiliegenden von Ihnen bescheinigten [illegible]lohnlisten berechnen wir Ihnen für verfahrene [illegible]lohnstunden in der Zeit vom 15.11. – 22.12.42:				
		lt. [illegible]lohnl. Nr. 7 v. 15.– 20.11.42				
	45	Polier- Std à 1,25		56,25		
	76	Maurer- " à 0,67		50,92		
				107,17		
		+ 43%		46,08	153,25	
		+ 25% für Überstunden				
	2,5	Maurer- Std à 0,17		0,43		
		+ 20%		0,09	0,52	
		lt. [illegible]lohnl. Nr. 8 v. 29.11.– 22.12.42				
	151,5	Polier- Std à 1,25		189,38		
	67	Maurer- " à 0,67		44,89		
				234,27		
		+ 43%		100,74	335,01	
		+ 20% für Überstunden				
	5	Polier- Std à 0,25		1,25		
		+ 20%		0,25	1,50	
		Insgesamt:		[illegible]	490,28	

[illegible]technisch richtig

8.6.43

12 MAI 1943

ARCHIWUM

BW 30/3[illegible]

(*Auschwitz-Birkenau Museum*)

Invoice of 31 December 1942 sent to the Auschwitz *Bauleitung* by the Kattowitz branch of Huta, outlining the hours of work to be paid for foremen and bricklayers employed at worksite 30c, Crematorium V, for the period 15 November to 22 December 1942.

(*Auschwitz-Birkenau Museum*)

Report of the work undertaken by a gang of 6 (including the foreman) employed by Huta, who 'fitted gas-tight doors' (Gastüren einsetzen) at Crematorium V on 16 and 17 April 1943. The foreman in charge of this work was called Zettelman.

As for Crematorium V, works had officially begun on 15 November 1942 and was handed over on 4 April 1943. However, it was not made operational until 18 April as there were still snag-works and various alterations required. There were no cost prices that survived the war, but it's probable that the costing of the crematorium was similar to that of Crematorium IV.

With the near completion of both crematoria the SS camp administration was more interested in their incineration capacity. Later that year a letter dated 28 June 1943 was sent by the Auschwitz *Bauleitung* to their superiors in Berlin. It was calculated that 768 corpses per unit in twenty-four hours, or a total of 1,536 per day for both crematoria could be achieved. This figure was, however, an educated guess, and authorities in Berlin took this calculation as a realistic estimate. They never took into consideration the practicability of the operation and the technical issues that followed. They never thought for one moment, in spite of professional advice from Topf & Sons, that when the crematoria were completed the SS would overwork the crematoria until they broke down.

Whilst the crematoria were still in their construction phase, shipments of Jews often had to be redirected to Treblinka and Sobibor. Treblinka itself was already functioning at full capacity and as a result trains were often backed up for hours, whilst those running the camp frantically tried clearing the Jews awaiting to go through for 'special treatment'.

Two *Bauleitung* officers consulting a drawing during a work detail. It shows the laying of the stone bed for a road between Crematoria IV and V in the summer of 1942. The officers are probably Karl Bischoff, head of the *Bauleitung*, and Walter Dejaco, Head of the Drawing Office. Behind Bischoff, on his right, is a civilian. probably an employee of Lenz & Co. one of the civilian firms working at Birkenau on the construction of the PoW camp. The company were specialist in ground works. (*Auschwitz-Birkenau State Archive/Yad Vashem*)

SS-Reichsführer Heinrich Himmler smiling with commandant Rudolf Höss during Himmler's two-day tour, 17–18 July 1942. (*Auschwitz-Birkenau State Archive/Yad Vashem*)

Four photographs taken in sequence which were part of a photo album from the camp's Political Department Identification Service, under the direct control of commandant Rudolf Höss. This was regarded as a significant visit, as Himmler was inspecting the expansion of the Auschwitz complex, including Birkenau and the IG Farben plant. SS officers Bernard Walter and Ernest Hofmann took the photos showing Himmler's tour of the IG Farben plant. Fritz Bracht, and Higher SS and Police Leader Ernst-Heinrich Schmauser and other personnel made a visit to Auschwitz via the airport at Kattowitz with Himmler. Touring the massive IG Farben site the *Reichsführer* appeared thoroughly impressed. From the Buna works they proceeded to tour a wastewater treatment plant. (*Yad Vashem, Auschwitz-Birkenau State Museum, Instytut Pamieci Narodowej*)

Himmler examines a building plan with Max Faust (wearing the fedora) during an inspection tour of the Monowitz-Buna building site. Max Faust worked as a site manager for IG Farben near Breslau in Silesia, initially during the construction. He first visited the site in January 1941. Here Faust is explaining to Himmler the progress of the construction work for the plant on 18 July 1942. (*USHMM*)

SS officers observing forced labourers. The first of the four Birkenau areas planned for construction was built in the village of Birkenau during the winter of 1941/1942 and during the remainder of 1942, and divided into two sectors, BIa and BIb. (*Yad Vashem*)

The southern entrance to the men's camp, under construction. Birkenau camp area measured in total 750 x 1,800m. Two roads leading from the east to the west divided the camp into three large construction sections (*Bauabschnitt*, abbreviated B) called B-I, B-II and B-III. The individual construction sections were divided into smaller sections denoted by lowercase letters. Each section had a special function that changed a number of times during the camp's operation. (*Yad Vashem*)

A comparison photograph taken by the author in August 2024 at Auschwitz-Birkenau showing the entrance between BIId Mens Camp (left) and BIIc Transit Camp for Jewish Women from Hungary (right). (*HITM couretesy of Auschwitz-Birknau State Archive*)

Two photographs taken of the barracks in the men's quarantine camp BIIa before construction of the surrounding barbed wire. (*Yad Vashem*)

Construction of some of the barracks in Birkenau. The first part of the construction of BIa and BIb began in late 1941 and eventually would comprise of 62 residential barracks (30 brick and 32 wooden), along with 10 barracks comprising of washrooms and toilets, 2 kitchens, 2 bathhouses, and 2 storage barracks. (*Yad Vashem*)

Three photographs showing the first model of the wooden guard towers that were erected at Auschwitz-Birkenau. These images were taken by the author during his visit to the site in August 2024. These guard towers were of a basic construction and were erected around the fences at Birkenau. There were four wooden piles that supported the observation platform surrounded by a railing and covered roof. These watch towers were often manned by two guards, one that operated the searchlight during night duties and the other armed with a machine gun. (*HITM courtesy of Auschwitz-Birkenau State Museum*)

Interior of an inmate barracks. The first drawing planned to accommodate 550 PoWs. This estimate was then crossed-out and corrected to house 744 prisoners with 62 bunks. The bunks were a permanent structure and built in three tiers. The base bunk was brick, and the other two wooden. The barracks did not have proper foundations and were supported by a thin layer of concrete, which could become wet and cold. Much of the construction of the barracks was to be built from wood. A German company had already designed the standard army horse stable barrack, and this would be produced and dispatched to Auschwitz as a kit where it could easily be erected and dismantled. It was argued that these prefabricated wooden huts could be assembled very rapidly with a gang of just thirty unskilled men led by one carpenter. In total 253 of these huts were assigned to Birkenau. (*Yad Vashem*)

In the middle of these wooden barracks there was an ineffective brick heating duct, heated at both ends occasionally by a brick stove. As strange as it was, during the planning process of these barracks part of the planning regulations outlined that the buildings had a heating facilitiy. However, the heating was totally inadequate and impractical, and often the stoves were never used due to the lack of fuel or materials for burning. (*Yad Vashem*)

Two photographs showing the construction of sewage purification pools to the south of Crematorium II. (*Yad Vashem*)

A photo of the construction of Crematorium II. Contracts for the building work for Crematorium II were awarded on 29 July 1942. It was not until early October 1942 that work on Crematorium II began, although no exact date has been found. (*Yad Vashem*)

Tiling of Crematorium II. Note in the foreground of the image on the right, next to the timber covered with snow, you can see the exposed wall of the underground gas chamber. Foundations and basement construction began probably at the end of October or in early November 1942. Huta, for instance, requested to carry out the damp proofing work on the basements as early as 12 August. Vedag was the company that undertook the damp proofing and gave a guarantee of two years. (*Yad Vashem*)

Construction of the steel reinforcements for Crematorium II undressing room roof, probably in early January 1943. During December 1942, work on the building had to he interrupted a number of times due to illness and bad weather. On 27 January 1943, the *Bauleitung* informed Huta in a letter that their engineer, Herr Stephan, had not used a special frost-protection liquid when pouring the concrete roof of the mortuary, despite the cold weather. At considerable cost and time, it was now being dug, which potentially delayed the handover date of Crematorium II. *Bauleitung* made it clear that Huta would take the consequences of the faults and had to complete the shell almost on time. (*Yad Vashem*)

Camp prisoners digging drainage ditch south of Crematorium II. (*Yad Vashem*)

Construction of Crematorium III. Contracts for the building work for Crematorium III were awarded on 29 July 1942, the same day as Crematorium II. (*Yad Vashem*)

Part of Crematorium III in scaffolding during the early winter of 1943. On Monday, 1 February 1943, a team of bricklayers, civilians and prisoners, working for Messrs Robert Koehler, finally completed the chimneys of Crematorium III. (*Yad Vashem*)

Construction of Crematorium III. On 1 March 1943 the contract for the roof of Crematorium III was awarded to Industrie Bau AG, following a quote of 9,418.04 RM. (*Yad Vashem*)

Construction of the roof of the undressing room of Crematorium III during the early winter of 1943. (*Yad Vashem*)

Above: Construction of Crematorium IV from the crematorium side. It shows one of the chimneys in scaffolding being constructed. For the building of Crematorium IV, there were no less than nine civilian firms that participated in their construction. Each company was given a specific role and job in the construction process. The shells were constructed by Huta of Kattowitz and Riedel & Sons of Bielitz. The roof was designed by Konrad Segnitz of Beuthen and built by Industrie-Bau AC of Bielitz. The chimneys were built by Robert Koehler of Myslowitz. Work on Crematorium IV had begun on 23 September 1942. A total of about eighty men worked on worksite 30b, sixty or seventy of them being prisoners, 20 of whom worked for Koehler on building the chimneys. (*Yad Vashem*)

Right: A photograph showing the second chimney of Crematorium IV completed. The contract for the construction of the four chimneys for Crematorium IV was awarded to Messrs Robert Koehler on 20 August 1942. It was agreed that the incineration capacity of the camp was to be increased to 52 muffles. (*Yad Vashem*)

Three photographs showing the construction of Crematoria III known as 'Worksite 30a'. The chimney is clearly surrounded by scaffold. The photographs were most likely taken in late January and early February 1943. (*Yad Vasham*)

Construction of Crematorium IV. Plans for Crematorium IV measured 67m x 12m, and comprised of a cremation area, which included a furnace room, a separating airlock, and a morgue. In total there were three different phases to the plans for this crematorium. The second phase of the plans were submitted in late 1942 of the drawing of the roof produced by Messrs Konrad Segnitz. The drawing showed a complete cremation installation with its furnaces and morgue and these areas were ventilated by six chimneys. Further modifications included the creation of two gas chambers which were designed to be used alternately. There was no undressing room at this stage of the planning and it was proposed a nearby undressing hut would be erected in order to facilitate the gassing process. (*Yad Vashem*)

A view of the construction of the whole south-side of Crematorium IV. Note that just to the left of the building is a temporary watchtower. The windows have just been installed. Works had officially begun on 15 November 1942. Order 9681 was made for 120,000 bricks. A total of 290,000 bricks were ordered for the construction. On 4 April 1943, Crematorium V was officially handed over to the camp administration, but the installation was still not deemed fully operational, since the gas-tight doors to the gas chambers were still to be fitted. Work on the doors was completed between 16 and 17 April by a civilian firm working for Huta. (*Yad Vashem*)

A photograph showing labourers working on the construction of what was known at Auschwitz-Birkenau as the Central Sauna building. The Central Sauna building had commenced construction in May and entered service in December 1943, following a number of minor alterations to its original plans. (*Yad Vashem*)

Construction of the foundations for the Central Sauna during the summer months of 1943. (*Yad Vashem*)

An SS officer and an engineer overseeing the construction of a sewage purification facility east of sector BIIa, summer 1943. (*Yad Vashem*)

A typical worksite inspection visit to Birkenau, probably taken in the summer of 1943. The SS officer appears to be Jothann who would soon become head of the *Bauleitung*. He is overseeing the construction of a sewage water treatment plant, which was located to the east of the external road running along Birkenau BIIa parallel with drainage during the second construction stage (BA II). (*Yad Vashem*)

An ornamental garden at the edge of Block BIIa. Construction on the second phase of the build known as BII began in 1942 and was not completed until the end of 1943. This area was divided into seven sectors comprising of wooden barracks. Sector BIIa comprised of sixteen residential barracks, three barracks with washrooms and toilets, and a kitchen barracks. Sectors BII b, c, d, and e each comprised thirty-two residential barracks, six barracks containing washrooms and toilets, and two kitchens. In sector BIIf there were seventeen residential barracks and one bathhouse barracks. Thirty barracks used mainly as warehouses were built in sector BIIg, along with one brick bathhouse (sauna). (*Yad Vashem*)

Four photographs taken in sequence by the author in August 2024 showing four brick buildings in B1a Women's camp. Thirty of these buildings were constructed in the first part of the camp, fifteen in sector BIa and fifteen in sector Bib. The first plans for these brick structures were drawn for the new Birkenau site on 7 October 1941 by Fritz Ertl, and approved by Bischoff on the following day. (*HITM courtesy of the Auschwitz-Birkenau State Archive*)

A photograph taken by the author in August 2024 showing one of the brick buildings in B1a Women's camp. Accompanying and assisting the author during his site visit of Birkenau were his friends Ian and Jayne Large who can be seen walking along the service road. (*HITM courtesy of the Auschwitz-Birkenau State Archive*)

Showing a view of the barracks at Birkenau during one of its construction phases in the winter of 1943. Note the small-gauge rail line travelling the full length of the camp carrying materials. By the spring of 1944 the camp's construction segments had been divided into sectors (camps) and separated by electrified barbed-wire fences. Guard towers surrounded the entire camp and a three-track railroad spur and unloading ramp went into operation in May 1944. A total of some 300 housing facilities, administrative, and barracks and buildings had been constructed including some ten miles of drainage ditches, thirteen miles of barbed-wire fencing, and over seven miles of roads within an area of some 140 hectares at Birkenau. (*Yad Vashem*)

Chapter IV

Operation of the Crematoria 1943

By 1943 Auschwitz-Birkenau was slowly being transformed into a factory of death which had all originated from the office of the *Zentral Bauleitung der Waffen-SS.* This SS-internal planning office under Bischoff was undoudtedly playing an important role in the state-organized mass murder of European Jews. Its construction management had designed, planned and willingly constructed buildings that would seal the fate of many thousands of innocent men, women and children being murdered in the structures that they had built. The year 1943 was a pinnacle year for the evolution of the camp and a major step towards the total implementation of what the SS referred to as 'special treatment'.

Only two years earlier, in 1941, the construction management comprised of thirty-four people, which was then subsequently increased to some ninety employees with various skills, comprising architects, draughtsmen, civil and electrical engineers, bricklayers, roofers, and ground workers. There were a variety of prisoners used for extensive planning and drawing tasks. In total, Auschwitz had around 140 SS members between 1941 and 1943. They organized the deployment of around 9,000 prisoners and 1,000 civilian workers. Planning decisions were under the supervision of twenty or so SS officers who all served at the camp.

The SS offices were organized into five departments, which comprised the following:

Construction management 1
Main camp (Hans Kirschneck): Expansion of the prisoner blocks, new construction of functional buildings in the command area, accommodation barracks and housing estates.

Construction management 2
Birkenau prisoner of war camp (Josef Janisch): Construction of 343 prisoner barracks, 158 functional barracks, four crematoria, gas chambers and morgues.

Construction management 3
Auschwitz industrial site (Werner Jothann): workshops DAW (Deutsche Equipmentwerke GmbH – German Equipment Factories), DEST (Deutschen

Erd- und Steinwerke GmbH – German Earth and Stone Works) and Friedrich Krupp AG (Fried. Krupp Aktiengesellschaft – Krupp heavy industries).

Construction management 4
Main economic camp of the Waffen-SS and troop economic camp Oderberg (Josef Pollok): magazine building and office barracks.

Construction management 5
Gut Freudenthal and Partschendorf (SS-Unterscharführer Mayer): Buildings for agricultural businesses – improvements from 1944 (Josef Frenk) the crematoria for the implementation of the final solution.

Yet, in spite of the expansion of the construction manangment offices of the *Bauleitung*, Höss sent a communication to Bischoff about his decision of wanting to withdraw Polish inmates from the staff of the offices. Bischoff was concerned about the commandant's decision as it would create serious consequences on the running of the offices, especially when some of the staff had already been removed and sent to the Eastern Front to fight. In a phone call to Höss Bischoff requested that he keep all the well trained workers. In total there were some 685 inmates distributed across the various sections of the construction offices, but then that number was soon increased to 789 at the request of the Department of Labour Deployment of the Main Camp. Bischoff was told to send Höss a current list of all the Polish inmates still employed in the Central Construction Office, outlining other foreign workers too. The list comprised of 379 persons, including 39 at the construction depot, 239 at workshops, 16 in transportation departments I and II, and 85 in the main contruction office. The numbers employed in the construction office contained 85 Poles, 8 Czechs, 1 Russian, 1 Polish Jew and 1 Czech Jew.

Bischoff made it clear that the list of people was indispensible for the enormous construction tasks ahead. He also said that in order to complete the crematoria in a timely manner including other buildings which would help serve the efficient running of the camp, he needed more labour due to the severe lack of construction workers. He therefore requested more personnel from Department IIIa. He asked for electricians, plumbers, carpenters, technicians, whitewashers, masons and blacksmiths. Without these additional specialised labourers, he made it known to Höss that the construction office would not be able to carry out their tasks. The commandant was totally aware of the importance of the construction office and he would sanction what they required.

Whilst Bischoff negotiated on the labour force for the construction office, in late January typhus once again spread throughout Birkenau, ravaging the prisoners and workforce. Worried that the disease would further delay the building of the four crematoria and spread to surrounding areas, on 8 February Höss issued an order to his subordinates telling them that:

> *'By order of the SS-Brigadeführer and Generalmajor der Waffen-SS Glücks, a total quarantine is issued for KL Auschwitz. The order of the group leader states as follows: Because of the high incidence of typhus, all permissions for furlough or leaves must be cancelled.'*

Another concern was that civilian workers too were becoming infected. It was agreed that all civilian workers living together with those who were ill would be quarantined for three weeks by order of the physician in charge. As for the majority of inmates that now fell ill or showed the least symptoms of the disease, they would be disinfected, or in other words sent directly to the gas chamber for 'special treatment'. After they had been '*disinfected*' their bodies would be disposed of in the same manner as the thousands of others who had perished in Bunkers I and II, in the open air cremations. Pit burning was still the chief method of corpse disposal in early 1943.

COPY/ORDER/

J A TOPF & SONS
Erfurt, 12th February 1943

SS and Police Central Construction Management
Oswiecim

CONCERNING: Crematoria 2 and 3, PoW camp

We acknowledge receipt of your telegram of 10th February reading as follows:

We once again confirm receipt of your order for five triple muffle furnaces, including, two electric lifts for the corpses and one provisional hoist for corpses. Also the order for a practical device for charging coal and a device for transporting ashes. You are to deliver the whole installation for Crematorium 3. We expect you to take the necessary steps to immediately dispatch all machines and parts. The complete installation must come into service on 10th April 1943.

J A TOPF & SONS

[certified a true copy]
Captain Kunin

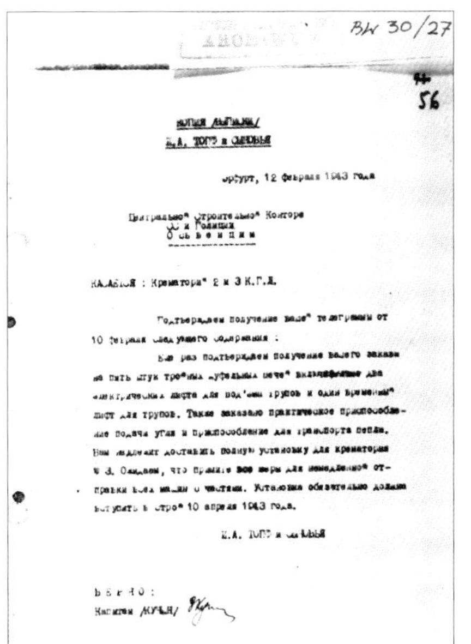
BW 30/27
56

(*Auschwitz-Birkenau Museum*)

On 12 February with the camp personel trying to contain the spread of typhus, Topf & Sons sent a letter concerning Crematoria II and III.

On 18 February, Kirschneck informed Messrs Industrie Bau AG, the company in charge of constructing the roof of Crematorium III, of an extension of 2 metres in the southern wing housing the waste incinerator. They requested them to send a quotation for the additional works.

Two days later Kirschneck reported to the camp 'Labour Office' that of the 200 prisoners sent to the construction sites of Crematoria II and III, only 40 were able to work due to typhus. On 19 February it was further reported that out of a labour force of 200 men, only 80 were able to work.

Auschwitz, am 6.3.1943

PANSTWOWE MUZEUM W OSWIECIMIU ARCHIWUM BW 30/25

Brftgb.: 24365/43/Jä/Lm

Betr.: KLa Auschwitz, Krem. II und III KGL, BW 30 u. 30 a
Bezug: Dort. Schreiben vom 22.2.43 D.IV. Prf.
Anlg.: - - -

Firma
T o p f und S ö h n e
E r f u r t

Auf Grund Ihres Vorschlages erklärt sich die Dienststelle einverstanden, dass der Keller 1 mit der Abluft aus den Räumen der 3 Saugzuganlagen vorgewärmt wird. Die Anlieferung und der Einbau der hierfür benötigten Rohrleitungen und der Druckluftgebläses muss schnellstens erfolgen. Wie Sie in o.a. Schreiben angeben, sollte die Ausführung noch in dieser Woche geschehen. Um Vergabe eines spezifizierten Kostenangebotes 3-fach für Lieferung und Einbau wird gebeten.

Desgleichen wird um Einsendung eines Nachtragsangebotes für die Umänderung der Entlüftungsanlage für den Auskleideraum gebeten.

Nach Eingang dieser Angebote wird Ihnen schriftlich Auftrag erteilt.

Der Leiter der Zentralbauleitung
der Waffen-SS und Polizei Auschwitz

SS-Sturmbannführer

Verteiler:
1 Bault. KL u.Landw.
2 Registr. KGL BW 30 u.30 a
1 Sachbearb.

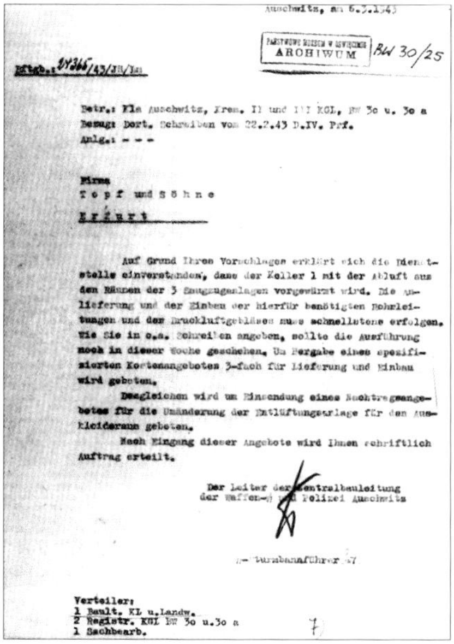

Correspondence register no. 24365/43/Jä /Lm
Auschwitz. 6/3/43
Subject: KL Auschwitz Crematoria II and II PoW camp, BW 30 and 30a
Reference: Your letter of 22/2/43 D.IV Prf
Enclosure: –

Topf & Sons
Erfurt

In accordance with your suggestion, the service agrees that cellar 1 should be preheated with the air coming from the rooms of the 3 forced draught installations. The supply and installation of the ductwork and blowers necessary to this end are to be effected as soon as possible. As you point out in your above mentioned letter, execution should commence this week. We would ask you to send in triplicate detailed quote for supply and installation.

At the same time, we would ask you to send an additional quotation for the modification of the air extraction installation in the undressing room.

After receipt of these quotations we shall send a written order.

Head of the Auschwitz Waffen-SS and Police
Central Construction Management
[Bischoff's initials]

SS Major [Jährling initials]

Distribution:
1 KL and Agriculture Bauleitung
2 Files KGL BW 30 and 30a
1 Official in charge

(*Auschwitz-Birkenau Museum*)

On 22 February the *Bauleitung* Drawing Office made further alterations for Crematorium III, producing a drawing with a front elevation, a side elevation and a plan of the ground floor. The alteration was in the annex wing and measured 12 metres in length.

On 26 February, a report was made concerning the terra cotta pipes for the drainage of Crematorium II and the supply of doors and windows for Crematorium III. It also briefly highlighted the entrance and future undressing room of Crematorium II and included a sketch showing the western access stairway.

At the end of February 1943 the five triple-muffle furnaces in Crematorium II were to be finally tested.

On 1 March the contract for the roof of Crematorium III was awarded to Industrie Bau AG, following a quote of 9,418.04 RM.

The following day, on Tuesday,, 2 March, a foreman from the firm, Riedel, reported that the concrete flooring had been laid in Crematorium IV. His daily report outlined that his labourers had covered the ground with hard fill and concreted in the gas chamber. Below is a time sheet filled out regarding works in Crematorium IV.

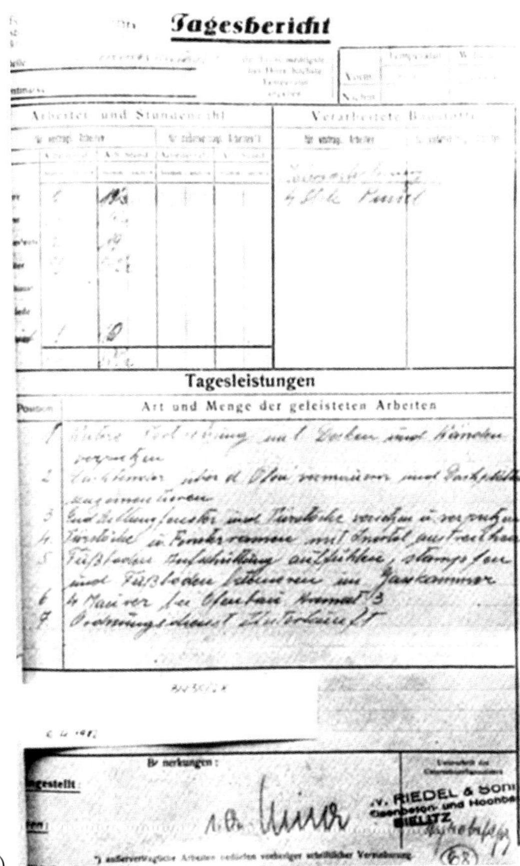

Tagesbericht

Tagesleistungen

Art und Menge der geleisteten Arbeiten

Bemerkungen:

J. RIEDEL & SOHN
Eisenbeton- und Hochbau
BIELITZ

(*Auschwitz-Birkenau Museum*)

A few days later on 4 March a report noted that 'forty-five *well-fleshed*' male corpses specially selected from a batch gassed in Bunker II were transported to Crematorium II for 'a trial run'. The incineration rooms were on the ground floor, while in the cellar there was a gas chamber and a mortuary. Inside the incineration room the bodies were cremated under the watchful eye of Prüfer and other engineers. For the next ten days the furnaces were run to dry them out whilst engineers completed the gas chamber and an elaborate ventilation system and air ducts. On 8 and 9 March, Messing worked eight hours a day on the air extraction system. On 10 March, it was reported that Messing worked for sixteen hours, testing the ventilation and air extraction systems of Crematorium II. These tests were in order to trial the efficiency of the ventilation, and the time needed to wait between the application of the toxic gas and the opening of the gas-tight door. Following a number of tests, it was noted that twenty to thirty minutes was sufficient to bring down the toxic gasses to a safe level so that the door could be opened. This would then allow for the safe removal of corpses from the chamber without the camp '*Sonderkommando*' being poisoned.

On 11 March, chief engineer Schulze obtained from Bischoff a certification outlining that the ventilation of the gas chamber was ready for service for the evening of 12 March. In fact, there was a delay in making the crematorium operational, and it was another twenty-four-hours before it was ready. The delay was due to additional parts for the ventilation system. During this period engineers calculated the consumption of coke needed for the furnaces. Also on the same day, three copies of the operating instructions for the three muffle furnaces of Crematorium II supplied by Messrs Topf were sent to the Kommandantur Administration. These instructions were identical to those already sent for Crematoriuum I.

On Saturday, 13 March, it was announced that crematorium II was officially operational and ready for 'special treatment'. During the evening of Sunday, 14 March, 1,492 women, children, and old people from the Krakow ghetto had been selected for the trial run at Crematorium II. Under the cover of darkness, the Jews were quietly led to a temporary undressing hut built next to Crematorium II in its north yard where they were ordered to undress, and kindly requested to keep their personal effects together for when they returned. They were then led naked in file down the western stairway with its metal guard rails to the basement of Crematorium II, through a doorway with a sign that read '*Bath and Disinfection Room*'. As they entered the room they could see that from the ceiling hung sieves mounted on pieces of wood or metal, which appeared to be shower heads. Once crammed inside, the airtight door to the room was slammed shut and secured by two latch bars, which were screwed tight.

So that the killing process could be observed, there was a specially designed peephole consisting of a double pane of glass. Through this opening the SS watched as 1 or 1.5kg of pale blue-green granulated Zyklon B was poured in from the roof by SS medical orderlies wearing gasmasks. It entered the room via four metal meshed hollow columns that protruded from the concrete ceiling. When the gas was dropped into the room the victims started screaming and panicking, but their death agonies were not heard for long because the Zyklon B used was forty times the lethal dose. In a few minutes, five at the most, the gas chamber fell silent. Once they were sure that all the victims were no longer moving the air extraction system was then switched on for at least twenty or thirty minutes so that it could suck out the poisoned air that was still in the chamber. The gas tight door was then unbolted and opened, and the gruesome task of extracting the dead women, children and old people by the *Sonderkommando* began immediately.

The corpses were then loaded three or four at a time on a temporary hoist, and sent up to the ground floor. Plans for the installation of an electric elevator had already been drawn-up. Once the bodies arrived on the ground floor of the incinerator room the *Sonderkommando* attached leather thongs to the bodies and pulled them along the concrete surface through shallow water to a point in front of the furnaces. They were then placed face up head to foot in threes on a metal 'corpse board' that ran on rollers and rammed into one of the muffles. It was predicted that the incineration process would probably take between forty-five minutes and one hour, but that evening the incinerators were only being run at half their capacity to prevent any technical problems. In total, preparation and gassing took two hours, but the incineration took nearly forty-eight hours.

The trial run had been regarded a complete success and a teletype message was dispatched from Auschwitz informing the SS headquarters that the new '*bathhouse*' had undertaken its first 'special action'. Eichmann, eager to get shipments moving, believed that all the Birkenau crematoria were now fully operational and ordered a transport of 3,000 Salonika Jews to Auschwitz. However, Crematorium II was only in its trial stage, whilst Crematoria III, IV and V, were still being constructed. Nevertheless, on 20 March the transport arrived, much to the frustration of the camp personnel. Out of the total 3,000 Jews that arrived on that Saturday, 417 men and 192 women were selected to work, whilst the other 2,191 deportees were sent directly for 'special treatment'. The camp authorities had decided to use Crematorium II again for the 'special action', in spite of technical concerns. The selected Jews were immediately passed through the '*bathhouse*', using the same procedure as before, but this time the ovens were worked to full capacity. It immediately became apparent that the building could not handle the amount of cremations and there was an electrical fire. The ventilation system for extracting the Zyklon B from the gas chamber also developed a problem, but it was agreed that the crematorium could not be closed down for repair.

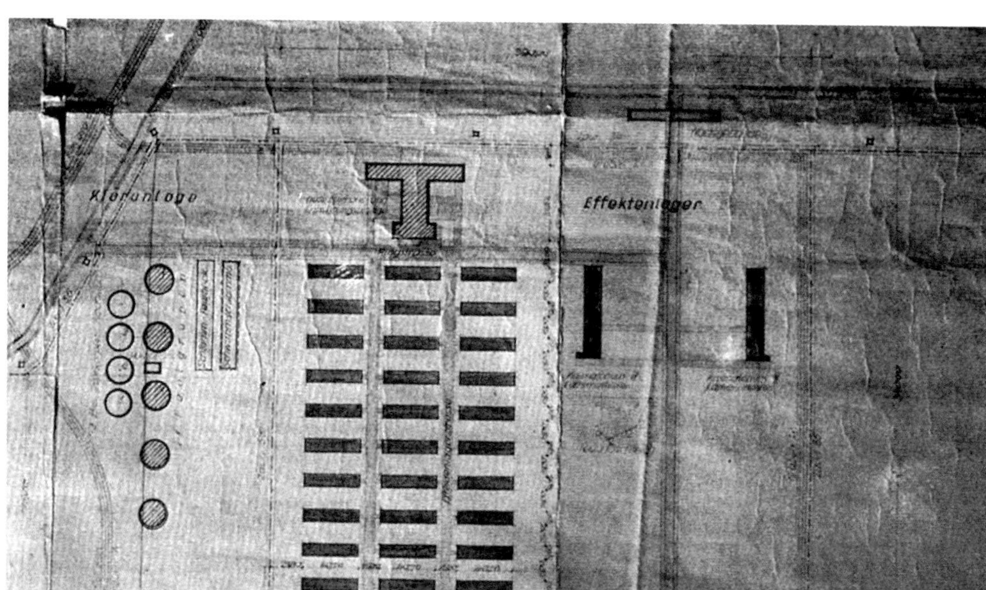

Part of an overall plan of Birkenau, drawn by the *Bauleitung*, drawing dated 20 March 1943, showing clearly Crematoria IV and V. To the south of Crematorium IV are the three rows of huts which were Canada II and the new Central Sauna which has been shaded. To the left of Canada II on the drawing is sewage treatment plant II, which was never completed, though part was made operational. (*Auschwitz-Birkenau Museum*)

On 22 March in a drastic attempt to reduce further damage to Crematorium II, the camp authorities insisted that the architects sign off Crematorium IV, whilst engineers tried to repair the crippled facility. When another Salonika transport arrived some 2,000 Jews were led to their death in Crematorium IV. The killing had been so swift that the camp authorities had not even had time to trial run the incinerators.

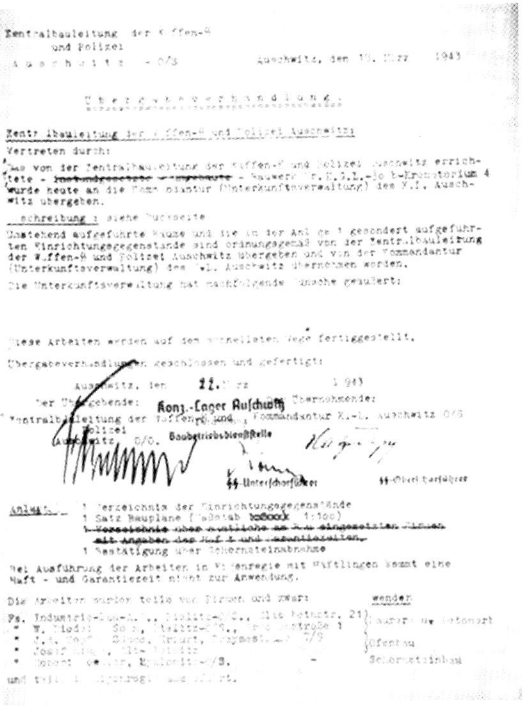

Zentralbauleitung der Waffen-SS
und Polizei
Auschwitz – O/S Auschwitz, den 19. März 1943

Übergabeverhandlung.

Zentralbauleitung der Waffen-SS und Polizei Auschwitz:
Vertreten durch:

Das von der Zentralbauleitung der Waffen-SS und Polizei Auschwitz errichtete – ~~[illegible]~~ – Bauwerk Nr. K.G.L.-Bo [illegible]-Krematorium 4 wurde heute an die Kommandantur (Unterkunftsverwaltung) des K.L. Auschwitz übergeben.

Beschreibung : siehe Rückseite

Umstehend aufgeführte Räume und die in der Anlage 1 gesondert aufgeführten Einrichtungsgegenstände sind ordnungsgemäß von der Zentralbauleitung der Waffen-SS und Polizei Auschwitz übergeben und von der Kommandantur (Unterkunftsverwaltung) des K.L. Auschwitz übernommen worden.

Die Unterkunftsverwaltung hat nachfolgende Wünsche geäußert:

Diese Arbeiten werden auf dem schnellsten Wege fertiggestellt.

Übergabeverhandlungen geschlossen und gefertigt:

Auschwitz, den 22. März 1943

Der Übergebende: Der Übernehmende:
Zentralbauleitung der Waffen-SS und Polizei Auschwitz O/O. Kommandantur K.-L. Auschwitz O/S

Konz.-Lager Auschwitz
Baubetriebsdienststelle

SS-Unterscharführer SS-Obersturmführer

Anlagen: 1 Verzeichnis der Einrichtungsgegenstände
1 Satz Baupläne (Maßstab ~~[illegible]~~ 1:100)
~~1 Verzeichnis über sämtliche am Bau eingesetzten Firmen mit Angaben der [illegible] und Garantiezeiten.~~
1 Bestätigung über Schornsteinabnahme

Bei Ausführung der Arbeiten in Eigenregie mit Häftlingen kommt eine Haft- und Garantiezeit nicht zur Anwendung.

Die Arbeiten wurden teils von Firmen und zwar: wenden

Fa. Industrie-Bau-A.G., Bielitz-O/S., [illegible] 21 } Maurer- u. Betonarb.
" W. Riedel & Sohn, Bielitz-O/S., [illegible]straße 1 }
" J.A. Topf & Söhne, Erfurt, [illegible] 7/9 } Ofenbau
" Josef [illegible], [illegible]
" Robert [illegible], [illegible]-O/S. – Schornsteinbau

und teils in Eigenregie ausgeführt.

The deed of transfer dated 19 March 1943 outlining the handing over of Crematorium IV to the camp administration as from 22 March. The signature on the left is that of the head of the *Bauleitung*, SS Major Bischoff. At the bottom of the page is the list of the five firms that had participated in the construction. The *Bauleitung* confirmed that where work had been carried out on its own account using prisoner labour there was no guarantee. This meant that the civilian firms had covered themselves and were not liable for future potential issues. (*Auschwitz Birkenau Museum*)

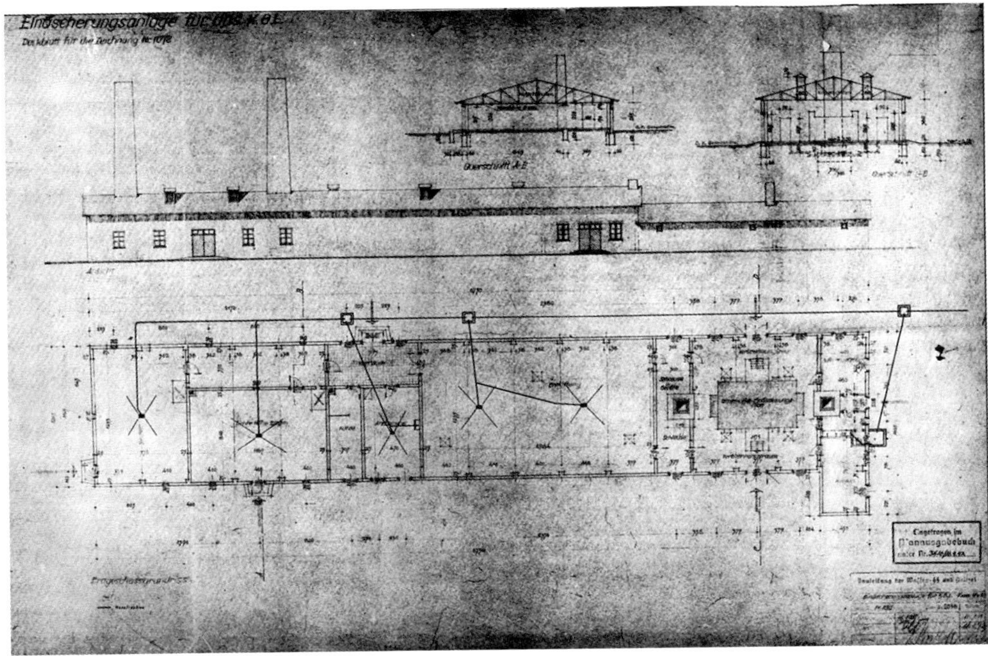

This plan view of crematoria IV and V shows north façade and two cross-sections. Crematorium IV became operational on 22 March, and Crematorium V on 4 April 1943. This plan was originally drawn on 11 January 1943 by Haftling 127 (Josef Sikora). As the drawing shows, the crematorium chambers are situated in the eastern parts of the building, whilst in the large open area is the undressing room. The western part of the structure includes three gas chambers. Note the walls on the left side of the chambers showing the opening hatches for the Zyklon B granules to be poured through. There were seven hatches and eight interconnected with the medium gas chamber and the smaller gas chamber. (*Auschwitz-Birkenau State Archives*)

In late March meetings were held in regards to erecting barbed wire fences around both Crematoria IV and V. On 7 April Huta sent a letter to the Auschwitz *Bauleitung*. In the letter Huta outlines '*that for the moment they cannot employ the additional 60 prisoners who were to join the 20 already working on the job, because the work has had to be interrupted because of obstacles (rails)*'. Consequently, the fence would not be erected until much later and the electric current switched on at 16:00 hours on 26 June 1944.

By the end of the month Crematorium II had been temporarily repaired and transferred over to the camp again. For the next few weeks the crematoria functioned relatively well. Crematorium IV was also run simultaneously during what was known

Description of building

General: Single storey building, partly over basement, comprising:

Basement: Corpse cellar 30.0 x 7.0[m] with ventilation and air extraction ducts, 1 gas tight door, 1 corpse cellar 50.0 x 7.93[m], wind break and vestibule, 1 gold processing room, 1 office with safe, 1 antechamber with lift [temporary goods hoist], 3 stairways, 1 [corpse] chute.

Ground floor: 1 wind break, 1 corridor, 1 dissecting room with table, 1 laboratory, 1 washroom, 1 WC, 1 [corpse] washing room, 1 incineration room with 5 3 muffle cremation furnaces and blower installation, with corpse charging trolley on rails, coal [in fact coke] or clinker trolley on rails, 1 brick separating wall for the ashes of corpses [outside yard], 1 motor room [in fact three], 1 waste incinerator room, 1 brick separating wall for waste [another outside yard], 1 fuel store, 1 capos room, 1 tool store [irons for firing and operating the furnaces], 1 room with urinal and WC [and shower], 1 prisoners' rest mom, 1 corridor, 1 stairway.

Roof space: 1 heraclite built room for prisoner accommodation, 1 loft with furnace room air extraction ducts, 1 loft with air extraction for the whole Crematoria and 1 temporary goods hoist.

External walls:	Brickwork with no facing
Internal walls:	Brickwork, plastered and whitewashed
Ceilings:	Ackermann reinforced parpends
Floor:	Concrete floor with cement screed
Stairways:	Reinforced concrete with cement screed
Roof:	Gable roof with dormers, tile covered
Windows:	Single glazing
Water supply	Basement and ground floor and drainage:
Lighting:	Electric lighting
Heating:	1 chimney installation 15.46 m high

(*Auschwitz-Birkenau Museum*)

as '*Salonika action*', but because it was worked so intensively the double four muffle furnace cracked. Eager to keep the crematoria running engineers were immediately contacted to try and attempt to repair the incinerator. To make matters worse, days later the internal lining of the chimney and the connecting flue to the incinerator of Crematorium II began to collapse. Whilst engineers tried to rectify the problem with Crematorium II, on 4 April Crematorium V was officially handed over to the camp administration, but the installation was still not deemed fully operational, since the gas-tight doors to the gas chambers were still to be fitted. Work on the doors was completed between 16 and 17 April by a civilian firm working for Huta.

Although difficult to read, this document gives a detailed description of Crematorium V in April 1943 for its official handover.

With Crematoria II and IV now functioning, in mid-April *SS-Sturmbannführer* Alfred Franke-Gricksch, adjutant to *SS-Obergruppenführer* Maximillian Von Herff, Head of the SS Central Personnel Office in Berlin, visited Auschwitz, where they witnessed the gassing of 2,930 Salonika Jews in Crematorium II. The procedure had gone very smoothly, but there were still technical issues with the crematoria and breakdowns. However, in spite of the set-backs and constant complaints between the architects and engineers, in just two months both installations had in fact liquidated some 30,000 victims from the '*Salonika action*', and 7,000 German, Polish and Yugoslavian Jews. Though these figures were seen by the SS as impressive, any hopes to increase the capacity were quickly dashed when both crematoria were shut down in May. Crematorium II was temporarily taken out of commission so that engineers could re-line the chimney, whilst Crematorium IV's incinerator was decommissioned. Following an inspection to the damage of Crematorium IV on 17 or 18 May, it was reported that the furnace was starting to crack. Also, the natural ventilation was noted as being unacceptable and dangerous. It was considered that Crematorium IV incinerator may need completely replacing. However, the building could still be effective as a gas chamber, but in order to make the ventilation more rapid, there were discussions about installing an extraction system that would be able to remove toxic air from the gas chamber within five minutes. Furthermore, there were plans to enlarge the Zyklon-B openings from 30x40cm to 40x50cm and to make the opening and closing easier and quicker.

Below is a letter dated 9 June 1943 from Messrs Topf & Sons to the Auschwitz Bauleitung following the meeting of 18 May 1943. It gave the cost of 2,510 RM for the supply of 2 air extraction installations for Crematoria IV and V. Two copies of Topf drawing D 59.620 were enclosed, showing the construction of the brick-built extraction ducts and plans for the suction duct, blower and pressure duct to be supplied by Topf. It was proposed that the electric motors to be supplied were 3.5 HP with a capacity run of 8,000m^3 per hour. This extraction system was never installed.

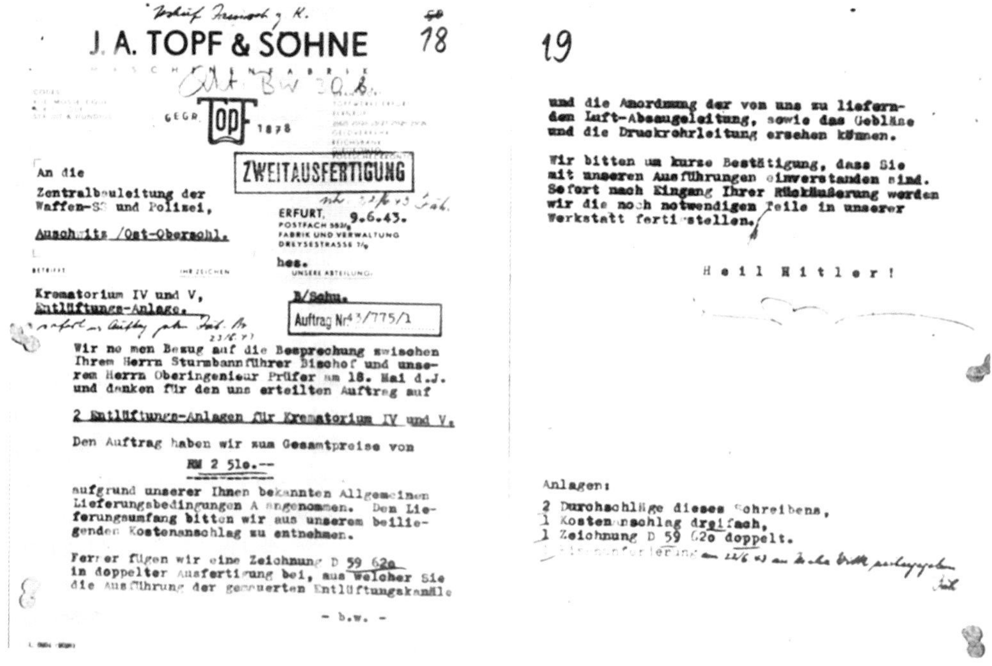

18

J. A. TOPF & SÖHNE

MASCHINENFABRIK

GEGR. TOPF 1878

ZWEITAUSFERTIGUNG

An die
Zentralbauleitung der
Waffen-SS und Polizei,
Auschwitz /Ost-Oberschl.

ERFURT, 9.6.43.
POSTFACH
FABRIK UND VERWALTUNG
DREYSESTRASSE

BETRIFFT
IHR ZEICHEN
hes.
UNSERE ABTEILUNG
D/Schu.

Krematorium IV und V,
Entlüftungs-Anlage.

Auftrag Nr. 43/775/1

Wir nehmen Bezug auf die Besprechung zwischen Ihrem Herrn Sturmbannführer Bischof und unserem Herrn Oberingenieur Prüfer am 18. Mai d.J. und danken für den uns erteilten Auftrag auf

2 Entlüftungs-Anlagen für Krematorium IV und V.

Den Auftrag haben wir zum Gesamtpreise von

RM 2 51o.--

aufgrund unserer Ihnen bekannten Allgemeinen Lieferungsbedingungen A angenommen. Den Lieferungsumfang bitten wir aus unserem beiliegenden Kostenanschlag zu entnehmen.

Ferner fügen wir eine Zeichnung D 59 62o in doppelter Ausfertigung bei, aus welcher Sie die Ausführung der gemauerten Entlüftungskanäle

- b.w. -

19

und die Anordnung der von uns zu liefernden Luft-Absaugeleitung, sowie das Gebläse und die Druckrohrleitung ersehen können.

Wir bitten um kurze Bestätigung, dass Sie mit unseren Ausführungen einverstanden sind. Sofort nach Eingang Ihrer Rückäußerung werden wir die noch notwendigen Teile in unserer Werkstatt fertigstellen.

Heil Hitler!

Anlagen:

2 Durchschläge dieses Schreibens,
1 Kostenanschlag dreifach,
1 Zeichnung D 59 62o doppelt.

(*Auschwitz-Birkenau Museum*)

However, the main gripe during the meeting was the incinerator issue which the SS themselves had caused. Topf engineer Prüfer outlined that his company should not incur the cost of constantly repairing a furnace whilst it was being flagrantly operated to full capacity. This was noted in the correspondence below, rubber stamped and received by the Auschwitz *Bauleitung*, 12 April 1943. It was initialled by Kirscheck and Jährling.

To the
Waffen-SS and Police
Central Construction Management

Auschwitz/East Upper Silesia

Subject:	Your ref.	Our division D IV
Crematorium IV PoW	Corres. reg.	Prf [Prüfer]
camp 30b	26419/43/Jä/Lm	
Your letter of 3/4/43		

In reply to your letter mentioned above, we would inform you that we have requested our site foreman, Herr Koch, to repair the fissures that have apparently recently appeared in the 8-muffle furnace in Crematorium IV. At the same time we have noted the agreement made between your Head of Construction, SS Major Bischoff and our chief engineer. Herr Prüfer, according to which we are to make good any defects in the cremation furnace built by us that should appear within 2 months after its coming into service, at no cost to you. This is naturally subject to the precondition that any defects that may appear are the result of faulty construction and not, for example, caused by overheating the furnace or damaging the internal lining with fire irons, etc.

As already mentioned, we have instructed our site foreman Koch to repair the damage that has occurred, which has no doubt been done in the meantime.

Ever at your service, please be sure of our best wishes,

Heil Hitler!

(Signed] J A Topf & Sons

Enclosures:
2 further copies of this letter.

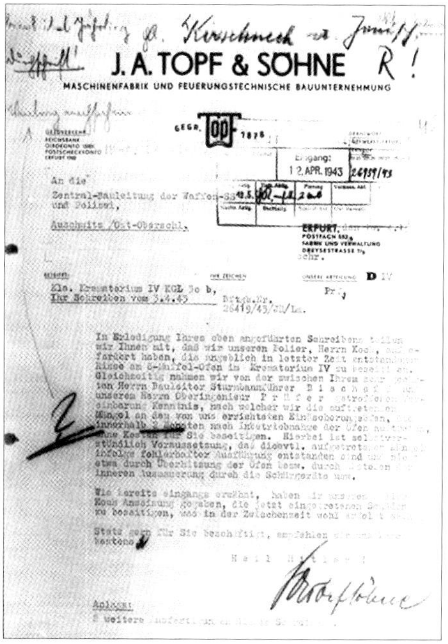
J. A. TOPF & SÖHNE
MASCHINENFABRIK UND FEUERUNGSTECHNISCHE BAUUNTERNEHMUNG
GEGR. 1878
Eingang: 12. APR. 1943 26959/43
An die
Zentral-Bauleitung der Waffen-SS und Polizei,
Auschwitz /Ost-Oberschl.
ERFURT,
POSTFACH 583,
FABRIK UND VERWALTUNG
DREYSESTRASSE 7/9
D IV
Pr.
Kl. Krematorium IV KGL 30 b,
Ihr Schreiben vom 3.4.43
Bftgb.Nr.
26419/43/Jä/Lm.

In Erledigung Ihres oben angeführten Schreibens teilen wir Ihnen mit, daß wir unseren Polier, Herrn Koch, aufgefordert haben, die angeblich in letzter Zeit entstandenen Risse am 8-Muffel-Ofen im Krematorium IV zu beseitigen. Gleichzeitig nahmen wir von der zwischen Ihrem sehr geehrten Herrn Bauleiter Sturmbannführer Bischoff und unserem Herrn Oberingenieur Prüfer getroffenen Vereinbarung Kenntnis, nach welcher wir die auftretenden Mängel an den von uns errichteten Einäscherungsöfen, die innerhalb 2 Monaten nach Inbetriebnahme der Öfen auftreten, ohne Kosten für Sie beseitigen. Hierbei ist selbstverständlich Voraussetzung, daß die evtl. aufgetretenen Mängel infolge fehlerhafter Ausführung entstanden sind und nicht etwa durch Überhitzung der Öfen bzw. durch [illegible] der inneren Ausmauerung durch die Schürgeräte usw.

Wie bereits eingangs erwähnt, haben wir unserem [illegible] Koch Anweisung gegeben, die jetzt eingetretenen Schäden zu beseitigen, was in der Zwischenzeit wohl erfolgt sein [illegible]

Stets gern für Sie beschäftigt, empfehlen [illegible]

Heil Hitler!

Anlage:
2 weitere Ausfertigungen [illegible]

(*Auschwitz-Birkenau Museum*)

With both the SS and Topf & Sons not agreeing to solve the issue operations of Crematorium IV, the furnace was taken out of service, but the gas chambers could still be used. The furnaces, however, of Crematorium II were still intact, but its chimney lining was damaged and the installation was shut down awaiting repairs. Below is a telegram that outlined the relining of the chimney of Crematorium II, dated 29 May 1943 and initialled by Bischoff and Kirschneck.

Address: Topfwerke Erfurt
Text: Construction drawings for Crematorium II chimney promised by Herr Prüfer, for Messrs Köhler not yet arrived. Request immediate dispatch as work had to cease.

Zentralbauleitung Auschwitz

[Bischoff' s initials]
SS Major

Distribution:
File BW 30 Krema II
Bauleitung PoW camp (SS Second Lieutenant Janisch)
Bauleitung KL (SS Second Lieutenant Kirschneck)
Technical Section Civilian Employee Jährling

(*Auschwitz-Birkenau Museum*)

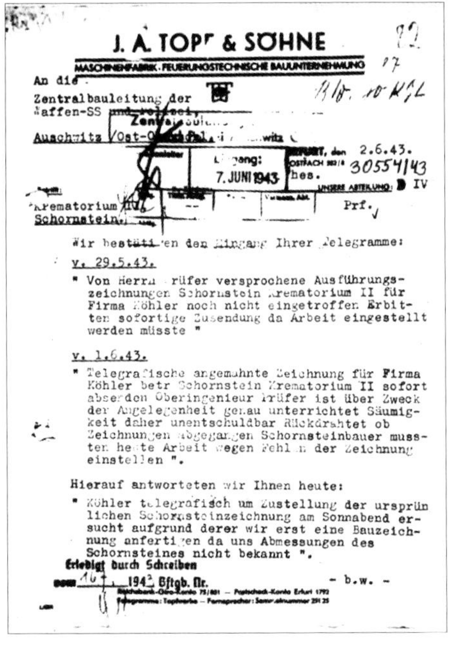

J. A. TOPF & SÖHNE
MASCHINENFABRIK · FEUERUNGSTECHNISCHE BAUUNTERNEHMUNG

An die
Zentralbauleitung der
Waffen-SS
Auschwitz Ost-O

Eingang: 7. JUNI 1943

ERFURT, den 2.6.43.
30554/43 hes.
UNSERE ABTEILUNG: D IV
Prf.

Krematorium II
Schornstein.

Wir bestätigen den Eingang Ihrer Telegramme:

v. 29.5.43.
" Von Herrn Prüfer versprochene Ausführungszeichnungen Schornstein Krematorium II für Firma Köhler noch nicht eingetroffen Erbitten sofortige Zusendung da Arbeit eingestellt werden müsste "

v. 1.6.43.
" Telegrafische angemahnte Zeichnung für Firma Köhler betr Schornstein Krematorium II sofort absenden Oberingenieur Prüfer ist über Zweck der Angelegenheit genau unterrichtet Säumigkeit daher unentschuldbar Rückdrahtet ob Zeichnungen abgegangen Schornsteinbauer mussten heute Arbeit wegen Fehlen der Zeichnung einstellen ".

Hierauf antworteten wir Ihnen heute:
" Köhler telegrafisch um Zustellung der ursprünlichen Schornsteinzeichnung am Sonnabend ersucht aufgrund derer wir erst eine Bauzeichnung anfertigen da uns Abmessungen des Schornsteines nicht bekannt ".

Erledigt durch Schreiben
- b.w. -

Messrs J A Topf & Sons

To
Auschwitz Waffen-SS and Police
Central Construction Management
Auschwitz. Eastern Upper Silesia

Received
7th June 43

ERFURT. 2/6/43
hes. 30554/43
Our Division D IV R,
Prf
Subject:
Crematorium II
Chimney

We acknowledge receipt of your telegrams:

Of 29:5.43 [Saturday]
"Construction drawings for Crematorium for chimney promised by Herr Prüfer for Messrs Köhler not yet arrived. Request immediate dispatch as work has had to cease."

Of 1/6/1943 [Tuesday]
"Send immediately drawing requested by telegram for Messrs Köhler concerning chimney Crematorium chimney II [.] Chief engineer Prüfer fully aware of the purpose of this request [.] Delay therefore inexcusable [.] Telegraph whether the drawings have been sent [.] Chimney constructor had to stop work today due to absence of drawing."

To which replied today:
"Requested Köhler by telegram Saturday [29 May] supply original drawing of chimney enable us produce construction drawing as we do not know dimensions of the chimney."

Replied in writing
PTO
[Friday] 16/7/1943 Correspondence register no.
[initialed] Kirschneck

(*Auschwitz-Birkenau Museum*)

As a result, the incineration capacity had dropped considerably and in order to cope with the amount of incoming transports destined for 'special treatment', the SS were required to increase the open air burnings once more. Only Crematorium I in the main camp and Crematorium V could provide limited support to the cremations.

To add to the cremation issues, the warmer weather and the lack of hygiene had increased again and those severely undernourished also died. In a number of meetings the importance of the health of the inmates was discussed. It was noted there were poor latrines, an unsatisfactory sewer system, and a lack of sick bays. There was opposition to the system of pits, as the high water table would cause further infection of the ground water. The head of the Central Construction Office had already indicated that the large disinfestation unit for Birkenau was already under construction and it was agreed that this would be a permanent solution for delousing all able-bodied prisoners before they entered the camp.

On 22 May in a speech to Hans Kammler, and other functionaries, Höss clarified the objective of Auschwitz-Birkenau. Those that had not been selected for 'special treatment', he said, were to be kept as healthy as possible and used for labour in the various armament firms.

A few days later the Auschwitz authorities took immediate action to improve the hygienic conditions of the camp. They were determined to reconstruct the sewage system, change the structure of the latrines, dig a main drainage ditch to the Vistula, and complete the disinfestation facilities known as the Central Sauna.

The first drawings for a central sauna had been drawn back in November 1942. The machinery to be installed in this building was to include four Topf disinfestation hot air chambers. The building was designed purely for sanitary treatment only of the prisoners that were selected for labour. They would have their hair cut, a medical examination, and be disinfected and showered. A disinfection process would also be applied to their clothing and personal artifacts.

However, the project was temporarily put on hold by the *Bauleitung* as the epidemic through the camp was being temporarily controlled, and the fact it was winter time. On 16 December 1942 Bischoff wrote regarding the need for clean water:

'As experience has taught, where large numbers of people are crowded together, the danger of infectious diseases from the consumption of impure water or as a result of inadequate hygiene due to shortage of water is very great. Therefore, in calculating the number of wells, the size of the pump aggregates and the pipe bores etc., a water requirement of 150 litres for each member of the troops and 40 litres for each prisoner is to be assumed. This amounts to a daily water requirement of 5,900m^3. Moreover, the installation of a chlorination plant for a quantity of water up to 50m^3 per hour is planned. The facility has 2 air/vacuum pumps with an output of 360l/m each, for clearing the siphoning lines, as well as an air compressor with output of 450l/min and 6 atmospheres of operating pressure for the pressurized air chambers. In order to supply the individual crematoria and other special facilities, approx. 15,900 running metres of pressure pipes of 50–500mm diameter with about 73 water valves and 73 underground hydrants are to be laid.'

The letter by Bischoff was an additional request to significantly reduce another wide-scale epidemic alongside plans for the Central Sauna facility. However, there was a funding problem with the Sauna and it was deemed less a priority than plans for water pipes and wells. Furthermore, construction of the four crematoria were given priority over any other building plans. Yet in spite of this priority, drawings of the Central Sauna were received in Berlin in January 1943. Following a lukewarm response to the submitted plans, there was still a requirement to go ahead with the construction. Initially, there were issues with the plans and it was deemed there was not adequate space for reception and waiting areas. After a number of revisions to the drawings, the alterations were re-submitted to the SS Main Economic and Administrative Office. By April it was deemed that the installation was now urgently required and even Höss himself outlined the necessity, reporting on the severe health situation in the Gypsy Camp (Birkenau Ba.IIe). The SS personnel in the camp were extremely concerned that there would be a resurgence of the epidemic during the summer months. However, following a number of meetings and discussions of the Sauna build, which would include disinfestation ovens supplied by Topf & Sons of Erfurt, and the autoclaves by another specialist firm in Munich, the new drawings were authorized. As a result of this a drainage drawing was produced in May 1943.

In fact, following the commencement of the construction of the new Central Sauna building, the *Bauleitung* once against stressed the deep concern of the health issues in Birkenau. There were two letters that mentioned the fight against rats and the increased number of corpses that had not been incinerated. In June and July 1943 it was highlighted by reports of pests, namely rats, carrying typhus. There were also rats reported in the prisoners' accommodation. It was for this reason that the camp personnel were urgently pushing for the completion of the Central Sauna, and rectifying the problems with the crematoria.

On 4 June Bischoff sent the plans of the Central Sauna facility to the SS WVHA and attached a letter, which read:

> *'The construction of the delousing and disinfection facility had to begin at once according to the original design, since immediate measures for disinfestation were required by the physician as well as the camp commandant, due to the occupancy of the camp, which was still under construction. After typhus broke out in the Gypsy camp, the construction of a disinfection facility became so urgently necessary that construction work within the framework of special construction measures, as ordered by SS Brigadeführer and Generalmajor of the Waffen-SS Dr. Eng. Kammler for the improvement of hygienic conditions, had to be begun at once. The work has meanwhile progressed to the point that a modification of the project would necessitate the complete demolition of the facilities already partially finished, and at the same time would further delay the completion date for facilities which are so vitally important … . The original design was prepared with the agreement of the camp commandant and the garrison physician. The large dressing and undressing rooms are absolutely necessary, since those coming in from an entire transport (approx. 2,000), which mostly arrive at night, must be locked up in one room until the next morning. Having the arrivals wait in the fully occupied camp is excluded due to the danger of transmission of lice.'*

Whilst engineers and construction workers set-to-work on the foundations of the new Central Sauna, work also began on extending the camp into a third section known as BIII. For some months the *Bauleitung* had put together a number of drawings for approval which planned to house an additional 60,000 prisoners in 188 barracks. The new section of the camp was nicknamed 'Mexico'. A total of four construction phases were planned in the course of the construction of Birkenau, of which BI and BII were built. Although a fence was erected quite quickly for the BIII segment, building on the area during the summer months of 1943 was slow due to heavy demands put on the construction workers in other areas of the camp. The *Bauleitung* were also pressed with mounting work which saw its offices revising various plans and drawings for a multitude of projects, many of which never came to fruition. In spite of the workload, many plans were approved and were selected in line of importance to the camp's needs and requirements. One drawing that was accepted in June 1943 was the camp's new watch towers. Below are blueprints showing two different sizes of watchtowers.

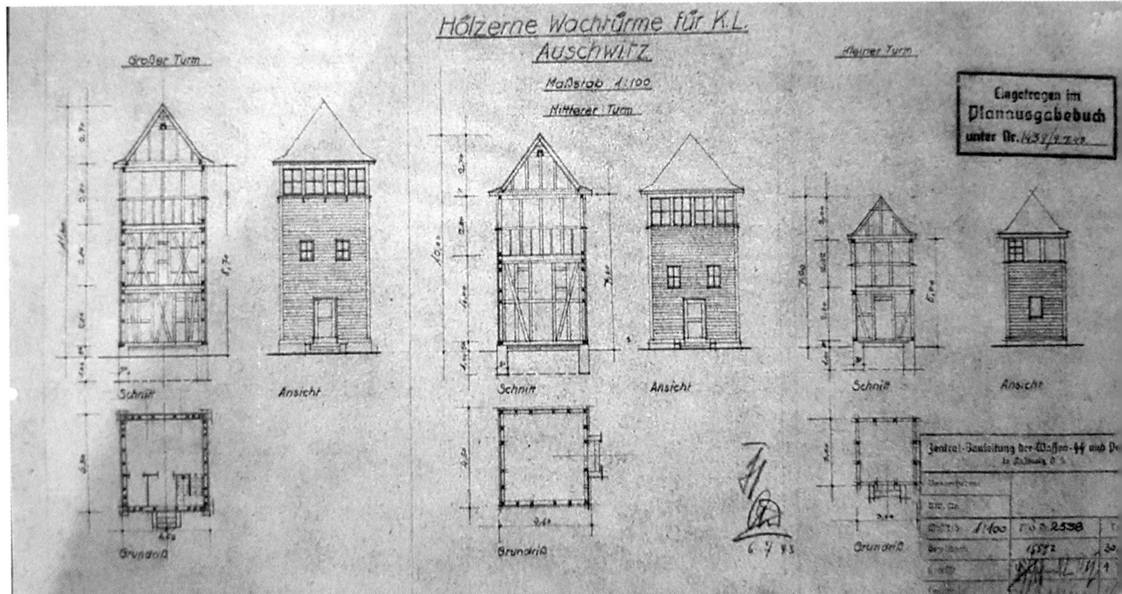

(*Auschwitz-Birkenau Museum*)

This blueprint, drawn and prepared by Haftling 15592 (Rudolf Kauer), shows a drawing of watchtowers designed in three sizes comprising of small, medium and large. Each of these structures was designed with glass windows and weatherboard cladding. They also included insulation with particle-cement board and even had an internal toilet and their own sceptic tank unit. (Auschwitz-Birkenau Archive)

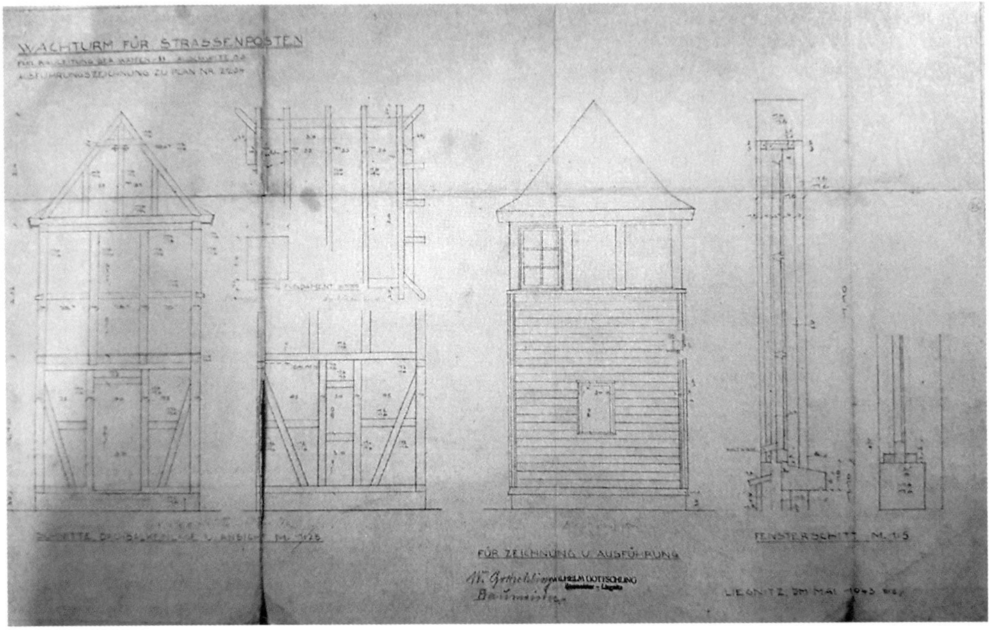

This blueprint drawing, drawn in Legnica (Liegnitz) for the *Bauleitung*, shows the small watchtower. These small structures comprised of a specially designed window as the cross-section on the right clearly shows. These structures were made by German companies and delivered prefabricated to the camp by rail. They were completed by the spring of 1944. The larger towers measured 4.5 x 4.5m at their base and were 11.6m high. Their design meant they were able to be converted. (*Auschwitz-Birkenau Museum*)

A photograph taken in February 2007 by the author showing one of the watchtowers. This view is from the former prisoner compound looking towards Crematorium I to the north. Between the watchtowers are two brick buildings that were constructed around 1918 and between 1940 and 1945 served the SS garrison and administration. (*HITM couretesy of Auschwitz-Birkenau State Archive*)

During mid-1943, with the rapid rise of people passing through Birkenau, the BIIg Canada facilities were erected. These 'Canada' storage buildings occupied several dozen barracks and other structures around the camp, and some 1,500 prisoners worked there in two shifts sorting through all the plundered Jewish goods that had arrived in the camp. The barracks were literally a treasure trove to the individual members of the SS. They had seen nothing like it, and many of them were unable to resist the temptation provided by these 'riches'. Supervision of the SS in Canada was surprisingly slack and as a result many actively participated in theft. SS officers too at Auschwitz were also personally benefiting from the accumulating wealth, including the commandant himself. Diamonds, gold, coins, currency was stolen. Large amounts of food and alcohol too were taken for personal use and sold on the black market. The bulk of the property stored in the Canada stores was sorted and then distributed from Auschwitz through an extensive distribution network that served many individuals and various economic branches of the Nazi regime.

Also during this period, plans for the SS barracks, hospital, and administrative barracks to oversee the counting of prisoners during roll call, were drafted and

Four photographs taken in sequence in August 2024 by the author of one of the watchtowers that were erected along the perimeter fence of BIIa Quantantine Camp for men. The window was specially designed to quickly be released and drop into a slot in the sill if the guard needed to fire his weapon from the tower. (*HITM courtesy of Auschwitz-Birkenau State Archive*)

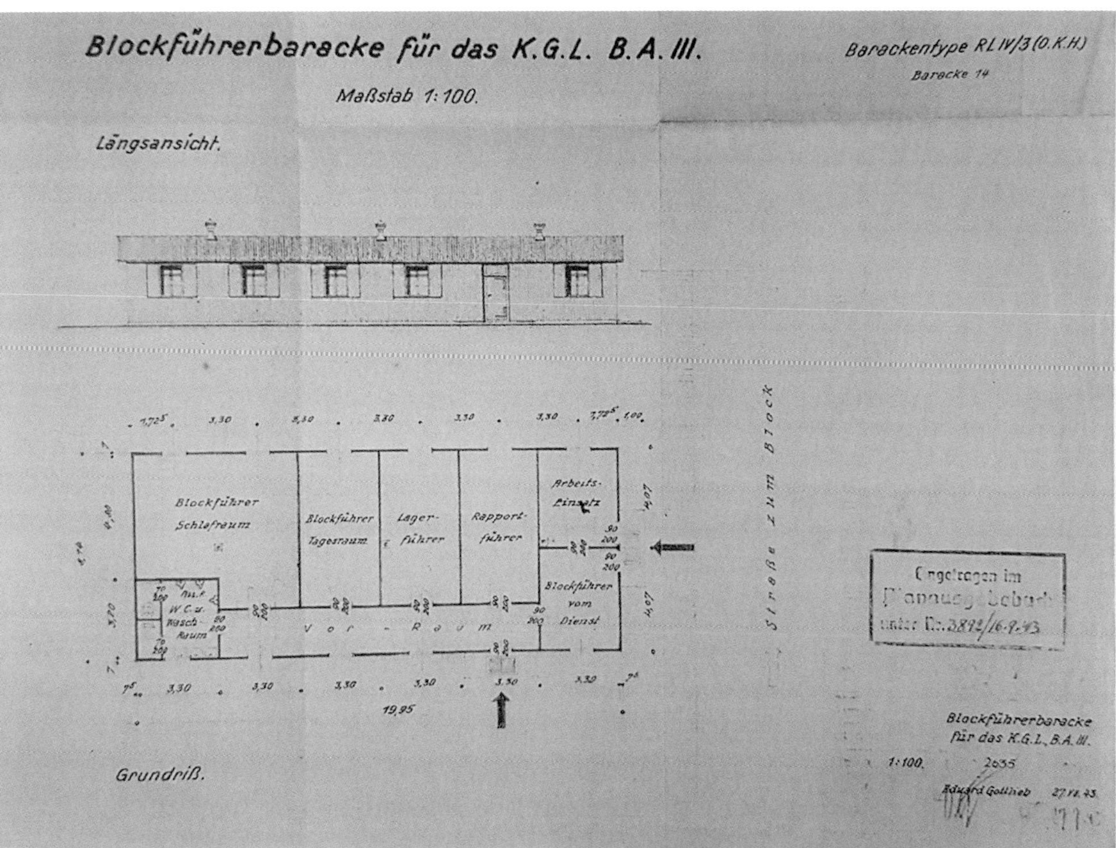

This drawing of a *Blockführerbaracke* for BAIII in Birkenau, was often the same barrack type used for administrative purposes. The Camp Leader or *SS-Lagerführer* and his non-commissioned Report Leader or *SS-Rapportführer*, oversaw counting of prisoners from these barracks during roll call. (*Auschwitz State Archives*)

approved to be built and extended. There were giant warehouses too, planned to hold potatoes along the railway line along what was termed the 'old Jewish ramp', which was on the main railway line.

Whilst plans to expand the camp were continued by the *Bauleitung*, throughout June there had been continuous technical problems with the existing crematoria. This included issues with the structures themselves and was blamed on wartime shortage of materials. As a result, the builders often had to economize during the construction of both Crematoria II and III, and they were of a less solid construction. The retort ovens also did not meet the requirements either. Prüfer made it clear to Höss that he felt let down by the poor quality of the build and the second-rate materials, categorically blaming the contractors for the breakdowns. However, in spite of these constant set-backs, by 24 June Crematorium III was finally transferred to the camp authorities. Below is the transfer deed correspondence of Crematorium III.

Waffen-SS and Police
Central Construction Management
Auschwitz
Auschwitz 24th June 1943
DEED OF TRANSFER

Auschwitz Waffen-SS and Police Central Construction Management
Represented by:

Worksite 30a of the PoW camp, Crematorium III built repaired modified by the Auschwitz Waffen-SS and Police Central Construction Management has this day been handed over to the Kommandantur (Accommodation Administration) of KL Auschwitz.

Description: see verso

The surrounding areas and the equipment installed, indicated separately in annex 1, have been duly handed over by Auschwitz Waffen-SS and Police Central Construction Management and taken over by the Kommandantur (Accommodation administration) of K L Auschwitz.

The Accommodation Administration expressed the following wishes:

This work was completed by the quickest method possible.

Deed of transfer completed and closed:

Auschwitz, 24th June 1943

The transferer	The transferee
Waffen-SS and Police	KL Auschwitz Kommandantur
Central Construction Management	Auschwitz Garrison Administration
Auschwitz, Upper Silesia	Buildings operation service
[signed Bischoff]	[Two illegible signatures]
SS Major	SS Sergeant Major SS Sgt
[initialed by Kirschneck]	

Annexes:
1 inventory of equipment
1 set of construction drawings (scale 1:200)
1 list of all firms having participated in construction with indication of length of liability and guarantee
1 certificate of acceptance for the chimney

Since the work was carried out on own account using prisoners, the length of liability and guarantee is inapplicable.

Bricklaying and concreting was done partly by Messrs Huta, partly by prisoners, the roofing by Industriebau A G of Bielitz, machinery and furnace installation by Messrs Topf & Sons of Erfurt, construction of the chimney by Messrs Köhler of Myslowitz. 2 year guarantee.

(Auschwitz-Birkenau Museum)

Bauleitung der Waffen SS u. Polizei
KGL - Auschwitz

Aufstellung

der bereits übergebenen Bauwerke an die Standortverwaltung

ARCHIWUM BW 30/25

Lfd. Nr.	[illegible] Nr.	Datum d. [illegible]	Bauwerk Nr.		Bezeichnung des Gebäudes	Meldung an [illegible]	von der Standort-verw. zurückgereicht
30	[illegible]	26. 3.43	[illegible] 14	3	Truppenunterkunft [illegible]	28 172/43/[illegible]	21.7.43 31229/43
31	[illegible]	[illegible] 3.43	" 14	7	" "	28 172/43/[illegible]/Co.	
32	[illegible]	[illegible] 3.43	" [illegible]	1	[illegible]matorium IV	[illegible] 172/43/[illegible]	21.7.43 31229/43
33	[illegible] 172/43/[illegible]	31. 3.43	" 30	1	" II	[illegible] 176/43/[illegible]	" "
35	[illegible]/43/[illegible]	31. [illegible].43	" [illegible]	4	[illegible]wirtschaftsbar. [illegible]	[illegible] 300/43/[illegible]/Co.	13.7.43
36	[illegible]	4.4.43	" [illegible]	1	[illegible]matorium V	[illegible] 663/[illegible] 1/Co.	21.7.43 31229/43
43	[illegible]	17. [illegible].43	" [illegible]	2	[illegible]	28 [illegible]75/43/[illegible]	" "
53	[illegible]	[illegible] 6.43	" 30	1	Krematorium III	[illegible]0/43/[illegible]	
[illegible]	[illegible] 43	15. [illegible].43	" [illegible]	5	[illegible]wirtschaftsbar[illegible]		

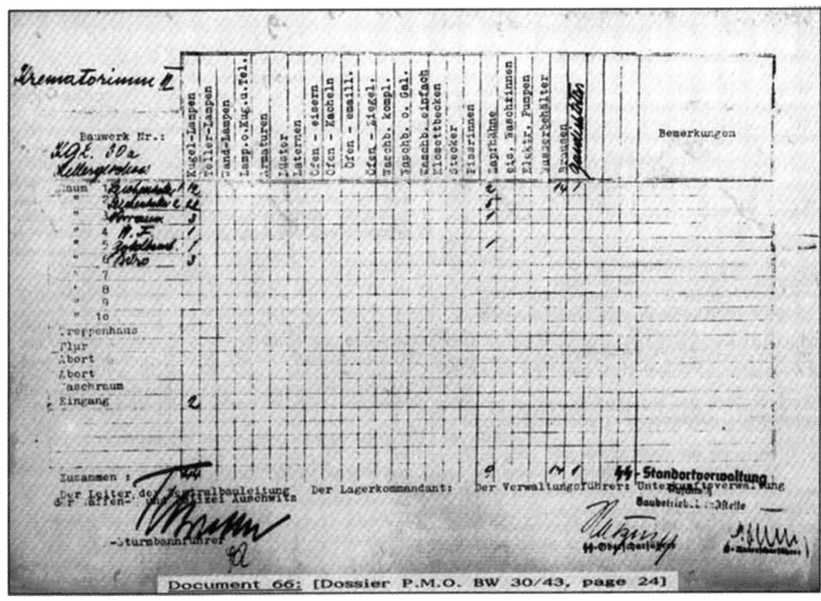

Krematorium II

Bauwerk Nr.: KGL. 30a

Kugel-Lampen | Teller-Lampen | Wand-Lampen | Lamp. o. Kug. u. Tel. | Armaturen | Lüster | Laternen | Öfen - eisern | Öfen - Kacheln | Öfen - emaill. | Öfen - Ziegel. | Waschb. kompl. | Waschb. o. Gal. | Waschb. einfach | Klosettbecken | Stecker | Pissrinnen | Zapfhähne | Sta. Waschrinnen | Elektr. Pumpen | Wasserbehälter | Brausen | Bemerkungen

Raum 1 – 10, Treppenhaus, Flur, Abort, Abort, Waschraum, Eingang

Zusammen:

Der Leiter der Zentralbauleitung d. W. Waffen-SS u. Polizei Auschwitz – Sturmbannführer | Der Lagerkommandant: | Der Verwaltungsführer: | SS-Standortverwaltung Auschwitz Unterkunftsverwaltung Baubetriebsdienststelle

Document 66: [Dossier P.M.O. BW 30/43, page 24]

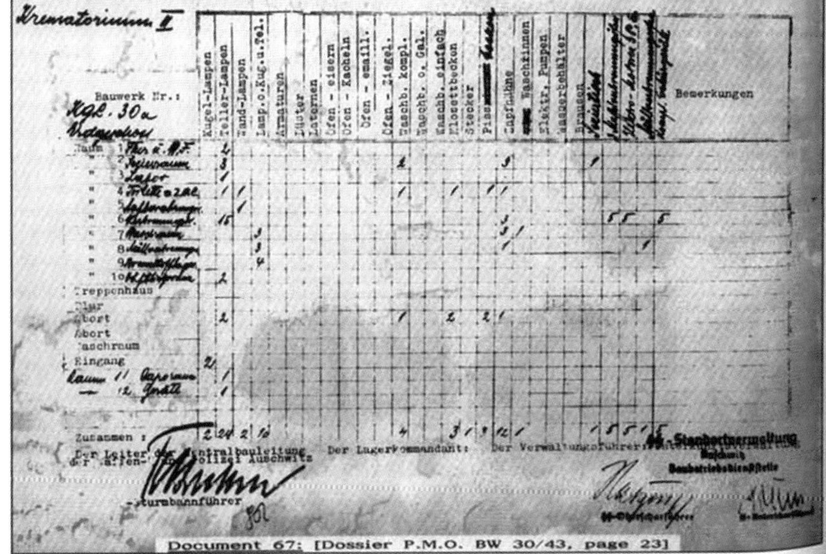

Krematorium II

Bauwerk Nr.: KGL. 30a

Kugel-Lampen | Teller-Lampen | Wand-Lampen | Lamp. o. Kug. u. Tel. | Armaturen | Lüster | Laternen | Öfen - eisern | Öfen - Kacheln | Öfen - emaill. | Öfen - Ziegel. | Waschb. kompl. | Waschb. o. Gal. | Waschb. einfach | Klosettbecken | Stecker | Pissrinnen | Zapfhähne | Sta. Waschrinnen | Elektr. Pumpen | Wasserbehälter | Brausen | Bemerkungen

Raum 1 – 10, Treppenhaus, Flur, Abort, Abort, Waschraum, Eingang

Zusammen:

Der Leiter der Zentralbauleitung d. W. Waffen-SS u. Polizei Auschwitz – Sturmbannführer | Der Lagerkommandant: | Der Verwaltungsführer: | SS-Standortverwaltung Auschwitz Baubetriebsdienststelle

Document 67: [Dossier P.M.O. BW 30/43, page 23]

Part of the register of buildings handed over by the Bauleitung to the camp administration. The entry for Crematorium III is on the second last line. (*Auschwitz-Birkenau Museum*)

By the end of June Auschwitz-Birkenau had an official daily incineration output of some 4,756 corpses. Yet, despite frequent requests by the engineers not to overload the crematorium, the Auschwitz authorities continued to operate the installations at their absolute limit. According to engineers' reports the furnaces were not being operated correctly, being constantly overheated, and it was suggested that the *Sonderkommando* were deliberately damaging the internal lining with their fire irons.

By 11 July the repair to Crematorium II chimney lining was completed. However, the *Bauleitung* were not happy and raised their concerns that they were being held liable for the defects that had delayed the operation of the crematorium. They also notified Topf that the under-floor flues from the furnaces to the chimney were showing serious defects and under the terms of the guarantee they should be repaired or replaced immediately.

Throughout the remainder of July and August recurring problems with the crematoria still continued to hamper operations. With all four crematoria running simultaneously, Auschwitz had a massive killing potential, and yet only two were in operation. Crematorium IV was out of service and Crematorium II had temporarily stopped working so it could be repaired. In fact, on 4 August Topf informed the *Bauleitung* that the permanent corpse lifts for Crematoria II and III were still not ready. Topf's subcontractor could not complete them because authorization had been refused. This consequently caused serious delays in corpse removal and plans were put into motion to get the problem solved.

As for the other Crematoria, Crematorium I was closed down altogether at the request of the Political Department, and as for Crematoria III and V, these two installations were running, but not at full capacity. Camp personnel attempted everything possible to try and speed up the process of killing, fearing the camp would become quickly overcrowded with those destined for 'special treatment'. In fact, reports had confirmed that between April and the end of September 1943, Crematoria II, III, IV, and V only worked for two months at full capacity. Only a quarter of their maximum capacity was used. Nonetheless, in the midst of all these problems an enormous amount of people were still sent to their deaths in all four crematoria during this time. In total between 160,000 and 210,000 victims were given 'special treatment'.

These actions, however hideous they were, were regarded as a complete success by the camp personnel in spite of the technical issues. In fact, in early August *SS-Hauptsturmführer* Hans Aumeier, representing the camp commandant, issued garrison order no. 31/43, and outlined the following:

'As recognition for the labour performed by all SS members during the special action of the last few days, the commandant has ordered that from 13:00 hours on Saturday evening, 7 August 1943, through Sunday, 8 August 1943, inclusive, there will be a rest from every operational duty.'

Yet, in spite the amount of killings that continued in Birkenau during the summer of 1943, there were heated discussions about the technical issues and inferior construction of the crematoria. As a result, the relationship between Prüfer and the *Bauleitung* had deteriorated, with the SS blaming him for the bad building of the crematoria.

On 13 September a letter was sent regarding the defective lining of the chimney of Crematorium II. The letter was concerning the costs incurred in having to replace the defective lining of the chimney and the reasons behind the defective chimney.

Auschwitz, [Monday] 13/9/1943

The system worked perfectly. Here chief engineer Prüfer this time designated the reason for the damage to the lining as being that the brickwork was bonded with lime mortar instead of refractory mortar, and also errors in the static calculations.

In reply to this, in the conversation on the following day with Herr engineer Koehler, who built this chimney according to the Topf & Sons drawings, stated that the lining was completely built with refractory mortar from the bottom to the top.

It was pointed out to Herr chief engineer Prüfer that with each visit he brought a new explanation for the reasons for the collapse of the chimney lining.

During his last visit but one, in the presence of the Commandant, he gave as the reason the great stresses caused by firing individual furnaces, which was not taken into account in the plans.

In the opinion of the Zentralbauleitung, this was in fact probably the main reason, and would be taken into account in the new Topf & Sons plans, in which the different rates of expansion of different parts of the lining would be allowed for by having openings such that they could slide with respect to one another.

Herr engineer Koehler declared during this conversation that the overloading of the chimney installation was the most important cause of the damage.

Since it had not been possible to completely settle the question of liability, Herr engineer Koehler for Messrs Robert Koehler, Myslowitz and Herr chief engineer Prüfer for Messrs Topf & Sons (subject to consultation with his superior) declared their agreement, in the interests of further good relations, to each assume 1/3 of the total extra cost, provided that for its part the Bauleitung was prepared to assume a similar sum. This total cost was provisionally estimated at 5,000 RM.

With this settlement, the reconstruction of the chimney lining in Crematorium II, PoW camp BW 30, is considered to be finally settled.

Read and approved
SS Second Lieutenant (Specialist)
SS Major

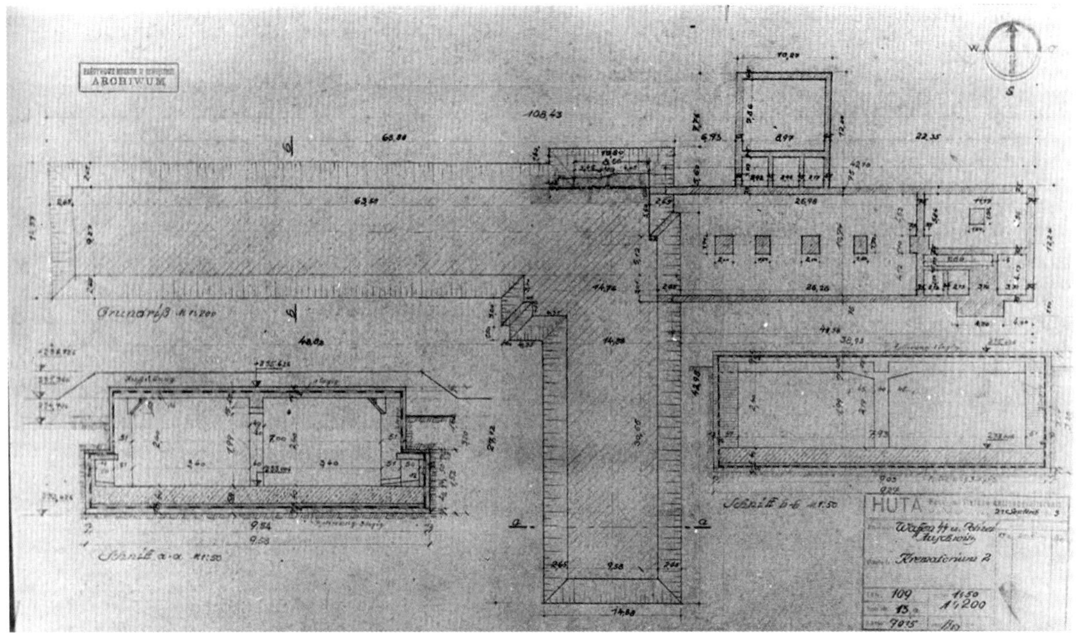

A plan of Crematorium II drawn on 21 September 1943. The drawing includes a cross-section of the undressing room and gas chamber. (*Auschwitz-Birkenau Memorial Archives*)

A plan of Crematorium II drawn on 24 September 1943. The drawing includes a cross-section of the underground chambers. (*Auschwitz-Birkenau Memorial Archives*)

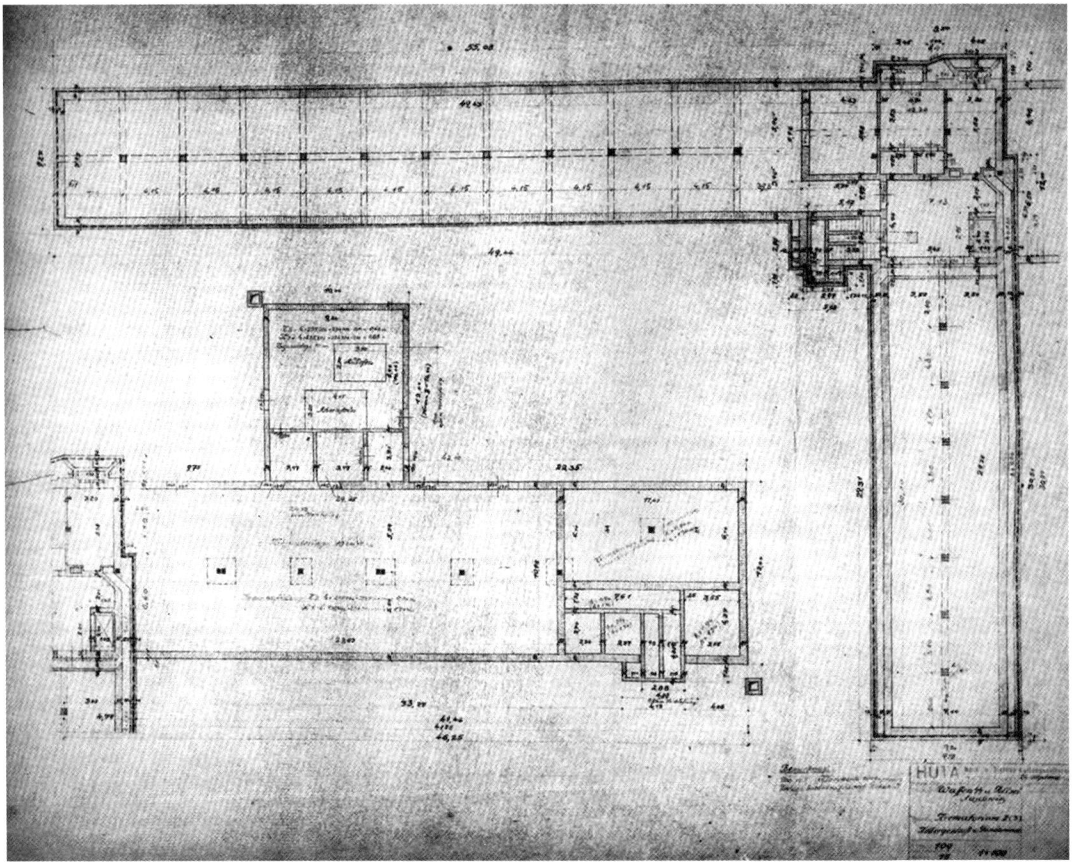

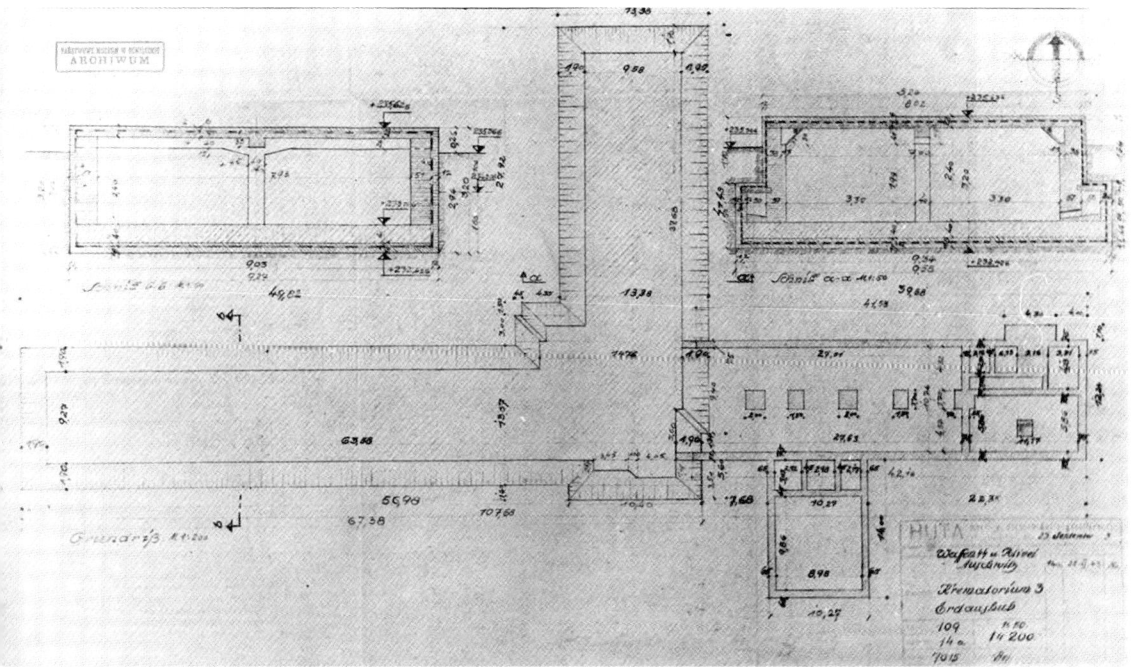

A plan prepared by the Huta Company and signed on 21 September 1943 showing two-cross sections of Crematorium III's underground chambers. (*Auschwitz-Birkenau Memorial Archives*)

On 2 November 1943, Huta sent the *Bauleitung* invoices for their work on Crematoria II and III. Four days later Bischoff, following a conversation with Höss, wrote requesting SS Major Joachim Caesar, head of the agricultural section of the camp, to supply various trees to be planted to conceal Crematoria II and III. The trees were an idea to make the area look less conspicuous to those working and being sent for processing. There were also plans that were given authorization for the creation of a formal garden in the northern area of Crematorium II.

Below is a letter dated 6 November 1943 regarding the delivery of trees and bushes for the establishment of a ring of greenery for Crematoria II and III.

Crematoria II and III, however were never camouflaged. However, camp personnel wanted hedges and trees to potentially hide not the actual buildings themselves, but the open pit incineration ditches that were dug behind Crematoria V and IV. There were plans to erect screening against the barbed wire using rush matting. However, due to the lack of materials, this would be done using branches cut from the nearby wood and installed against the barbed wire.

Elsewhere in the camp construction continued on various buildings. The Central Sauna building that had commenced construction in May and June entered service in December 1943 following a number of minor alterations to its original plans.

6th November 1943

39533/43/Kam/J

Subject:	Delivery of plant material for the establishment of a ring of greenery for Crematoria I [II] and II [III] in the PoW camp
Reference:	Conversation between Camp Commandant SS Lieutenant Colonel Hoess and SS Major Bischoff
Enclosure:	—

Head of the Agricultural Service
SS Major (Specialist) Caesar
KL Auschwitz, Upper Silesia

By order of Camp Commandant SS Lieutenant Colonel Hoess, Crematoria I [II] and II [III] in the PoW camp are to be provided with a ring of greenery to constitute a natural separation from the rest of the camp.

To implement this measure, the following plant material is necessary, to be taken from forestry stocks:

200	deciduous trees 3-5m high
100	deciduous trees 1½-4m high
300	spruce and pine trees 1½-4m high
and 1000	assorted bushes 1-2½m high

from the nurseries.

You are requested to make these plants available to us.

Head of the Auschwitz Waffen-SS and Police
Central Construction management
[initialed] Jothann
SS Lieutenant (Specialist)

Distribution:
1 SS Second Lieutenant (S) Dejaco
1 SS Major Bischoff 1 Registration
1 SS Sergeant Kamann

(Auschwitz-Birkenau Museum)

A narrow-gauge rail line has been laid and a supply train can be seen pulling earth during excavations near Crematorium II in the winter of 1943. (*Yad Vashem*)

A photograph of Crematorium III. Between May and the beginning of July 1944, some 200,000 to 250.000 Hungarian Jews were murdered in the gas chambers and incineration furnaces of both Crematoria II and III. (*Auschwitz-Birkenau State Museum/Yad Vashem*)

View of the east side and south end of Crematorium IV in April 1943, taken from the '*Bauleitung Album*'. In mid-May 1943 the Crematorium IV furnace started to crack due to being overworked. Also the natural ventilation was noted as being unacceptable and dangerous. It was considered that the Crematorium IV incinerator needed replacing. However, the building was still deemed effective as a gas chamber. Yet in spite of the technical issues, the crematorium played a pivotal part in the camp's operation, especially during 1943. (*Auschwitz-Birkenau State Archive/Yad Vashem*)

The same image as before, this time showing the general layout plan of Crematorium IV. This building was officially handed over by the *Bauleitung* in working order on 22 March 1943. (*Auschwitz-Birkenau State Archive/Yad Vashem*)

A photograph showing the south side and east end of Crematorium V partly concealed by birch trees. Because of the location of both Crematoria IV and V both buildings were nicknamed by the SS personnel the 'forest crematoria'. This image was probably taken during the Hungarian operation. Note the evidence of soot from the chimneys. It was inside these birch trees that Hunargian Jews awaited their fate. (*Yad Vashem*)

View of the furnace room of Crematorium III. It shows the Topf three-muffle incinerators just after the building was transferred to the camp authorities. At the end of January 1943 engineers Topf & Sons outlined in a letter to the *Bauleitung* that the installation of the five three-muffle incineration furnaces could be completed within five weeks. They hoped the ovens would be in service by mid-April. Deed of transfer for Crematorium III was finally handed over on 24 June 1943. (*Yad Vashem*)

A row of ovens in one of the crematoria at Auschwitz. It shows the Topf & Sons' three-muffle incinerators. (*Yad Vashem*)

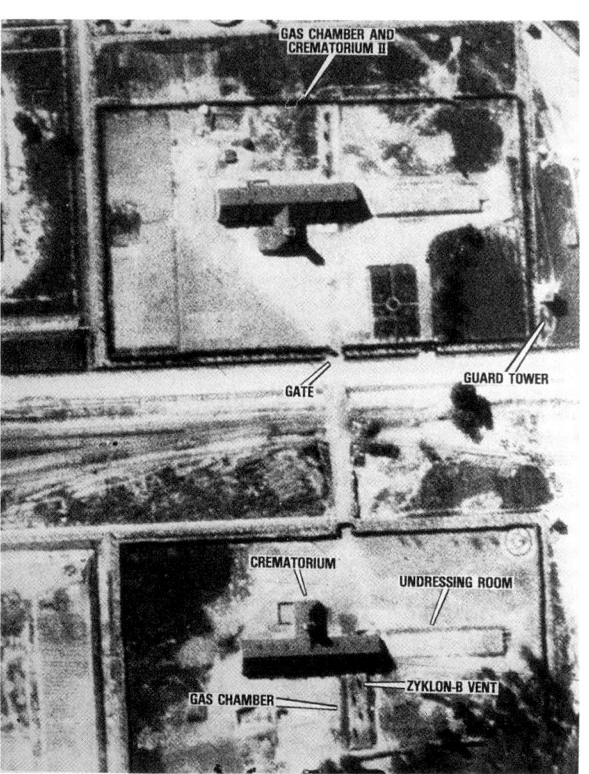

An oversized aerial reconnaissance photograph of Birkenau showing crematoria II and III gas chambers and undressing rooms. From April 1943 those selected for death entered the north yard of Crematorium II, walked along the northern side of the undressing room along its whole length and proceeded down the western stairway before entering an undressing room. The whole operation was now completed underground. Once they were undressed they were channelled through a double door at the far end of the undressing room along a short corridor and through the entrance hall into the gas chamber. (*NARA – The National Archives and Records Administration*)

Chapter V

Frenzied Killing 1944

By early November 1943, the transports into Birkenau became much larger, and the people selected for work as well as death increased massively. On 10 November Pohl arrived at Auschwitz from his offices in Berlin for an important meeting with commandant Höss. During their conversation Pohl outlined the future developments of Auschwitz-Birkenau. For some time Pohl had been negotiating with numerous businesses in order to expand the Auschwitz empire into a system of satellite camps located on industrial sites. Already there was the Buna camp at Monowitz, the Jawischowitz camp near the mines at Brzeszcze, a small shoe factory camp in Chelmek and a number of other camps being erected. In total there were 33,000 prisoners working in the satellite camps. The SS enterprises were very lucrative indeed, taking an average of two million marks each month. Due to the sheer size of the enterprise, Pohl said, the command of the Auschwitz-Birkenau complex and its satellite camps were to be divided up into three command groups. Pohl said that in view of the unavoidable changes to the system at Auschwitz and the fact that the responsibility was too much for one person, it was with reluctance that Höss would be removed from his post as commandant. However, in view of his service and his accomplishments at the camp, he was offered a choice of either becoming the commandant of Sachsenhausen concentration camp, or a promotion joining the staff of Pohl's Economic Office.

On 1 December Höss decided on taking the position as the newly appointed chief of Department DI – Central Office of the political section within the WVHA. He succeeded in *SS-Standartenführer* Artur Liebehenschel's post, who had succeeded Rudolf as commandant of Auschwitz. Rudolf's deputy was *SS-Obersturmführer* Johannes Otto, and they both worked very closely with the Deputy of concentration camps, *SS-Standartenführer* Gerhard Maurer. In Höss's new position his main task was improving the concentration camp system, and this would also include visiting Auschwitz.

By the end of 1943 further modifications of Crematorium II was undertaken. This included dividing the chambers into two by constructing a wall. No documentary evidence was mentioned by the *Bauleitung*, but it was more than likely undertaken by the Crematoria administration. One of the main reasons for the dividing wall was probably to reduce the number of people being gassed. This would effectively reduce overloading which in turn would limit the pressure on the cremation furnaces which ultimately would cause more breakdowns. Initially it was estimated that 2,000 people were being crammed into the chambers and by dividing it into 1,000 people at a time the SS thought this would avoid technical issues. The division of Crematorium V was also planned. It is unknown if the Crematorium III chamber was divided, but it's possible this would have been planned.

From late December 1943 until April 1944, Crematoria II and III were reported to have run without any major technical issues, but they were not operated at full capacity. Crematoria IV and V were still out of service. In preparation of the arrival of larger shipments of Jews, notably from Hungary, the SS Crematoria Administration prepared four buildings in readiness.

During the last two weeks of March parts of Crematorium II was still not prepared for the large shipment of Jews. The access stairway to the underground undressing room for instance was not completed, so a temporary stable hut was erected on a north-south line in the north area of the building. Jews destined to be processed in Crematorium II entered the hut, were told to undress and emerged naked at the southern end and then disappeared into the northern stairway of the Crematorium. From here they were led in to the gas chamber, the door was then slammed shut and the hapless people inside were gassed.

In early April the stairway was completed and the hut was dismantled. Those that were chosen to be processed then entered the northern area of Crematorium II, walked along the northern side of the undressing room, and then proceeded to go down into the western stairway complete with its metal guard rails, and entered the main undressing room. The whole operation was concealed and once the people undressed, they went through the double doors at the far end of the undressing room along a small corridor and then into the gas chamber.

On 13 April 1944, the metal working shop received an urgent order for the repair of twenty furnace doors and ten scrapers for Crematoria II and III. On 1 June the shop received an order to repair thirty furnace doors for Crematoria IV and V and for 4 slicers. It appears that this order for the furnace doors of Crematoria IV and V probably suggested that these crematoria may have functioned during the large shipments from Hungary, or at least for a short period during this operation. Both crematoria were still under repair in April and there was an order by the SS to dig five incineration ditches nearby and to reactive Bunker 2/V immediately for the operation. There was a possibility that due to the mass operation from Hungary in May, that Crematoria IV and V were reactivated in order to increase the killing capacity. Temporary repairs did allow Crematorium V to run more or less satisfactorily, however, there were incineration issues where the chimney to Crematorium IV needed to be completely rebuilt.

Operation Höss

After Höss's arrival it did not take long before he got himself formally acquainted with the camp once again. The day he arrived the commandant of Auschwitz I, *SS-Obersturmbannführer* Artur Liebehenschel, was relieved of his command, and was replaced by *SS-Hauptsturmführer* Richard Baer.

Both Höss and Baer worked very closely together. A lot had changed at Auschwitz-Birkenau since Höss's departure. Liebehenschel had divided the camp into three independent camps, giving *SS-Sturmbannführer* Friedrich Wilhelm Heinrich Hartjenstein the largest part to command – which was Birkenau. Both men had worked well together, but like Liebehenschel, Hartjenstein was not a brutal commander. During Höss's inspection of Birkenau with Baer, he was perturbed by the general running of the camp and filed a dissatisfied report to the RSHA in Berlin. When Eichmann arrived from Budapest to make a formal inspection of Birkenau he was incensed that Hartjenstein had not fulfilled his orders. Though the incineration installations at Crematorium V were not properly in service because the ovens were being filled with special fireclay paste, the open-air cremation ditch that had been hastily dug behind the gas chamber in order to compensate for the low incineration output was standing idle. As a result, the gassed victims were piled outside, waiting to be burnt. It was decided that Hartjenstein would be relieved of his command and transferred as commandant to the Natzweiler concentration camp in the Alsace region of France. Hartenstein's replacement was none other than Höss's first ever adjutant and an old veteran of the concentration camp system, *SS-Hauptsturmführer* Josef Kramer. Kramer arrived at Auschwitz on 8 May, when he immediately took up his duties as the new *Lagerführer* of Auschwitz II-Birkenau. Living conditions in the Birkenau camp were as bad as ever with disease and plagues of rats everywhere. The stench of faeces, urine, and filth coupled with the constant smell of burning corpses made every newcomer sick to their stomach. With the immense overcrowding and the severe lack of food, hundreds were perishing every day. But in spite of the terrible conditions Höss and his camp personnel had no time to think about the welfare of the living, he was already busily making preparations for the arrival of the Hungarian Jews.

The first transport of Hungarian Jews, consisting of 1,800 people, had arrived in Birkenau in early May, but many more convoys over the ensuing weeks were expected. In preparation for their arrival, camp personnel set to work and prepared Crematorium V to be put into operation again. An engineer's report, however, confirmed that Crematorium V's furnaces were still damaged, and because of their slow incineration rate they had replaced them in late April and activated the five small incineration ditches that had been dug. In order to compensate for the huge numbers of transports expected over the coming weeks it was suggested to reactivate Bunker II and designate it as Bunker 2/V. So that they could facilitate the process of murder quickly and effectively Höss made *SS-Hauptsturmführer* Otto Moll in charge of all four Crematoria, and assigned a special squad to enlarge the inside of the crematoria. From Crematorium V a special track was laid between the building and the pits so that the corpses could be loaded onto trolleys and disposed of quickly. As for the other killing installations, they were also overhauled, including Crematoria II and III, which received new elevators connecting the gas chambers with the incineration rooms. Even the walls of the changing rooms and the gas chambers were given a fresh coat of paint.

To assist the smooth arrival of the Hungarian Jews and to provide a direct link between the Auschwitz station and the crematoria, the train lines were extended through the main entrance of Birkenau with plans to run them right up to Crematoria II and III. In a letter sent to the Central Construction Office by the German construction railway company Schlesische Industriebau Lenz & Co. dated 2 February 1944, it outlined the construction of the rail line into Birkenau.

Night and day hundreds of prisoners were set to work laying the three-way railway track through the camp, and constructing the loading and unloading ramps. By the second week of May the railway line was completed and the finishing touches were made to the ramps. From these ramps Höss would now coordinate the destruction of the Hungarian Jews, now code-named '*Aktion Höss*'.

The first major Hungarian transports steamed their way through to Auschwitz on 15 May. Once they arrived the train pulled over the new spur through the gate into Birkenau and halted at the ramps. Here at the ramps '*Aktion Höss*' was put into operation. First the Jews were unloaded from the cattle trains. Once the Jews were unloaded they were immediately separated into two columns, one of women and children; the other of men. A selection was then carried out by one or two SS medical doctors and the two columns were divided into four columns: two of women and children, and two of men. Those unfit for labour were sent straight ahead toward the crematoria, whilst all able-bodied workers were either interned in Auschwitz or were retained ready at a moment's notice to be transferred to other camps in the Reich. The selection for labour in each transport varied daily, sometimes it was as low as 10 per cent, or as high as 50 per cent. But the majority of Jews that arrived through the gates of Birkenau were immediately sent through to the 'bathhouses' to their death. After selection on the ramps, groups classified unfit for work were marched on foot, whilst those too weak to walk were transported by truck to either Crematoria II or III.

Roughly, there were 3,300 people arriving per day, sometimes that figure even rose to 4,300. On 20 May, for instance, one convoy arrived with an average of 3,000 people of whom some 1,000 were able, and 2,000 were unable to work. The following day on 21 May two convoys were reported to have arrived from Hungary with 6,000 people, of whom 2,000 were able to work and the remainder were directly sent to their death. During that day both the incinerators of Crematoria II and III were being serviced so the victims from the transport were disposed of in the three incineration ditches next to Crematorium V. Though the specially-built track from the Crematorium to the pits had been laid, it was never used because it was considered an inconvenience. Instead, the *Sonderkommando* had to drag the corpses directly from the gas chamber to the pits.

The process of being killed was relatively quick once the Jews had gone through into the crematoria. For instance, between 1,000 and 1,500 people could be crammed into the chambers of Crematorium II. Once inside, the gas-tight door was closed and secured by two latch bars, which screwed shut. The lights were then probably turned off. This often caused panic among those trapped inside and what followed were screams and people crying. On the roof, an SS medical orderly wearing a gasmask then poured 1 or 1.5kg of Zyklon B into each of the four chimneys. After a short period of time all the victims fell silent and were dead. The air filtration system was then switched on for up to 30-minutes. The gas-tight doors were then opened and the work began immediately of extracting the corpses. The bodies were taken from a lift at the end of the furnace room. Before the installation of electric lifts a temporary hoist was erected. Prior to the bodies being cremated, the site dentist then pulled out the gold teeth, whilst the barbers sheared off the hair of the women. The *Sondercommando* then dragged the corpses along the ground through a shallow water trough to the furnaces. The pulsed air blowers on the side of the furnaces were then switch on and the furnaces were started up. The gassing of up to 1,500 people took a whole day to complete. The process was laboriously slow and as a result there were bottlenecks in the process of people waiting to be gassed. Both Crematoria II and III were working at capacity trying to destroy those that went through. The cremation process could take some 36-hours.

As more convoys arrived daily at Birkenau from Hungary, Höss was kept continuously informed on their progress. Regularly he visited Birkenaum where he watched the selections, and was even seen observing the burning of the corpses in the open-air ditches, ensuring that they were being disposed of quickly, ready for the next arrival. Almost daily the chimneys of Crematoria II and III were visible from almost all over the Birkenau camp and there can be little doubt that everyone that arrived in the camp from the unloading ramp could see the black smoke bellowing skyward. As for Crematorium V, this area was surrounded by the birch wood and was not visible to the arriving Jews. However, the incineration ditches that were dug behind it were regularly burning, which suggested that the crematoria furnaces were defective or not operating. Regarding Crematorium IV, this building was partly obscured by trees, but most people in the area could see smoke rising from the nearby incineration ditches located some 400m west of Crematorium IV. Once again this suggested that Crematorium IV's furnaces were not working properly or were completely out of action.

The transports varied daily, but from the very beginning of the '*Aktion*' until midnight on 28 May, it has been reported that some 184,049 Jews had arrived in Auschwitz in 58 trains. Within a period of just two weeks approximately 122,700 persons that were deemed unsuitable for forced labour were subsequently sent to their death. Birkenau was effectively gassing over 8,000 Jews on average each day. For the Auschwitz authorities the numbers were no less impressive, for it was the most sustained mass killing so far in the history of the camp, and only comparable to the scale of murders undertaken at Treblinka during July and August 1942.

In order to ensure that the camp would not degenerate into chaotic disorder, Höss increased the number of *Sonderkommando* that were working in shifts in the four crematoria. By the end of May there were nearly 900 of these people living and working in the crematoria. The whole of this horrific operation was supervised by only a handful of SS men. The sight of women and children going to their death had become such a common feature at Auschwitz that very often these SS men would stand around, chatting and joking among themselves. Many of them had become extremely hardened to the brutality of overseeing the killings, and there were no reports ever filed of any SS having any kind of psychological breakdown.

Throughout June more trains continued to arrive from Hungary. Though the operation was a success, the high numbers gassed began to exceed the official incineration capacity, and as a result the crematoria began overflowing with the dead. Many victims were already being burned in the pits nearby to cope with the high amount of corpses, but Moll, who oversaw the liquidation of the Hungarian Jews, assured his superiors that the '*Moll Plan*' would be achieved swiftly and successfully.

Over the coming weeks the orgy of destruction escalated. Thousands of Hungarian Jews continued their one-way passage to the crematoria, including valuable labour. No matter how gruesome the outcome was for these hapless Hungarian Jews during the summer of 1944, Höss had created the perfect killing factory on an industrial scale. All four crematoria were now working more or less on a daily basis, killing thousands each day. The ovens continued to work at full capacity and the incineration ditches were being used day and night. The frenetic gassings and burnings carried on for days and weeks, regardless of the deteriorating military situation. During July an average of 3,500 each day were arriving at the ramps, with more than three-quarters of the new arrivals being sent directly to the crematoria for 'special treatment'. In no less than eight weeks Höss had masterminded the killing of more than 320,000 Hungarian Jews. The numbers were massive, but reports from Budapest confirmed that the deportations were to be suspended. By the end of July, with the number of transports dwindling, the Hungarian operation ended. Just before Höss left Auschwitz on 29 July and returned to Berlin, Baer was given command of the garrison. Höss knew that Auschwitz had finally evolved, and it was now left in the capable hands of the new commander to start making plans to liquidate whole sections of Birkenau. One particular section that had been discussed before Höss 's departure was the gypsy camp. At its peak there were estimated to be some 23,000 gypsy men and women in the camp. However, thanks to overcrowding combined with the lack of food and water, disease had quickly spread throughout the camp killing 20,000 of the 23,000 gypsies. Those remaining were rounded up on the night of 2 August and marched off to the crematoria and gassed.

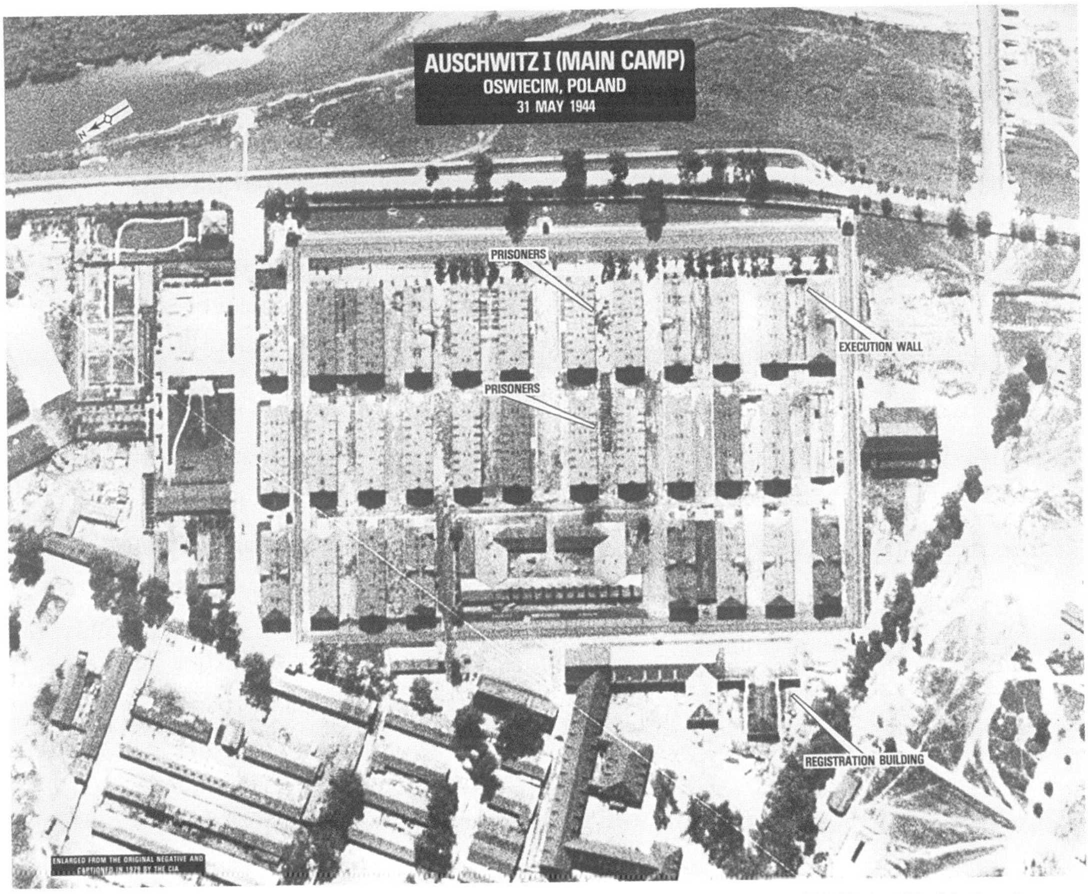

An aerial reconnaissance photograph showing Auschwitz I on 31 May 1944. (*NARA – The National Archives and Records Administration*)

An aerial reconnaissance photograph showing both Auschwitz I and Birkenau. (*NARA – The National Archives and Records Administration*)

A throng of men, women and children are seen after disembarking from their transport. They will have been told to leave their possessions on the ramp so they could be selected and taken to the showers to be cleaned. The trucks on the service road which leads down to the gates at Crematoria II and III were mainly used for collecting the personal possessions left on the ramp. They sometimes assisted in transporting those people too old or sick to walk to the gas chambers. Crematorium II can just be seen in the distance at the end of the service road. (*Yad Vashem/Auschwitz-Birkenau Museum*)

A relative comparison photograph taken by the author in August 2024. The original is slightly elevated as the photographer is standing in one of the railway cars. (*HITM courtesy of Auschwitz-Birkenau State Archive*)

Two photographs taken in sequence during the Hungarian Operation in the summer of 1944 showing the mass disembarkation of Jewish men women and children, all holding onto their bundle of belongings. Note in the distance Crematoria II (left) and III (right). (*Yad Vashem/Auschwitz-Birkenau Museum*)

A relative comparison photograph taken by the author in August 2024. The original is elevated as the photographer is standing on one of the railway cars on the rail line to the right. (*HITM courtesy of Auschwitz-Birkenau State Archive*)

Hundreds of Jewish men, women and children can be seen on the ramp waiting for selection. Note German officers and guards on the ramp preparing for the selection process. The prisoners dressed in the familiar striped concentration camp garments were tasked with collecting valuables and clothing. These were known as 'clearing-up commandos' or *Aufräumungskommando*. They were also known as 'Kanada commando'. These special units confiscated the property of the transportees and sorted them for storage in the warehouse complex known as 'Canada'. Note the long column of Jews selected for death walking along the service road down towards the crematoria at the base of the camp. (*Yad Vashem/ Auschwitz-Birkenau Museum*)

Jews have disembarked from a cattle car, some still clutching their possessions. They are waiting to be selected. Some of the people can visibly be seen wearing the Star of David stitched to the left breast of their clothing. Note the service road is empty as no selections have been undertaken at this stage. Crematorium II can clearly be seen at the end of the road at the base of the camp. (*Yad Vashem/Auschwitz-Birkenau Museum*)

In preparation for selection following disembarking onto the ramp. SS personnel can be seen along with 'clearing-up commandos'. Note Crematorium II in the distance. (*Yad Vashem/Auschwitz-Birkenau Museum*)

A closer look at Crematorium II, which is clearly visible from the unloading ramp. Strange though it may seem, in spite of the 'ring of greenery' order given by commandant Höss to conceal the crematorium with trees and foliage, nothing has been done to camouflage the building from view. Just a few days after the commencement of the Hungarian Operation, on 21 May 1944, both incinerators Crematoria II and III were shut down and had to be serviced. Consequently, victims from the transports that day were disposed of in the three incineration ditches next to Crematorium V. Though the specially-built track from the crematorium to the pits had been laid it was never used because it was considered an inconvenience. (*Yad Vashem/Auschwitz-Birkenau Museum*)

SS guards walk along the arrival ramp following a transportation of Hungarian Jews. What follows is the clearing up operation by the Kanada Commandos. The Birkenau arrival ramp was completed only weeks before this photograph was taken. Prior to the third ramp being constructed the deportation trains arrived at a ramp that was half a mile away. Now trains could pull into Birkenau, allowing the killing machine to function more efficiently. Crematoria II and III can be seen in the far background. (*Yad Vashem/Auschwitz-Birkenau Museum*)

A close-up view of both Crematoria II and III at the base of the camp. In preparation for the Hungarian Operation, on 9 May, Höss announced a series of directives. He ordered that the expansion of the platform and the three-track rail connection in Birkenau be sped up. He also instructed that the inactive cremation ovens in Crematorium V be put into operation. Next to the crematoria he ordered gangs to dig five crematoria pits (three large and two smaller ones). These will be used for the incineration of corpses. He also ordered that Bunker 2 is to be put back into operation and incineration trenches are to be dug nearby. Barracks were to be constructed for use as changing rooms. Höss promoted the commander of Gleiwitz I, SS Otto Moll, as Director of all Crematoria. (*Yad Vashem/Auschwitz-Birkenau Museum*)

Jews from Subcarpathian Rus undergo a selection on the ramp. In the distance the infamous gates of Birkenau built a couple of years earlier can be seen. (*Yad Vashem/Auschwitz-Birkenau Museum*)

Many of the men in this photograph appear elderly. SS medical personnel would send them to the gas chambers where they were usually killed and cremated on the same day. Here this image shows men being selected to walk along the service road to join others that have been selected for death and were being guided to one of the crematoria. (*Yad Vashem/Auschwitz-Birkenau Museum*)

A relative comparison photograph taken by the author in August 2024. (*HITM courtesy of Auschwitz-Birkenau State Archive*)

On the ramp following their arrival at the camp, mothers with their children will soon be selected for death. (*Yad Vashem/Auschwitz-Birkenau Museum*)

Women and children at the base of the ramp preparing to be sent either to Crematoria II or III. (*Yad Vashem/Auschwitz-Birkenau Museum*)

Two photographs showing mothers with their children selected to be murdered during the Hungarian Operation. (*Yad Vashem/Auschwitz-Birkenau Museum*)

Two photographs showing women and children making their way to one of the Crematoria during the Hungarian Operation. The majority of Jews that arrived through the gates of Birkenau were immediately sent to their death. There were roughly 3,300 people per day arriving, sometimes that figure even rose to 4,300. On 20 May, for instance, one convoy arrived with an average of 3,000 people of whom some 1,000 were able, and 2,000 were unable to work. The following day, 21 May, two convoys were reported to have arrived from Hungary with 6,000 people of whom 2,000 were able to work and the remainder were directly sent to their death. During that day both the incinerators of Crematoria II and III were being serviced so the victims from the transport were disposed of in the three incineration ditches next to Crematorium V. (*Yad Vashem/Auschwitz-Birkenau Museum*)

Jewish women and children from Subcarpathian Rus who have been selected for death walk toward the gas chambers. Crematorium III can be seen behind them. By the end of June Birkenau had an official daily incineration output of some 4,756 corpses. Yet, despite frequent requests by the engineers not to overload the crematorium, the Auschwitz authorities continued to operate the installations at their absolute limit. According to reports the furnaces were not being operated correctly, being constantly overheated, and it was suggested that the *Sonderkommando* were deliberately damaging the internal lining with their fire irons. By early July the transports to Birkenau had become much larger and the number of people selected for death increased massively. (*Yad Vashem/Auschwitz-Birkenau Museum*)

An elderly lady appears to be walking along the service road to join the large queue preparing to be gassed in one of the crematoria. (*Yad Vashem/ Auschwitz-Birkenau Museum*)

Although tragic and upsetting this is the only photograph taken between Crematoria IV and V. This image shows an elderly woman, quite possibly separated from either her husband or family, with three men assisting her. They are walking towards Crematorium V. Note in the background the north side of Crematorium IV. In spite of the concealment by trees, you can just observe the double door and two windows of the furnace room. (*Yad Vashem/Auschwitz-Birkenau Museum*)

Opposite bottom and above: Three photographs showing Subcarpathian Rus who have been selected for death waiting in a clearing near a grove of trees before being led to the gas chambers. This series of photographs was taken near Crematoria IV and V. Although the 'Hungarian action' was the most sustained mass killing so far in the history of the Auschwitz camp, and was comparable to the scale of murders carried out at Treblinka during July and August of 1942, it was also the most problematic for the murderers. There were so many Jews that had been selected to die that frequently hundreds of women and children, including the old, had to sit and wait for some considerable time outside the compound of the crematoria before being ordered to undress and be led through the crematoria to their death. (*USHMM/Yad Vashem Museum*)

Females selected for labour are seen leaving the camp's Central Sauna after being showered and re-clothed. The Central Camp Sauna, or 'bathhouse', as the SS named it, was purely designed for the mass disinfection of clothing and for the extermination of insects in clothing. The building was situated in sector BIIg (Kanada II), near Crematoria IV and V. (*USHMM/Yad Vashem*)

Prisoners of the *Aufräumungskommando* ('order commandos'), nicknamed 'Canada Commandos', sort through a mound of personal belongings confiscated from the arriving transport of Jews from Subcarpathian Rus. The primary tasks of these special units were to assist in camp duties such as unloading Jews from trains, with the assistance of the order commandos (*Aufräumungskommando)*, who were a group of recruited Jews that were used to unload the confiscated property of the transports. They were tasked with collecting transport possessions and sorting them for storage in the warehouse complex known as 'Canada'. (*Yad Vashem/Auschwitz-Birkenau Museum*)

Prisoners in the Canada Commandos unload the confiscated property of a transport of Jews. The camp prisoners came to refer the looted property as 'Canada', associating it with the riches symbolised by Canada. The members of this commando were almost exclusively Jews. 'Canada' storage facilities occupied several dozen barracks and other buildings around the camp. The looted property was funnelled from Auschwitz through an extensive distribution network that served many individuals and various economic branches of the Third Reich. (*USHMM/Yad Vashem*)

A photograph probably taken in June 1944 of *SS-Obergruppenführer* Oswald Pohl during an official visit to Auschwitz, accompanied by Auschwitz Commandant Richard Baer who had previously served as his adjutant. In the background between Baer and Pohl is Karl Bischoff. (*USHMM*)

A US Air Force aerial reconnaissance photograph taken on 26 June 1944 during the Hungarian Operation. It shows Auschwitz I and Birkenau. The photo shows no activity from the four crematoria. This was probably because the last shipment of Hungarian Jews had arrived on 18 June 1944, and the next batch of trains was not until two days later on 28 June 1944. (*National Archives and Records Administration – NARA*)

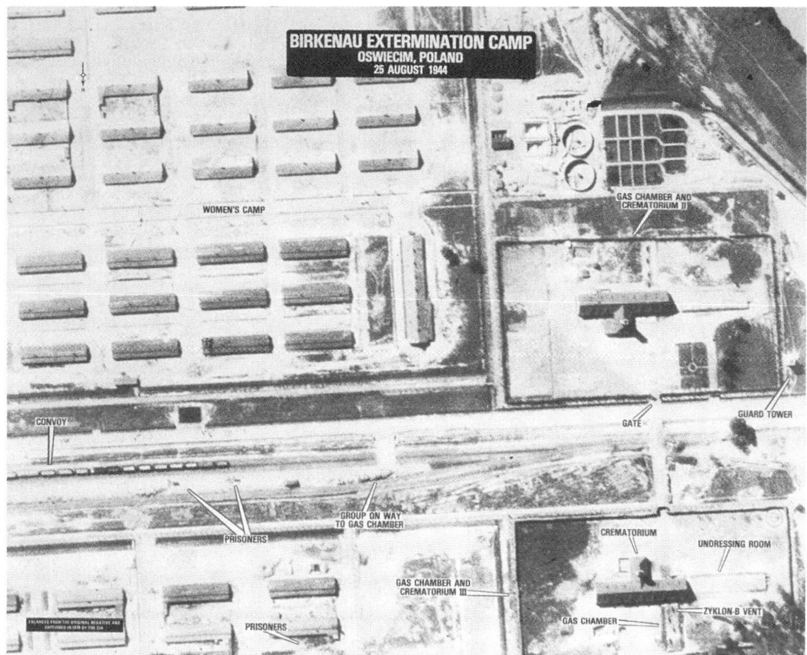

A US Air Force aerial reconnaissance photograph taken on 25 August 1944 shows Auschwitz-Birkenau camp, highlighting the location of Crematoria II and III. No incineration action can be seen in the crematoria. However, on 20 August 1944 five transports had arrived in the camp. (*NARA – The National Archives and Records Administration*)

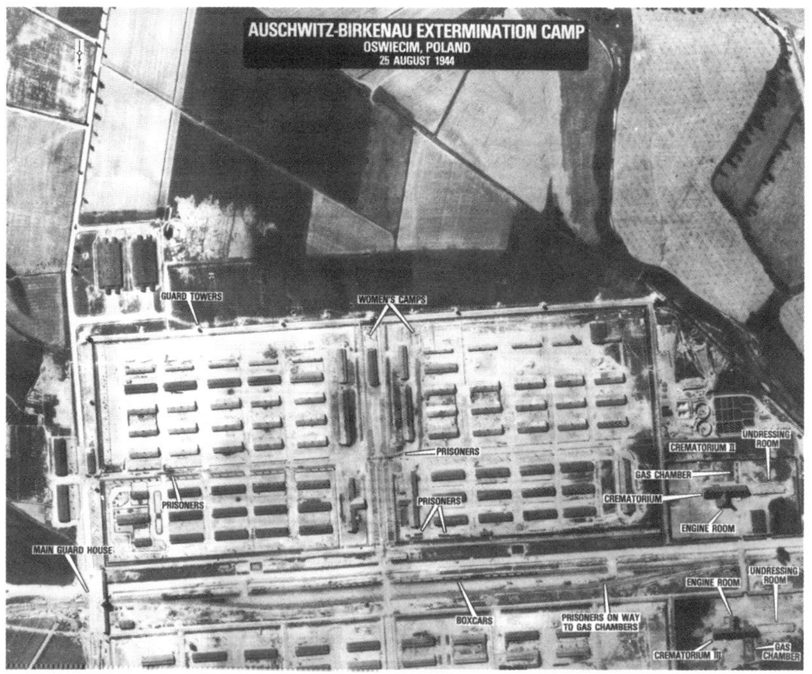

An aerial reconnaissance photograph taken on 25 August 1944 shows Auschwitz-Birkenau camp, highlighting the location of Crematoria II and III including a train, guard towers and people walking in the direction of the gas chambers. (*NARA – The National Archives and Records Administration*)

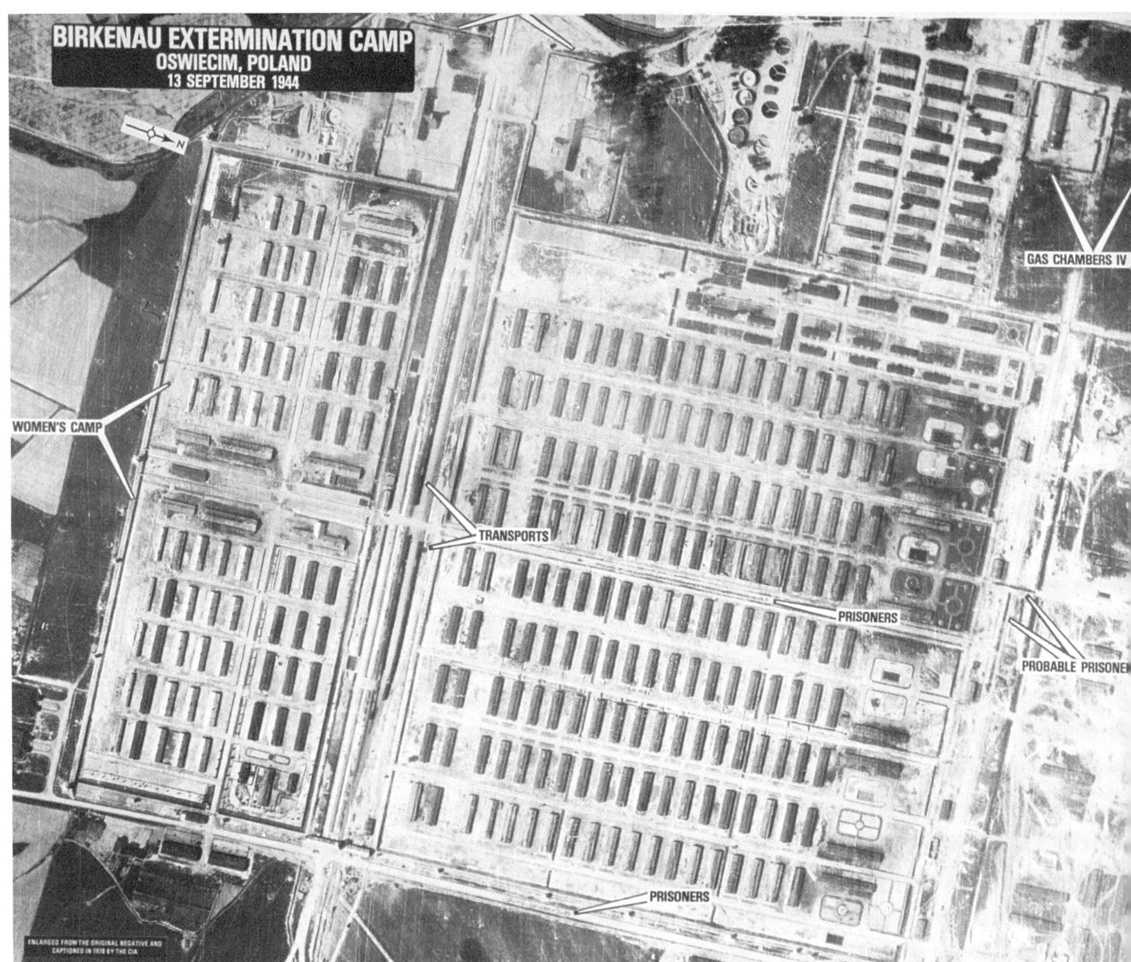

An aerial reconnaissance photograph taken on 13 September 1944 shows Auschwitz-Birkenau camp. It highlights the location of Crematoria IV and V including a train. However, no transports arrived that day, except 300 Jewish children from Kovno that were gassed the day before. The image may suggest that this train, which is pure speculation, had remained on the line from the day before. (*NARA – The National Archives and Records Administration*)

An aerial reconnaissance photograph taken on 25 August 1944 showing Auschwitz I. It highlights Crematorium I, various buildings including the Hoss villa, the commandant's offices, prisoner registration building, and the infamous penal block 11. (*NARA – The National Archives and Records Administration*)

An aerial reconnaissance photograph taken on 29 November showing Auschwitz I. (*NARA – The National Archives and Records Administration*)

Aftermath

In spite of the frenzied killing at Auschwitz-Birkenau during the summer of 1944 the military situation on both the Eastern and Western Fronts had deteriorated considerably. Out in the East, German troops were fighting frantically to stem the Russian onslaught and by incredible efforts and bitter fighting they had managed to slow down their enemy. But the whole German position in the East was now cracking, and any hope of repairing it was made almost impossible by crippling shortages of troops. To make matters worse, the Russians were now fighting on Polish soil east of Warsaw. Also, due to the American bombing on the IG Farben Buna Factory at Monowitz and on Auschwitz I on 13 September, the old crematorium, unused since the construction of the four crematoria at Birkenau, was converted into an air shelter, not for those incarcerated, but for the patients of the SS hospital. The drawing below by the Bauleitung drawn by prisoner 57347 on 21 September outlines the conversion of the old crematorium into an air raid shelter for the SS hospital with an operating theatre, chemical toilet, existing sewer complete with air lock.

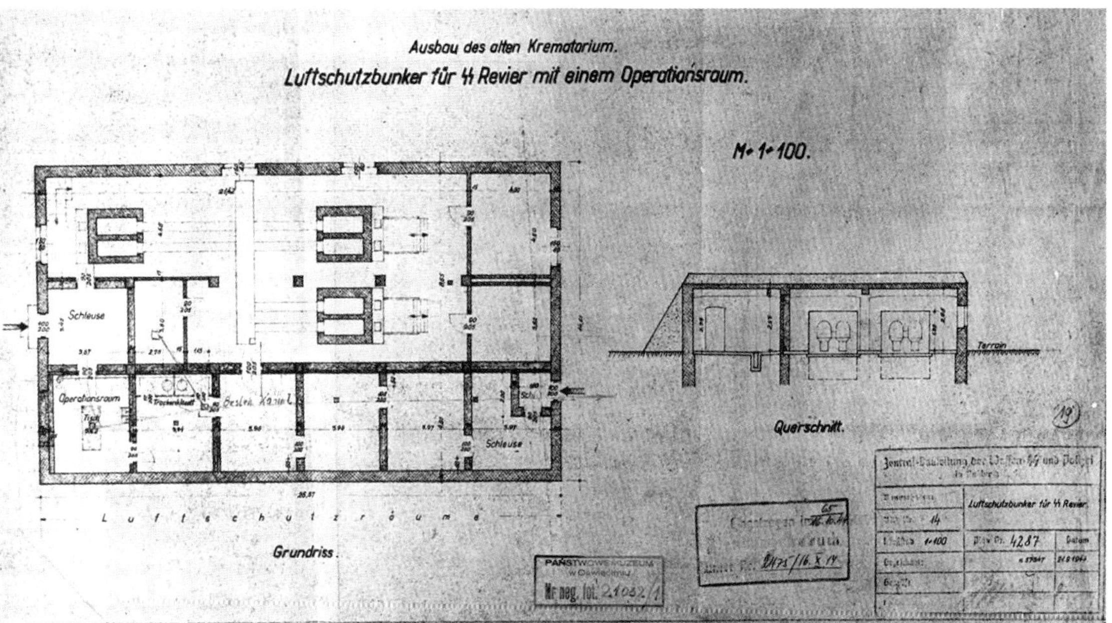

(*Auschwitz-Birkenau Museum*)

On 6 September, as further battles in Poland intensified, Himmler suddenly ordered the liquidation of Auschwitz, including plans for the complete destruction of all four crematoria, including Bunkers I and II. The order emphasised that all the personal effects from the warehouses, as well as building material and equipment, were to be transported by motor vehicle and train back to the *Reich*. Half of the 150,000 prisoners that were held captive in Auschwitz, most of them Poles and Russians, were to be moved to concentration camps in the west. Places like Buchenwald, Bergen-Belsen, Dachau, Flossenbürg, Gross-Rosen, Mauthausen, Natzweiler, and Ravensbrück were to receive the Auschwitz prisoners. In the surrounding sub-camps too those fit enough to be evacuated were ordered to be forced marched back to Germany and used as slave labour. This also included prisoners that had been working for the *Bauleitung*, who were transferred to other camps.

As news of the liquidation of the camp became common knowledge among the inmates, members of the *Sonderkommando* squad in charge of Crematorium IV rose in revolt on 7 October. According to an SS report gathered after the revolt, young Jewish women workers had been smuggling small packets of gunpowder out of the Weichsel-Union-Metallwerke, a munitions factory in an industrial area between the main camp of Auschwitz I and Auschwitz II. The plan was to destroy the gas chambers and the crematoria by launching an uprising. What followed were some members of the *Sonderkommando* attacking a number of the SS personnel. A fire was then started and this spread to the roof of the crematorium. As a result of the uprising some 280 *Sonderkommando* members were killed in Crematoria IV and V, 171 in Crematorium III, and 1 in Crematorium II. In total 452 members of the *Sonderkommando* were killed. During these events, three German camp guards were also killed.

Following the revolt, Crematorium IV was closed-down and would no longer be used as a gassing or crematorium facility. By this time there were reports of the Red Army advancing through Poland and action was required urgently to close-down the Birkenau facility altogether. As a result, the *SS-Bauinspecktion Schlesien* (Building Inspection Silesia) was moved from Katowice to Breslau. It was here that the German forces were hoping that they would hold back the Soviet advance. The Gross Rosen camp was an administrative hub for some ninety-seven subcamps, and it was to here that truck loads of documents comprising the Auschwitz *Bauleitung* archive were moved for safety.

Whilst the *Bauleitung* archive was being packed away at Gross Rosen, at Auschwitz Himmler ordered that the Birkenau killing apparatus be dismantled in a rushed effort to conceal what they had done there. During early January 1945 the incineration ditches too were cleared and levelled, and pits which had been filled with ash and the crushed bones of murdered prisoners were emptied and covered with fresh turf and other plantings. Crematorium I in the main camp had been turned into an air raid shelter and the chimney and the holes in the ceiling in which the Zyklon B had been thrown were removed. All the furnaces of Crematoria I, II, III and IV were dismantled and usable parts transported to other camps. On the night of 17 January some 58,000 prisoners were evacuated from Monowitz and the Auschwitz sub camps, with about 20,000 coming from the Auschwitz-Birkenau camp alone. Very few were evacuated by train, with the majority of them being forced into the snow and marched in freezing night-time temperatures westward towards Germany. As they shuffled along the icy road, behind them the night sky lit with flashes and the distant sounds of Russian gun fire rumbled across the horizon. Anyone, including children, unable to keep pace with the mass exodus was shot and their murdered corpses left at the roadside. The scenes were utterly terrible.

Amidst the chaotic evacuation order, the small groups of SS left behind at Auschwitz were given instructions for the demolition of the crematoria, including Bunkers I and II. After having blown up the remaining shells of Crematoria II and III in the early afternoon of 20 January, six days later they dynamited Crematorium V. As for Crematorium IV, this building had been demolished after it had been damaged by fire following the revolt in October 1944 by the *Sonderkommando*. During the demolition of the crematoria special SS units murdered around 700 prisoners at Birkenau and nearby sub-camps.

As news of the Red Army advanced along the main road from Krakow, the guards were ordered to destroy the last of the camp's documents, blue-prints, and drawings, to set fire to the Canada stores, and to liquidate the remaining prisoners in the camp. However, more concerned with saving their own lives than following orders, the SS guards fled the camp, leaving the soldiers of the First Ukrainian Front to liberate Auschwitz and its sub camps.

On their arrival in Birkenau, Russian soldiers found various structures destroyed including the crematoria. Crematorium IV was a contorted slab of concrete, whilst Crematorium V was a pile of twisted rubble with parts of protruding metal. Almost immediately soldiers were set to work in order to clear the rubble in an effort to find the furnaces still intact. However, all the furnaces of Crematoria I, II, III and IV had been hastily removed. It appeared that there was no trace of the human suffering and murder that had existed at these sites until a gas-tight door with no peephole was found almost virtually intact at Crematorium V. After further investigation three shutters for Zyklon-B introduction openings were found, but it could not be determined which crematoria they belonged to due to the extensive damage to the sites. At Crematorium V, after further clearing the site of rubble, part of the metal components of the furnace frame was found.

Evidence comprising of documents and drawings of Crematoria IV and V were found, but there was no extensive information. This was not because the evidence had been destroyed or lost, but purely the fact that these two crematoria saw little operation during their existence at Birkenau. Unlike Crematoria II and III, which were in constant use, the evidence from these documents, letters, various correspondence and drawings backs this proof.

Therefore, it suggests that, during the homicidal operation at Birkenau, Crematorium IV perhaps served as a testing basis for the other crematoria. Although Crematorium V was almost deprived of its furnaces due to ongoing technical issues, the building did play a pivotal part in the camp's operation during 1943. Over a period of some two months this crematorium was the only building used for gassing and cremating those totally unfit for work. However, when Crematorium III was completed and Crematorium II brought back into service, Crematorium V was decommissioned and kept in reserve as a gas chamber, but then brought back into operation for the Hungarian action in the summer of 1944. In service, the building operated as a gassing facility and used the nearby open-air cremation pits to burn the murdered victims due to the fact that the crematorium's furnaces were inoperative.

The total numbers of hapless victims that were ultimately destroyed at Crematoria IV and V is uncertain due to the lack of documentary evidence and the constant technical issues with both buildings. For Crematorium V the estimated figure is probably about 15,000 and the number for Crematorium IV probably about 20,000, but these numbers cannot be calculated and could be underestimated.

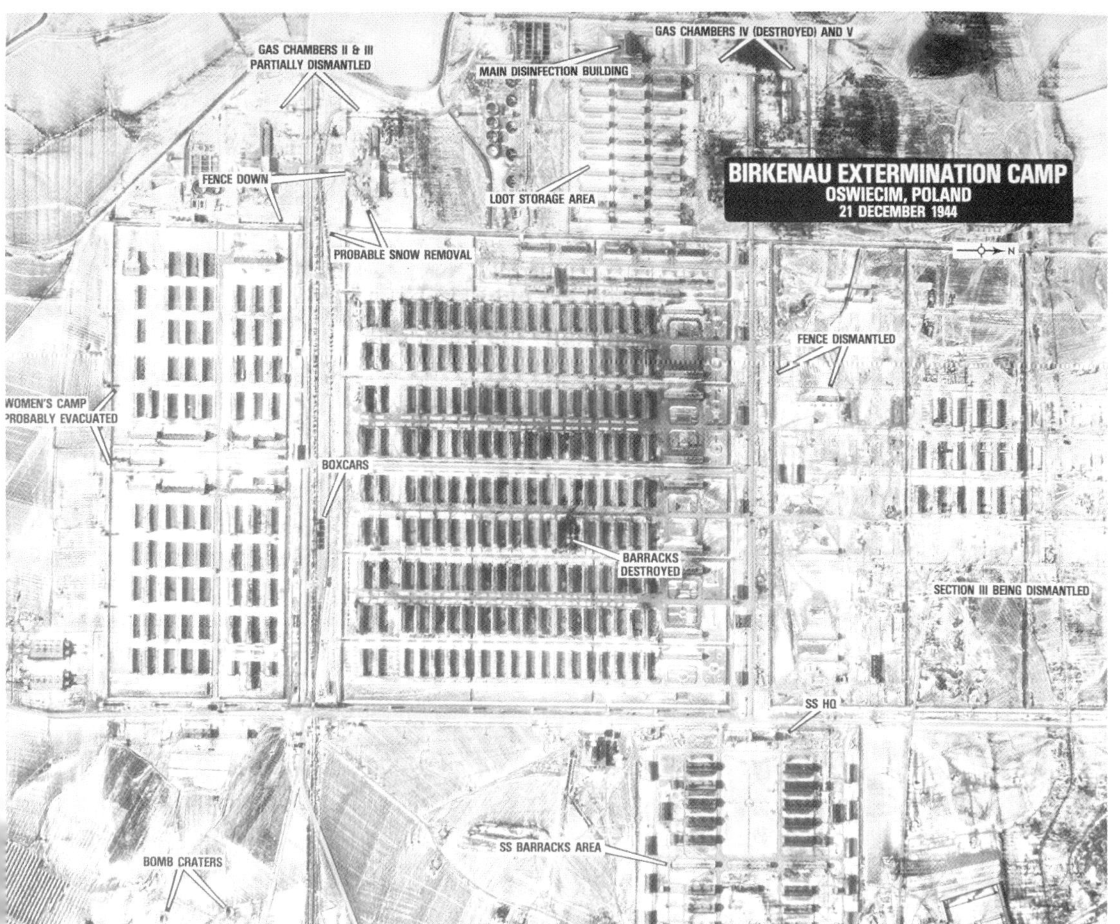

An aerial view taken on 21 December 1944 showing the destruction of the Auschwitz-Birkenau camp by SS personnel and camp *Kommandos* in expectation of the arrival of Soviet troops. A month later, the SS personnel that were left behind at Auschwitz were given instructions for the demolition of the crematoria, including Bunkers I and II. After having blown up the remaining shells of Crematoria II and III in the early afternoon of 20 January, six days later they dynamited Crematorium V. As for Crematorium IV, this building had been demolished after it had been damaged by fire following a revolt in October 1944 by *Sonderkommando* and it can be seen in the aerial photo. During the demolition of the crematoria special SS units murdered around 700 prisoners at Birkenau and nearby sub-camps. (*NARA – The National Archives and Records Administration*)

An aerial reconnaissance photograph taken on 21 December showing Auschwitz I, Birkenau and the surrounding area. (*NARA – The National Archives and Records Administration*)

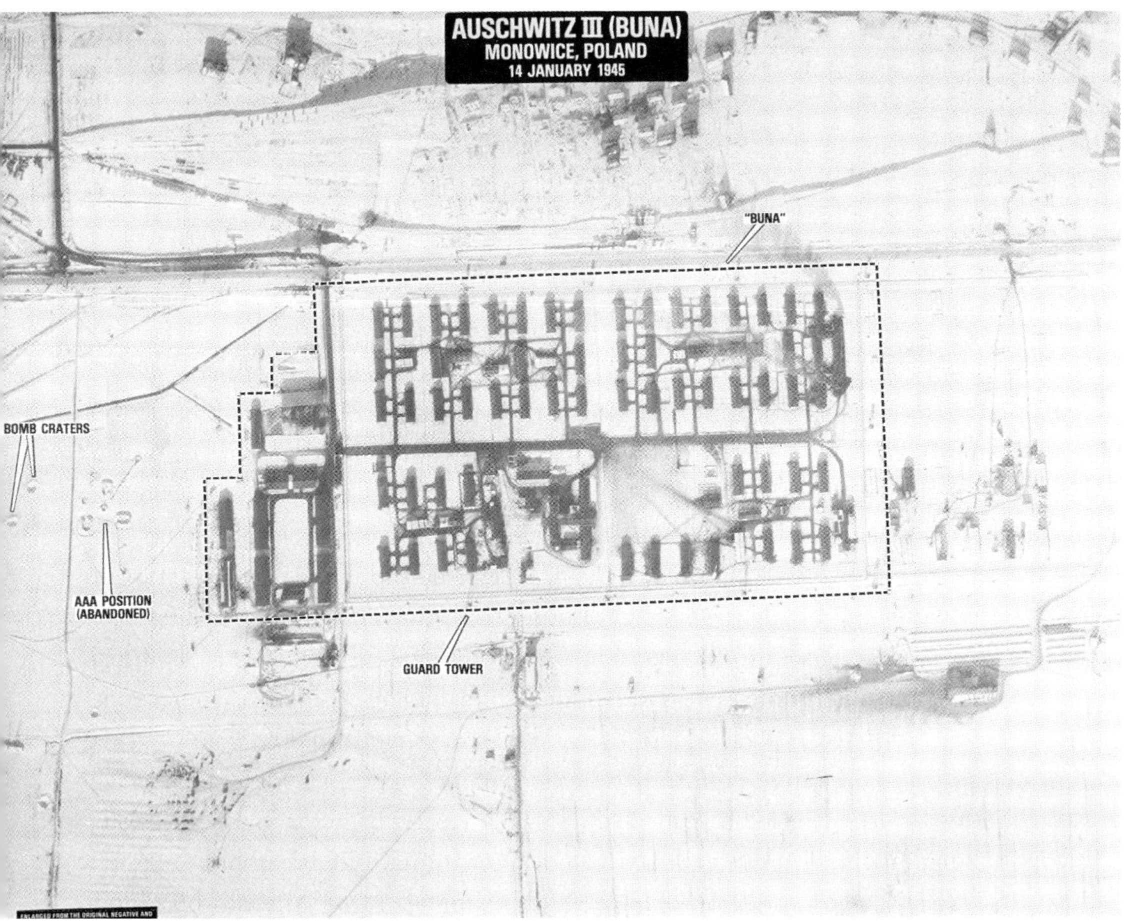

An aerial reconnaissance photograph taken on 14 January 1945 showing Auschwitz III (Buna plant). (*NARA – The National Archives and Records Administration*)

GAS CHAMBER IV
DESTROYED 7 OCT 1944
GAS CHAMBER V
GAS CHAMBER III
FENCE DOWN
GAS CHAMBER II
GUARD TOWERS
DISMANTLED
SECTION II
SECTION I (WOMEN'S CAMP) EVACUATED
SECTION III DISMANTLED
SS BARRACKS
QUARANTINE CAMP
EVACUATED
SECTION I PARTIALLY DISMANTLED
BIRKENAU EXTERMINATION COMPLEX
OSWIECIM, POLAND
14 JANUARY 1945
TO AUSCHWITZ I

An aerial reconnaissance photograph of Birkenau taken on 14 January 1945. It shows much of the camp evacuated and areas partially dismantled, including the destroyed crematoria. Thirteen days later the camp was liberated by the Red Army. (*NARA – The National Archives and Records Administration*)

A Russian photograph showing the liberation of Auschwitz I. The children are wearing adult-size prisoner jackets, and child survivors of Auschwitz are led by relief workers and Soviet soldiers through a narrow passage between two barbed-wire fences.

Joyful photograph showing prisoners liberated at the Auschwitz main camp gate.

Russian soldiers converse with inmates inside Auschwitz-Birkenau. On 27 January 1945, at 15:00, the Soviet 322nd Rifle Division arrived at Auschwitz. In the surrounding area there had been some heavy fighting around Monowitz, Birkenau and the Auschwitz main camp. What greeted the soldiers was 'pure horror'. Many of these soldiers were battle-hardened men that had fought viciously through Ukraine and into Poland and were used to seeing death. However, they were shocked at the appalling sight as they entered the camps. Red Army general Vasily Petrenko, commander of the 107th Infantry Division, said, 'I who saw people dying every day was shocked by the Nazis' indescribable hatred toward the inmates, who had turned into living skeletons. I read about the Nazis' treatment of Jews in various leaflets, but there was nothing about the Nazis' treatment of women, children, and old men. It was in Auschwitz that I found out about the fate of the Jews'. Some 7,000 prisoners had been left behind, the majority of which were weak, malnourished and very sick. Most of the inmates were middle-aged adults or children younger than 15-years-old. Soldiers found 600 corpses that had died in the barracks and stable huts. In the Canada Stores at Birkenau and at Auschwitz main camp, they counted 370,000 men's suits, 837,000 articles of women's clothing, and seven tonnes of human hair. At the Monowitz camp, there were about 800 survivors. Soldiers of the Soviet Sixtieth Army, which was part of the 1st Ukrainian Front, liberated the camp.

Appendices

Appendix 1

Planning and Construction Office: The SS Main Economic and Administrative Office, May 1940

Headed by *SS-Oberführer* Hans Kammler

Five Sections Each
Main Department II/I: General affairs relating to construction
Main Department II/2: Accounts Department
Main Department II/3: General Construction
Main Department II/4: Special Construction

Six Sections Each
Main Department II/5: Central Inspection of Construction
Main Department II/6: Planning Departments
Main Department II/7: Specialist Technical Department

One Section Each
Department II/Ro: Raw Materials Office
Department II/K: Vehicles

Appendix 2

The SS Economic and Administrative Main Office, 1 February 1942
(*SS-Wirtschafts- und Verwaltungshauptamt* – SS-WVHA)

Headed by *SS-Oberführer* Kammler

Office Group C was organized into six offices:

- C I: General Construction
- C II: Special Construction
- C III: Specialist Technical Department
- C IV: Artistic Special Department
- C V: Central Construction Inspection Office
- C VI: Building Maintenance and Business Administration

Office Group D was headed by *SS-Brigadeführer* and Major General of the Waffen-SS Richard Glücks.

The WVHA was under the command of the *SS-Gruppenführer* and Lieutenant General of the Waffen-SS Oswald Pohl.

Appendix 3

The Central Construction Office, January 1943

The Central Construction Office was divided into five construction offices and fourteen departments.

Central Construction Office of the Waffen-SS and Police Auschwitz

Headed by: *SS-Hauptsturmführer* Bischoff

Above Ground Construction

Drawing up of all construction designs for the Construction Offices of the concentration camp.

Civil Engineers

Construction management, construction strategy and all construction requirements.

Below Ground Construction

Planning and construction of streets, water purification plants and sewer pipes. This included water collection construction and construction of railway lines, bridges, etc.

Below Ground Construction Engineers

SS-Oberscharführer Strang, construction assistant
SS-Sturmmann Krause, mason
SS-Unterscharführer Fränzen, paver
SS-Unterscharführer Gerhard, paver
SS-Untersturmführer Schenk, underground technician

Irrigation

Planning for well digging and surveys, water purification points, water tanks and supply of water. Budget for works: 1,600,000 RM.

Irrigation Engineers

SS-Rottenführer Schuhknecht, stonecutter
SS-Schütze Schwab, Tiefbau technician
SS-Untersturmführer Eggeling, agrarian engineer
Civilian employee Wolf, smith

Surveying

Planning and surveying for general repairs, including water channels, a dam plant on the Sola River, water supply, draining and pumping, plus building projects relating to general water projects. Budget for works: 14,700,000 RM.

Surveyors

SS-Rottenführer Dragoni, subforeman pumping
SS-Rottenführer Schmid, subforeman drainage
SS-Schütze Fischer, surveyor
SS-Untersturmführer Töfferl, civilian engineer
SS-Untersturmführer Wallergang, agronomist

Planning

Planning and designs of buildings including existing buildings and designs for the Construction Offices' concentration camp, including farming and industrial construction.

Planners

SS-Schütze Gierisch, architect
SS-Schütze Splitt, building designer
SS-Untersturmführer Dejaco, architect
Civilian employee Schimmel, construction expert
Civilian employee Walther, architect
Civilian employee Werkmann, architect

Raw materials and purchases

Purchase and planning of raw materials for transport for construction projects.

Material Purchasers

SS-Oberscharführer Arloth, technical trader
SS-Sturmmann Kunert, food trader
SS-Unterscharführer Bracht, trader
SS-Unterscharführer Hoffmann, carpenter
SS-Unterscharführer Pruchnik, employee
SS-Unterscharführer Wilk, trader

Construction Depot I

Warehousing including administration, distribution of materials and tools for construction projects.

SS-Oberscharführer Stiller, trader
SS-Unterscharführer Holz, trader

Construction Depot II
Administration of Construction Depot Posen
Civilian employee Niendorf, farmer

Administration
Accounting and reporting including stock control of weapons, plus matters concerning all accommodation.

SS-Scharführer Betzinger, trader
SS-Unterscharführer Giesenberg, trader
SS-Unterscharführer Weislav, fur worker

Registry
SS-Unterscharführer Putzker, hotel employee
Civilian employee and trader Uttinger

Telephone communication
SS-Rottenführer Cerne, regional employee
SS-Unterscharführer Nitsche, banker mason

Ordnance
SS-Rottenführer Steinert, smith

Transportation
Maintenance and repair of the following:

- Two railcars
- Eleven motor buses
- Seventy-two construction machines
- Motor cars
- Forty-five horse-drawn carts

Drivers
SS-Scharführer Kögel
SS-Schütze Depta
SS-Sturmmann Bärwolf
SS-Sturmmann Rosenauer

SS-Sturmmann Seitner
SS-Unterscharführer Bergmann
SS-Unterscharführer Kling
SS-Unterscharführer Olschar

Technical department
Planning and installation of electrics, transformer station, heating stations, heating plant, machine construction for concentration camp including farming and electrical workshop with 165 inmates.

Technicians
SS-Sturmmann Beck, expert mechanic
SS-Unterscharführer Swoboda, electrics technician
Civilian employee Bendorff, electrics technician
Civilian employee Jährling, heating technician

Manpower Employment Department
Lodgings and employment for both civilian work force and concentration camp inmates.
Estimated numbers:

- 1,000 civilians
- 8,000 inmates

Employment Staff
SS-Rottenführer Steinstrasser, gardener
SS-Unterscharführer Hochscherf, testing employee
SS-Unterscharführer Pantke, manufacturing director in a furniture factory

Workshops
Supervision of the inmate workshops, which included the following workers per shop:

- 190 x cabinet shop
- 22 x glazier shop
- 232 x locksmith shop
- 76 x painters

Carpenter: *SS-Schütze* Blanke
Head of Shop: *SS-Unterscharführer* Kywitz
Painter: *SS-Rottenführer* Dengler

Carpentry and Roofing Shop

- 77 x self-employed carpenters and roofers
- 1,919 x inmates undertaking carpentry work, maintenance, barracks assembly, etc.

Head of Carpentry
SS-Rottenführer Lugert
SS-Unterscharführer Vieth

Landscaping
Gardens including all garden construction projects.

Head Gardener
SS-Unterscharführer Kamann

Secretaries
Civilian female employee Quitzau

CONSTRUCTION OFFICES

I. Construction Office of the Waffen-SS and Police Auschwitz, concentration camp Auschwitz and farming Auschwitz

Heads of Construction
Farming Auschwitz
Construction Assistant: *SS-Sturmmann* Lubitz
Construction Expert: *SS-Scharführer* Jäger
Construction Expert: *SS-Unterscharführer* Kirschnek
Designer: *SS-Schütze* Genur
Joiner: *SS-Hauptscharführer* Wiechmann
Mason: *SS-Unterscharführer* Oschinski
Secretary: Civilian Employee Lehmann

II. Construction Office of the PoW Camp

Heads of Construction
New construction, installation and constructing accommodations which comprised of the following:

- 343 x accommodation barracks
- 158 x barracks for amenities e.g. laundry, storehouses, infirmary, etc.
- 4 x crematoria
- 4 x mortuary chambers
- 16 x troop barracks

- 6 x workers barracks
- 6 x latrine barracks
- 11x barracks for offices, infirmary and general supplies.
- 2 x emergency electrical generators
- 3x transformer buildings

Architect: *SS-Untersturmführer* Peetz
Carpenter: *SS-Hauptscharführer* Böttjer
Designer: Civilian employee Uhl
Designer: *SS-Unterscharführer* Ulmer
Engineer: *SS-Unterscharführer* Janisch
Engineer: *SS-Untersturmführer* Kastner
Mason: *SS-Sturmmann* Scheffel
Mason: *SS-Schütz* Sihorsch
Secretary: Civilian employee Lippert
Works Supervisor: *SS-Oberscharführer* Kayser

III. Construction Office Industrial area Auschwitz – Krupp factory halls including construction of the Construction Depot Auschwitz.

Heads of Construction
Sheds, office buildings, plant for Krupp, etc.

SS-Unterscharführer Penn
SS-Sturmmann Jothann
SS-Rottenführer Wolff

IV. Construction Office Main Economic Camp of the Waffen-SS and Police and Troop Economic Camp Oderberg
Construction:
1 x warehouse barrack with basement
1 x office barrack, potato bunkers

V. Construction Office Works and Estate Freudenthal and Estate Partschendorf

Heads of Construction
2 x warehouse barracks for machines and fruit juices
2 x accommodation barracks for foreign civilian workers

Construction Assistant: *SS-Unterscharführer* Mayer

Appendix 4

List of Private Companies Assisting in Construction and Maintenance of Auschwitz

- Ader, Gustav
- AEG, Kattowitz, Holtzestrasse 23
- Anhalt Hoch- und Tiefbau AG, Baugeschäft, Berlin S W 11. Schönebergerstrasse 13
- Bahmbetr. Werke, Auschwitz
- Berhold, Robert, Gleisarbeiten, Gleiwitz
- Bolney, Speditionsfirma
- Boos, Friedrich, Zentralheizungen, Köln-Bichendorf, Helmholzstrasse 6167
- Brand, Carl, Halle/Saale, Platz der SA 10
- Continentale Wasserwerkgesellschaft GmbH, Berlin-Charlottenburg, Hardenbergstrasse 1
- Deutsche Bau-AG, Breslau, Charlottenstrasse 54–56
- Ekonomia, Bielitz O/S, Grünewaldstrasse 7
- Falk, Carl, Gleiwitz O/S, Gustav Freitag Allee 13
- Godzik, Karl K.G., Gleiwitz O/S, Miethe Allee 6
- Gottschling, Wilhelm, Baumeister Liegnitz O/S, Timmelmann-strasse 20
- Grabarz, Georg, Blitzableiteranlagen, Gleiwitz
- Herschel, Hermann, Gellersdorf am Quais, über Laubau
- Heyduck, Alois, Malermeister, Gleiwitz O/S
- Hirt, Hermann, Nachf., Eisenbetonbau, Breslau 13, Auguststrasse 147
- Huta Hoch- and Tiefbau-AG, Kattowitz O/S, Friedrichstrasse 19
- Industrie-Bau AG, Bielitz O/S, Elisabethstrasse 21
- Keil, Alfred, Baugeschäft, Gleiwitz O/S, Teucherstrasse 10
- Kermel, Wilhelm, Elektroinstallation, Kattowitz, Direktionsstrasse 3
- Kluge, Josef, Hoch-, Tief- u. Eisenbetonbau, Baugeschaft, Alt-Gleiwitz O/S, Labanderweg 59
- Knaut, Kanalisation
- Koehler, Robert, Ing., Bauunternehmung, Myslowitz O/S
- Kohlengrube, Brzeszcze
- Lenz Co. A.G.
- Lepski & Co., Bunzlau O/S, Löwenbergerstrasse 24–25
- Maschinenfabrik, Augsburg-Nürnberg (MAN), Augsburg
- Niegel, Fritz, Ofenbaugeschäft, Beuthen O/S, Stefanstrasse 6
- Petersen, Friedrich, Berlin-Pankow. Görstrasse 47a

- Prestel, Helmut, Sosnowitz O/S, Schoppinitzerstrasse 3
- Reckmann, Richard, Cottbus, Kaiser-Wilhelm-Platz 55
- Richter, Debica, Generalgouvernement
- Richter, Hermann, Tiefbau, Rohrsen bei Hannover
- Riedel u. SOHN, W., Eisenbeton- und Hocbbau, Bielitz O/S, Brükkenstrasse 1
- Schlesische Industriebau Lenz u. Co. AG, Kattowitz, Grundmannstrasse 23
- Segnitz, Konrad, Baugeschäft, Beuthen O/S, Lindenstrasse 38
- Spirra, Franz, Oppeln-Wilhelmstahl O/S, Hafenstrasse 24
- Strauch, Richard, Ing., Werchow b/Galau N.L., Alte Weichselstrasse 62
- Topf u. SÖHNE, Erfurt, Dreisestrasse 7–9
- Triton, Tiefbauunternehmung, Kattowitz O/S, Königshüttestrasse 87
- Vedag, Vereinigte Dachpappen-Fabriken, Breslau 1, Elferplatz 1a
- Wagner, Walter, Gleiwitz O/S, Grüne Waldstrasse 7
- Wodak, Hans, Bauingenieur and Brunnenbaumeister, Beuthen O/S, Gymnasialstrasse 20
- Zementfabrik, Golleschau

Appendix 5

Civilian Workers

From 13 May 1942 civilian workers were employed to support the private companies at Auschwitz. Below is a report list that Bischoff had to present on the use of manpower employed and used at Auschwitz.

1 April 1942
8,418 men
2,994 women

30 June 1942
8,688 men
3,406 women

30 September 1942
8,851 men
3,472 women

31 March 1943
Labour Registry Statistics Abu 4a first registered monthly, then quarterly, the variations in worker manpower: 20,292 registered male workers

30 June 1943
19,711 registered male workers

30 September 1943
20,472 registered males

31 December 1943
20,677 registered males

31 March 1944
21,275 registered males

30 June 1944
21,620 German workers
5,595 foreign workers

30 September 1944
21,885 German workers
6,664 foreign workers

31 December 1944
4,535 German workers
8,070 foreign workers

Appendix 6

List of Members of the Central Construction Office of Auschwitz, 25 November 1941

Bischoff, Karl
Arloth, Willibald Kunert, Karl
Bärwolf, Hans Kywitz, Walter
Beck, Walter Lubitz, Heinz
Blanke, Heinrich Lugert, Hans
Cerne, Albin Manhart, Ignaz
Dejaco, Walter Nestripke, Friedrich
Dengler, Hans Nitsche, Johann
Eggeling, Karl Olschar, Josef
Engler, Hans Pantke, Kurt
Ertl, Fritz Pruchnik, Rudolf
Fenrich, Josef Putzker,
Fränzen, Reinhard Scheffel, Rolf
Gertl, Schmid, Helmut
Giesenberg, Heinz Steinert, Georg
Hochscherf, Steinstrasser, Hans
Hoffmann, Heinrich Stiller, Alfred
Holz, Max Swoboda, Heinrich
Janisch, Josef Taddiken, Fritz
Jarzombek, Stefan Thoma, Walter
Jothann, Werner Ulmer, Karl
Kamann, Dietrich Vieth, Hermann
Kastner, Fritz Weislav, Franz
Kayser, Otto Werner, Paul
Kling, Armin Wilk, Paul
Kofler, Hans Wolff, Johann
Krause, Max Wolter, Frit

Appendix 7

List of Members of the Central Construction Office of Auschwitz, 15 December 1942

SS-*Oberscharführer* Arloth Williams
SS-*Sturmmann* Bärwolf Hans
SS-*Sturmmann* Beck Walter
SS-*Unterscharführer* Bergmann Georg
SS-*Scharführer* Betzinger Ewald
SS-*Hauptsturmführer* Bischoff Karl
SS-*Schütze* Blanke Heinrich
SS-*Hauptscharführer* Böttjer Heinrich
SS-*Unterscharführer* Bracht Fritz
SS-*Rottenführer* Cerne Albin
SS-*Untersturmführer* Dejaco Walter
SS-*Rottenführer* Dengler Hans
SS-*Schütze* Depta Romuald
SS-*Rottenführer* Dragoni Livio
SS-*Untersturmführer* Eggeling Karl
SS-*Untersturmführer* Ertl Fritz
SS-*Schütze* Fischer Anton
SS-*Unterscharführer* Fränzen Reinhard
SS-*Schütze* Genur Arpad
SS-*Unterscharführer* Gerhard Erwin
SS-*Schütze* Gierisch Martin
SS-*Unterscharführer* Giesenberg Heinz
SS-*Unterscharführer* Hoffmann Heinrich
SS-*Unterscharführer* Holz Max
SS-*Untersturmführer* Janisch Josef
SS-*Scharführer* Jäger Arthur
SS-*Sturmscharführer* Jothann Werner
SS-*Unterscharführer* Kamann Dietrich
SS-*Unterscharführer* Kastner Fritz
SS-*Oberscharführer* Kayser Otto
SS-*Untersturmführer* Kirschneck Hans
SS-*Unterscharführer* Kling Armin
SS-*Sturmmann* Kofler Hans
SS-*Scharführer* Kögel Kurt

SS-*Sturmmann* Krause Max
SS-*Sturmmann* Kunert Karl
SS-*Unterscharführer* Kywitz Walter
SS-*Sturmmann* Lubitz Heinz
SS-*Rottenführer* Lugert Hans
SS-*Unterscharführer* Nitsche Johann
SS-*Unterscharführer* Olschar Josef
SS-*Unterscharführer* Pantke Kurt
SS-*Untersturmführer* Peetz Rudolf
SS-*Unterscharführer* Penn Fritz
SS-*Untersturmführer* Pollok Josef
SS-*Unterscharführer* Pruchnik Rudolf
SS-*Sturmmann* Rosenauer Leonhard
SS-*Sturmmann* Scheffel Rolf
SS-*Untersturmführer* Schenk Ewald
SS-*Rottenführer* Schmid Helmut
SS-*Rottenführer* Schuhknecht Walter
SS-*Schütze* Schwab Roland
SS-*Schütze* Sihorsch Franz
SS-*Sturmmann* Seitner Rudolf
SS-*Schütze* Splitt *Erich*
SS-*Rottenführer* Steinert Georg
SS-*Rottenführer* Steinstrasser Hans
SS-*Oberscharführer* Stiller Alfred
SS-*Oberscharführer* Strang Hermann
SS-*Unterscharführer* Swoboda Heinrich
SS-*Unterscharführer* Thoma Walter
SS-*Untersturmführer* Töfferl Hermann
SS-*Unterscharführer* Ulmer Karl
SS-*Unterscharführer* Vieth Hermann
SS-*Unterscharführer* Weislav Franz
SS-*Untersturmführer* Wallerang Bernhard
SS-*Hauptscharführer W*iechmann Heinz
SS-*Unterscharführer* Wilk Paul
SS-*Rottenführer* Wolff Johann
SS-*Untersturmführer W*olter Fritz

Appendix 8

List of Members of the Central Construction Office of Auschwitz, January 1943

SS-*Oberscharführer* Arloth Techn. Kaufmann
SS-*Sturmmann* Bärwolf Kraftfahrer
SS-*Sturmmann* Beck Masch. Tech.
SS-*Unterscharführer* Bergmann Kraftfahrer
SS-*Scharführer* Betzinger Kaufmann
SS-*Hauptsturmführer* Bischoff
SS-*Schütze* Blanke Schreiner
SS-*Hauptscharführer* Böttjer Zimmerer
SS-*Unterscharführer* Bracht Kaufmann
SS-*Rottenführer* Cerne Gauleitungsangest.
SS-*Untersturmführer* Dejaco Architekt
SS-*Rottenführer* Dengler Maler
SS-*Schütze* Depta Kraftfahrer
SS-*Rottenführer* Dragoni Vorarbeiter f. Entwäss.
SS-*Untersturmführer* Eggeling Kulturbauing.
SS-*Untersturmführer* Ertl Bauing.
SS-*Schütze* Fischer Vermessungsing.
SS-*Unterscharführer* Fränzen Pflasterer
SS-*Schütze* Genur Zeichner
SS-*Unterscharführer* Gerhard Pflasterer
SS-*Schütze* Gierisch Architekt
SS-*Unterscharführer* Giesenberg Kaufmann
SS-*Unterscharführer* Hochscherf Kontrollangest.
SS-*Unterscharführer* Hoffmann Schrein
SS-*Unterscharführer* Holz Kaufmann
SS-*Scharführer* Jäger Bautechn.
SS-*Untersturmführer* Janisch Dipl. Ing. Neubau
SS-*Sturmmann* Jothann Hochbautechniker
SS-*Unterscharführer* Kamann Gärtner
SS-*Untersturmführer* Kastner Bauing.
SS-*Oberscharführer* Kayser Bauaufseher
SS-*Untersturmführer* Kirschnek Hochbautechn.
SS-*Unterscharführer* Kling Kraftfahrer
SS-*Sturmmann* Kofler Gauleiterangest.
SS-*Scharführer* Kögel Kraftfahrer

SS-*Sturmmann* Krause Maurer
SS-*Sturmmann* Kunert Lebensmittelhändler
SS-*Unterscharführer* Kywitz Werkleiter
SS-*Sturmmann* Lubitz Hilfsbauführer
SS-*Rottenführer* Lugert Zimmerer
SS-*Unterscharführer* Mayer Bauführer
SS-*Unterscharführer* Nitsche Steinschleifer
SS-*Unterscharführer* Olschar Kraftfahrer
SS-*Unterscharführer* Oschinski Maurer
SS-*Unterscharführer* Pantke Betriebsleiter
SS-*Untersturmführer* Peetz Architekt
SS-*Unterscharführer* Penn Bauunternehmer
SS-*Untersturmführer* Pollok
SS-*Unterscharführer* Pruchnik Beamter
SS-*Unterscharführer* Putzker Hotelangestell.
SS-*Sturmmann* Rosenauer Kraftfahrer
SS-*Sturmmann* Scheffel Maurer
SS-*Untersturmführer* Schenk Tiefbautechn.
SS-*Rottenführer* Schmid Vorarb. f. Drainage
SS-*Rottenführer* Schuhknecht Steinhauer
SS-*Schütze* Schwab Tiefbautechn.
SS-*Sturmmann* Seitner
SS-*Schütze* Sihorsch Maurer
SS-*Schütze* Splitt Bauzeichner
SS-*Rottenführer* Steinert Schlosser
SS-*Rottenführer* Steinstrasser Gärter
SS-*Oberscharführer* Stiller Kaufmann
SS-*Oberscharführer* Strang Bauführer
SS-*Unterscharführer* Swoboda Elektrotechn.
SS-v*Unterscharführer* Thoma Kaufmann
SS-*Untersturmführer* Töfferl Bauing.
SS-*Unterscharführer* Ulmer Zeichner
SS-*Unterscharführer* Vieth Zimmerer
SS-*Untersturmführer* Wallergang Kulturbaumeis
SS-*Unterscharführer* Weislav Lederarbeiter
SS-*Hauptscharführer* Wiechmann Tischler
SS-*Unterscharführer* Wilk Kaufmann
SS-*Rottenführer* Wolff Maurer
SS-*Untersturmführer* Wolter Bauing
Z.A. Bendorff Elektrotechn

Z.A. Götsch Schreibkraft
Z.A. Jährling Heiz Techn.
Z.A. Lehmann Schreibkraft
Z.A. Lippert Schreibkraft
Z.A. Niendorf Landwirt
Z.A. Partsch Schreibkraft
Z.A. Quitzau Stenotypistin
Z.A. Schimmel Bauzeichner
Z.A. Teichmann Bauführer
Z.A. Uhl Zeichner
Z.A. Uttinger Kaufmann
Z.A. Wachs Innenarchitekt
Z.A. Walther Architekt
Z.A. Werkmann Architekt
Z.A. Wolf Schlo

List of Members of the Central Construction Office of Auschwitz, 2 July 1943
SS-*Sturmbannführer* Bischoff Karl
SS-*Unterscharführer* Bracht Fritz
SS-*Untersturmführer* Dejaco Walter
SS-*Untersturmführer* Eggeling Kurt
SS-*Unterscharführer* Engler Hans
SS-*Rottenführer* Fabian Gerhard
SS-*Rottenführer* Fehnrich Josef
SS-*Unterscharführer* Fränzen Reinhard
SS-*Unterscharführer* Gerhard Erwin
SS-*Unterscharführer* Giessenberg Heinz
SS-*Schütze* Grandl Walter
SS-*Rottenführer* Hecht Willi
SS-*Unterscharführer* Hegert Emil
SS-*Unterscharführer* Holz Max
SS-*Unterscharführer* Horn Gustav
SS-*Scharführer* Jäger Arthur
SS-*Rottenführer* Jähner O
SS-*Untersturmführer* Janisch Josef
SS-*Rottenführer* Jarzombek Stefan
SS-*Obersturmführer* Jothann Werner
SS-*Unterscharführer* Kaman Dietrich
SS-*Rottenführer* Kessler Emil
SS-*Untersturmführer* Kirschnek Hans

SS-*Unterscharführer* Kofler Hans
SS-*Oberscharführer* Kögel Kurt
SS-*Sturmmann* Krause Max
SS-*Unterscharführer* Linnert Robert
SS-*Sturmmann* Lubitz Heinz
SS-*Sturmmann* Lubusch Eduard
SS-*Unterscharführer* Manhardt Ignaz
SS-*Sturmmann* Mazanek Friedrich
SS-*Sturmmann* Nestripke Friedrich
SS-*Sturmmann* Neuber Guido
SS-*Unterscharführer* Nitsche Johann
SS-*Unterscharführer* Oschinski Hans
SS-*Unterscharführer* Pantke Kurt
SS-*Unterscharführer* Penn Fritz
SS-*Rottenführer* Pohl Heinrich
SS-*Untersturmführer* Pollok Josef
SS-*Rottenführer* Schuhknecht Walter
SS-*Rottenführer* Schünner Alfred
SS-*Schütze* Sihorsch Franz
SS-*Rottenführer* Siegmund Kurt
SS-*Hauptscharführer* Stiller Alfred
SS-*Unterscharführer* Swoboda Heinrich
SS-*Sturmmann* Taddiken Fritz
SS-*Unterscharführer* Weislav Franz
SS-*Sturmmann* Werner Paul
SS-*Untersturmführer* Weznitza Erich
SS-*Unterscharführer* Wilk Paul
SS-*Unterscharführer* Wolff Johann
Z.A. Czembor Hildegard
Z.A. Dauner Ernst
Z.A. Jährling Rudolf
Z.A. Käfer Hugo
Z.A. Machus Walter
Z.A. Mosch Alois
Z.A. Müller Erich
Z.A. Neumann Wanda
Z.A. Niendorf Fritz
Z.A. Plaskura Wladislaus
Z.A. Reichelt Rud

List of Members of the Central Construction Office of Auschwitz, 1 September 1944

SS-*Sturmmann* Becker Hugo
SS-*Oberscharführer* Betzinger Ewald
SS-*Hauptscharführer* Böttjer Heinrich
SS-*Unterscharführer* Bracht Fritz
SS-*Unterscharführer* Brinkmann Rudolf
SS-*Obersturmführer* Eggeling Kurt
SS-*Sturmmann* Eisele
SS-*Unterscharführer* Fabian Gerhard
SS-*Unterscharführer* Fränzen Reinhard
SS-*Unterscharführer* Gerhard Erwin
SS-*Unterscharführer* Grandl Walter
SS-*Oberscharführer* Häuser Jakob
SS-*Rottenführer* Hecht Willi
SS-*Unterscharführer* Hegert Emil
SS-*Sturmmann* Henche Hugo
SS-*Untersturmführer* Hoffmann Karl
SS-*Unterscharführer* Holz Max
SS-*Rottenführer* Jähne Otto
SS-*Unterscharführer* Jarzombek Stefan
SS-*Obersturmführer* Jothann Werner
SS-*Unterscharführer* Kamann Dietrich
SS-*Unterscharführer* Kastner Fritz
SS-*Rottenführer* Kessler Emil
SS-*Obersturmführer* Kirschnek Hans
SS-*Hauptscharführer* Kögel Kurt
SS-*Obersturmführer* Krauss
SS-*Rottenführer* Krause Max
SS-*Oberscharführer* Krogman Helmut
SS-*Unterscharführer* Krug Heinrich
SS-*Unterscharführer* Lenksfeld
SS-*Rottenführer* Lichtl Heinrich
SS-*Unterscharführer* Linnert Robert
SS-*Sturmmann* Lippert
SS-*Unterscharführer* Lubitz H
SS-*Unterscharführer* Manhart Ignatz
SS-*Unterscharführer* Meissner Emil
SS-*Unterscharführer* Müller Paul

SS-*Unterscharführer* Nestripke Friedrich
SS-*Sturmmann* Neuber Guido
SS-*Unterscharführer* Nitsche Hans
SS-*Unterscharführer* Nordmann Alfons
SS-*Unterscharführer* Olscher Josef
SS-*Unterscharführer* Pantke Kurt
SS-*Oberscharführer* Penn Fritz
SS-*Rottenführer* Pohl Heinrich
SS-*Sturmmann* Prenk Josef
SS-*Unterscharführer* Schäfer
SS-*Unterscharführer* Schinner Alfred
SS-*Rottenführer* Schuhknecht Walter
SS-*Rottenführer* Schwarz Hans
SS-*Obersturmführer* Semenov Nikolai
SS-*Unterscharführer* Siegmund Kurt
SS-*Unterscharführer* Sihorsch Franz
SS-*Unterscharführer* Swoboda Heinrich
SS-*Unterscharführer* Taddiken Fritz
SS-*Sturmmann* Wack u. Borowitz
SS-*Oberscharführer*v Wegner
SS-*Unterscharführer* Weislav Franz
SS-*Oberscharführer* Wilk Paul
SS-*Unterscharführer* Wolff Johann
SS-*Oberscharführer* Zwenty Fritz
Z.A. Beller Walter
Z.A. Jährling Rudolf
Z.A. Käfer Hugo
Z.A. Krall Josef
Z.A. Kuhn Herbert
Z.A. Mischke Lucie
Z.A. Papesch Georg
Z.A. Plaskura Wladislaw
Z.A. Reichelt Rudolf
Z.A. Vanmarke Philibert
Z.A. Wesser E

Appendix 9

List of Officers Appointed to Auschwitz-Birkenau, 1940–1945

Adolf Krömer
Alois Kurz
Alfred Meimeth
Alfred Schemmel
Alfred Trzebinski
Alfons Verbruggen
Alois Kurz
Andreas Rieck
Armand Langermann
Armand Kudriawtzow
Arie Moehlmann
Artur Liebehenschel
Artur Plorin
August Schlachter
August Christian Arnold
Benno Adolph
Bruno Beger
Bruno Pfütze
Bruno Weber
Eduard Krebsbach
Eduard Wirths
Edmund Brauning
Emil Stocker
Eduard Drees
Elimer Luder Precht
Erich Frommhagen
Erich Sautter
Erwin von Helmersen
Franz Bodmann
Franz Lucas
Franz Xaver Maier
Fritz Wolter
Friedrich Turek
Friedrich Schluter
Franz Xaver Kraus
Franz Stenger
Friedrich Engelbrecht
Friedrich Entress
Friedrich Seidler
Fritz Ertl
Fritz Klein
Franz Halblieb
Friedrich Hartjenstein
Franz Hössler
Franz Johann Hofmann
Gerhard Gerber
Georg Kudriawtzow
Georg von Sauberzweig
Georg Dietrich Grunberg
Georg Gussregen
Georg Franz Meyer
Guntrum Pflaum
Hans Aumeier
Hans Schindler
Hans Karl Moser
Hans Weymann
Heinrich Plaza
Heinz Ritzheimer
Helmet Schippel
Helmet Vetter
Herbert Wuttke
Hans Conrad
Hans Stark
Hans Erich Merbach
Hans Hermann Kremer
Hans Stark
Henry Storch
Heinrich Tager
Heinz Thilo
Hans Kirschneck
Hans Muslow
Hans Münch
Hans Wilhelm Koenig
Hans Schurz
Heinrich Ganninger
Heinrich Josten
Heinrich Schwarz
Herbert-Gunther Kramer
Heinz Kühler
Heinz Schattenberg
Horst Fischer
Johann-Detlef Bartels
Josef Mengele
Josef Pollok
Joachim Caesar
Johann Schwarzhuber
Johann-Detlef Bartels
Josef Kollmer
Josef Kramer
Johann Desch
Josef Simon
Julius Sauer
Karl Bischoff
Karl Wotke
Konrad Wiegand
Karl Eggeling
Karl Storde
Karl Heinz Teuber
Kitt Bruno
Kurt Klipp
Kurt Uhlenbrook
Karl-Josef Fischer
Karl Fritzsch
Karl Höcker
Karl Hoffmann
Karl Ernest Möckel
Karl Heimann
Ludwig Baumgatner

Ludwig Böhne
Max Ehser
Max Popiersch
Max Gebhardt
Max Sell
Max Meyr
Maximilian Grabner
Max Muller
Otto Heidl
Otto Ludwig Schulz
Paul Kreuzmann
Paul Muller
Otto Blaschke
Otto Brossmann
Otto Brossmann
Oskar Dienstbach
Otto Stoppel
Otto Emil Reinicke
Richard Baer
Roland Albert
Rudolf Wagner
Rudolf Beer
Robert Mulka
Raimond Ehrenberger
Reinhold Schneier
Reinhard Thomsen
Rudolf Höss
Rudolf Horstmann
Rudolf Orlich
Robert Neumann
Siegfried Schwela
Theodor Kratzer
Theodor Lange
Thomas Paulsen
Victor Capesius
Victor Zoller
Valentin Meyer
Vincenz Schöttl
Walter Polenz
Walter Schmidetzki
Werner Rohde
Werner Zorn
Wilhelm Bayer
Wilhelm Reischenbeck
Wilhelm Ziemssen
Willy Pinnow
Willi Rieck
Walter Dejaco
Walter Urbanczyk
Werner Zorn
Wilhelm Burger
Willy Frank
Willi Schatz
Wilhelm Siegmann
Walter Goebel
Walter Schütz
Werner Jothan
Willibald Jobst
Wilhelm Schulte

Appendix 10

List of Construction Sites at Auschwitz Concentration Camp, 31 March–15 July 1942

1 *Bauleitungskosten*
2 *Geländeankauf*
3 *Frauenzweiglager*
4 *Häftlingsreviergebäude/Strassenbau Industriegelände* (Krupp-Werkhallen)
4 *Raisko, Werkbaracken*
5 *Häftlingszellengebäude*
6 *Hauptwache*
7 (HWL) *Prov. Kartoffellagerhalle*
7 (HWL) 2 *Magazinbaracken*
7A *Häftlingsunterkunftsgebäude* 41
7B *Blockführerbaracke*
8 *Wachtürme*
8 (HWL) *Prov. Kartoffelbunker*
8E *Instandesetzungsarbeiten an Wohnhäuser in Budy und Raisko*
9 *Kanalisation*
11 *Krematorium*
11a *Neuerstellung Schornstein Krem. K.L.*
12 *Häftlingseffektenkammergebäude*
13 *Kommandanturgebäude*
14 *Revier- und Kantinengebäude*
17A *Mannschaftsgebäude* 1
17B *Mannschaftsgebäude* 2
17C 4 *Mannschaftsunterkunftsbaracken*
17C 4 *Mannschaftsbaracken für die Kommandantur*
17D 13 *Mannschaftsunterkunftsbaracken*
17D/1 *Stabs- und Mannschaftsbaracke*
17D/2-13 12 *Mannschaftsbaracken*, 4 *Wasch- und* 4 *Abortbaracken für die Wachtruppe*
18 *Kraftfahrzeuggarage/Garagenerweiterung für die Kommandantur*
19 (BH) *Häftlingswerkstätten*
20A *Häftlingsunterkunftsgebäude* 1
20B *Häftlingsunterkunftsgebäude* 2
20C *Häftlingsunterkunftsgebäude*
20D *Häftlingsunterkunftsgebäude* 4
20E *Häftlingsunterkunftsgebäude* 5
20F *Häftlingsunterkunftsgebäude* 6

20G *Häftlingsunterkunftsgebäude* 7
20H *Häftlingsunterkunftsgebäude* 8
20J *Häftlingsunterkunftsgebäude* 9
20K *Häftlingsunterkunftsgebäude* 10
20L *Häftlingsunterkunftsgebäude* 11
20M *Häftlingsunterkunftsgebäude* 12
20N *Häftlingsunterkunftsgebäude* 13
20O *Häftlingsunterkunftsgebäude* 14
20P *Häftlingsunterkunftsgebäude* 15
20Q *Häftlingsunterkunftsgebäude* 16
20R *Häftlingsunterkunftsgebäude* 17
21 *Strassenbau Praga-Halle/Führerheimstrasse*
23A *Garage der Werkstätte/Transformatorenstation*
23B *Notstromaggregatgebäude*
24 *Kommandantenwohnhaus*
26A *Feldscheune*
26B (LW) 3 *Feldscheunen*
27 *Wohnhäuser für verheiratete Unterführer (Haus Rekord)*
27A *Haus Nr.* 27
28 *Aufnahmebaracke mit Entlausung und 4 Effektenbaracken*
29 *Wasserversorgungsanlage*
29A *Neubau eines Wasserturmes*
29B *Wasserleitungen und Aufbereitungsanlage*
30A *Kraftfahrzeugwerkstatt*
30B *Tankanlage für die Kommandantur*
31 *Wirtschaftsgebäude für die Kommandantur*
32A *Zivilarbeiterkan tinenbaracke*
32B *Zivilarbeiterunterkunftsgebäude*
32C 6 *Stück Zivilarbeiterunter kunftsbaracken und 4 Abortbaracken*
32D 1 *Zivilarbeiterkantinenbaracke*
32E 1 *Zivilarbeiterwirtschaftsbaracke*
32F 2 *Zivilarbeiterwaschbaracken*
32G 2 *Zivilarbeiterabortbaracken*
32H *Zivilarbeiterlager für Italiener/Zivilarbeiterlager für die Krupp A.G.*
33A *(LW) Stallanlagen/Scheunenfundament*
33B *Schlachthaus mit Molkerei/Schlachthauserweiterung*
33Ba *Pferdestallbaracke für Schlachtvieh*
33C *(LW) Prov. Gewächshausanlage Raisko*
34 *Badenanstalt*

35 *Schule mit Kindergarten*
36A *Führerheim*
36B *Wohnhäuser für verheiratete Führer und Führerunterkünfte*
36C *Wohnausausbau für den Leiter der landwirtschaftlichen Betriebe Auschwitz/Ausbau eines bestehenden Rohbaues*
36D 4 *Führerunterkunftsbaracken*
37A *Bauleitungsbaracke (alte)v*
37B *(BH) Bauleitungsbaracke (neue)*
37C *(BH) Bauleitungsunterkunfts- und Wirtschaftsbaracke*
37D *Garage (zerlegbar) für die Bauleitung*
37E *Bauleitungsbaracke* 3
38 *Garage (zerlegbar) für die Kommandant ur/Fahrzeug- und Gerätehalle*
38A *Zentralgaragenhof*
39 *Prov. SS-Unterkünfte/SS-Unterkünfte ausserhalb des Lagerbereiches*
40 *SS-Unterkunft "Deutsches Haus"*
40A *Einrüstung eines Generalquartiers*
41 *Schutzhaftlagereinfriedigung*
42 *Häftlingsküchenbaracke/Alte Häftlingsküchenerweiterung/Neue Häftlingsküchener weiterung*
43 *Häftlingskantinenbaracke*
44 *Sportplatzanlage*
45 *Schiessstandanlage*
46 *Frachtenstundung*
49 *Elektrische Aussenanlagen Freileitungsnetz/Elektrische Zuführungen*
50 *Bauhof*
50 *(BH) Bauhofstofflagerungschuppen*
50 *(BH) Pferdestallbaracken für Baustofflagerung*
51 *Pferdestallung*
54 *Gärtnerische Anlagen*
55 2 *Wohn- und Arbeitsbaracken*
56 3 *Unterkunftsbaracken für Arbeitskommandos*
57 2 *RAD- Wohnhäuser*
58 5 *Baracken für Sonderbehandlung der Häftlinge*
59 12 *Baracken zur Unterbringung von Häflingseffekten usw.*
60 2 *Baracken zur Unterbringung von Häftlingselektrikern usw.*
61A *Behelfswerkstätten*
61B *Zimmerei-Werkstatt*
61C 7 *Baustofflagerschuppen*
63 *(LW) 4 Hofscheunen*

64 *(LW) Gewächshausanlage Raisko*
65A *(LW) Entenzuchtstall Harmense*
65B *(LW) 21 Kückenaufzuchtställe*
65B *bis (LW) Geflügelzuchtställe*
65C 8 *Hühneraufzuchtställe für je 100 Hühnerv*
65D 16 *Hühneraufzuchtställe für je 50 Hühner*
65E *(LW) 18 Herdbuchställe*
66 4 *Kartoffellagerhäuser*
67 *SS-Unterkunft, Reithalle und Viehställe in den ehemaligen Praga-Werken in Birkenau*
68 *(LW) Laboratorium*
68A *Hygien. Laboratorium*
68B *Laboratorium in Raisko. Ausbau eines Rohbaues in Raisko*
69 *Fohlenhof*
70 12 *Weideviehunterstände*
71 *(LW) ca. 35 Pferdstallbaracken*
71A *Abfohlstall*
71B *(LW) Wirtschaftshof Babitz*
72 2 *Rindviehställe*
73A *Gutshof*
73B *Gutshof*
74 15 *Pferdestallbaracken*
75 5 *Wachbaracken*
76 *(LW) Grastrockenanlage*
77 *Unterkünfte für die Hundestaffeln*
78 *(LW) Dämpfanlage für Schweinemästerei*
79 *Meliorationen im Interessengebiet (Landw.)*
80 *(LW) Schweineställe in Budy*
81 *Hyg.Untersuchungsställe*
82 *Durschschleusungsanlage für Zivilarbeiterlager I*
83 *Haus 184 für sanitäre Zwecke für die Truppe*
84 *Zisternen im Gelände des K.L.*
85 *Haus Nr. 154 (Postamt II)*
86 *Vernehmungsbaracke Politische Abteilung (bei Krematorium)*
87 *Baracke II für Politische Abteilung (am Krema)*
88 *(LW) Wohnhausausbau (2 Stücke) in Raisko/Raisko Haus 60*
89 *Baracke für Häftlinge III*
90 2 *Baracken für Landwirtschaft (Sonderproduktion)*
92 *Luftwaffenbaracke für Politische Abteilung*
93 *Sonderbaracke B für das K.L.*

94 2 *Baracken O.K.H. 290/6 (Schulelagerung)*
95 5 *Kartoffellagerhallen bei der Rampe*
96 1 *Krautsilos*
100 *Häftlingsunterkunftsgebäude 18*
101 *Häftlingsunterkunftsgebäude 19*
102 *Häftlingsunterkunftsgebäude* 20
103 *Häftlingsunterkunftsgebäude* 21
104 *Häftlingsunterk unftsgebäude* 22
105 *Häftlingsunterkunftsgebäude* 23
106 *Häftlingsunterk unftsgebäude* 24
107 *Häftlingsunterkunftsgebäude* 25
108 *Häftlingsunterkunftsgebäude*
109 *Häftlingsunterkunftsgebäude*
110 *Häftlingsunterkunftsgebäude*
111 *Häftlingsunterkunftsgebäude*
112 *Häftlingsunterkunftsgebäude*
113 *Häftlingsunterkunftsgebäude*
114 *Häftlingsunterkunftsgebäude*
115 *Häftlingsunterkunftsgebäude*
116 *Häftlingsunterkunftsgebäude* 26
117 *Häftlingsunterkunftsgebäude* 27
118 *Häftlingsunterkunftsgebäude* 28
119 *Häftlingsunterkunftsgebäude* 29
120 *Häftlingsunterkunftsgebäude* 30
121 *Häftlingsunterkunftsgebäude*
122 *Häftlingsunterkunftsgebäude*
123 *Häftlingsunterkunftsgebäude*
124 *Häftlingsunterkunftsgebäude*
125 *Häftlingsunterkunftsgebäude* 31
126 *Häftlingsunterkunftsgebäude* 32
127 *Häftlingsunterkunftsgebäude* 33
128 *Häftlingsunterkunftsgebäude* 34
129 *Häftlingsunterkunftsgebäude* 35
130 *Häftlingsunterkunftsgebäude*
131 *Häftlingsunterkunftsgebäude*
132 *Häftlingsunterkunftsgebäude*
133 *Häftlingsunterkunftsgebäude*
134 *Häftlingsunterkunftsgebäude* 36
135 *Häftlingsunterkunftsgebäude* 37

136 *Häftlingsunterkunftsgebäude* 38
137 *Häftlingsunterkunftsgebäude* 39
138 *Häftlingsunterkunftsgebäude* 40
139 *Häftlingsunterkunftsgebäude*
140 *Häftlingsunterkunftsgebäude*
141 *Häftlingsunterkunftsgebäude*
142 *Häftlingsunterkunftsgebäude*
143 *Häftlingsunterkunftsgebäude*
144 *Häftlingsunterkunftsgebäude*
145 *Häftlingsunterkunftsgebäude*
146 *Häftlingsunterkunftsgebäude*
147 *Häftlingsunterkunftsgebäude*
148 *Häftlingsunterkunftsgebäude*
149 *Häftlingsunterkunftsgebäude*
150 *Häftlingsunterkunftsgebäude*
151 *Häftlingsunterkunftsgebäude*
152 *Häftlingsunterkunftsgebäude*
153 *Häftlingsunterkunftsgebäude*
154 *Häftlingsunterkunftsgebäude*
155 *Häftlingsunterkunftsgebäude*
156 *Häftlingsunterkunftsgebäude*
157A *Häftlingssicherung swerkstattgebäude* 1
157B *Häftlingssicherung swerkstattgebäude* 2
157C *Häftlingssicherung swerkstattgebäude* 3
157D *Häftlingssicherung swerkstattgebäude* 4
157E *Häftlingssicherung swerkstattgebäude* 5
158 *Eingangsgebäude mit Türm/Schutzhaftlagereingangsgebäude*
160 *Wäscherei- und Aufnahmegebäude mit Entlausungsanlage und Häft-lingsbad*
160a *Kurzwellen-Entlausungsanlage*
161 *Fernheizwerk/Fernheizkanal*
162 *Häftlings-Wirtschaftsgebäude*
166 *Ausbau von Häuser für bombengeschädigte SS-Angehörige im Interes-sengebiet K.L.*
167 *Instandesetzungsarbeiten an den durch Bomben beschädigten Gebäuden und Aussenanlagen im Interessengebiet des Konzentrationslager Auschwitz*
172 *Wirtschaftsbaracke für die Wachtruppe*
173 *Kommandantur und Kommandanturunterkunftsgebäude*
174 *Kommandanturwachgebäude*
200 5 *Wachtürme*
201 *Hauptsammlerkanal mit Kläranlage*

202 *Alarmanlage*
203 *Blitzschutzanlage*
204 *Telefonanlage*
205 *Behelfsanlage*
206 *Feuerlöschanlage*
207 2 *Saunaanlagen/Sauna bei Revierbaracke*
207a 1 *Saunaanlage für Landwirtschaft in Raisko*
208 *Gleisanschluss*
209 *Behelfsbrücke über die Sola*
209a *Verbindungsstrasse zur Solabrücke*
210 *Einfriedungen*
211 *Transformatorenstation*
212 *Hauptinsgem*

List of Construction Sites at Birkenau, 9 April 1943
1 *Bauleitungskosten*
2 *Drainierung des Geländes/Geländeankauf, Erschliessung des Grundstücks*
3a 30 *Gefangenenunterkunftsbaracken im Quarantänelager BA I*
3b 24 *Gefangenenunterkunftsbaracken BA I*
3c 60 *Gefangenenunterkunftsbaracken BA II*
3d 75 *Gefangenenunterkunftsbaracken BA II*
3e/f 111 *Krankenbaracken im K.G.L. BA III*
4a 2 *Wirtschaftsbaracken im Quarantänelager BA I und 2 Wirtschaftsbaracken (Teeküchen) BA I*
4b 3 *Vorratsbaracken im Quarantänelager BA I*
4c 9 *Wirtschaftsbaracken BA II*
4d 9 *Vorratsbaracken BA II*
4e 9 *Wirtschaftsbaracken BA III*
4f 9 *Vorratsbaracken BA III*
5a *Entlausungsbaracke I im Quarantänelager BA I*
5b *Entlausungsbaracke II im Quarantänelager BA I*
6a 5 *Waschbaracken im Quarantänelager BA I/Wasch- und Abortbaracken 1-5*
6b 14 *Waschbaracken im Quarantänelager BA II*
6c 14 *Waschbaracken im Quarantänelager BA III*
7a 5 *Abortbaracken im Quarantänelager BA I*
7b 15 *Abortbaracken BA II*
7c 14 *Abortbaracken BA III*
8a 1 *Leichenbaracke im Quarantänelager BA I*
8b 2 *Leichenbaracken BA II*

8c 2 *Leichenbaracken BA III*
9 *Quarantänlager-Eingangsgebäude einschl. Trafogebäude BA I*
10 *Kommandanturgebäude BA II*
11 *Wachgebäude BA II*
12a 11 *Revierbaracken BA II*
12b 12 *Baracken für Schwerkranke BA III*
12c 3 *Revierbaracken BA I*
12d 12 *Blockführerbaracken BAII u. BA III*
12e 2 *Quarantänebaracken, ausserhalb FKL BA I*
12f 2 *Blockführerbaracken BA I*
13 47 *Wachtürme aus Holz/Häftlingsunterkunftbaracken*
14 *Barackenlager für die Wachtruppe BA II/Wirtschaftbaracken*
14a 16 *Unterkunftsbaracken BA III*
3 *Waschbaracken BA III*
1 *Prov. Sauna BA III*
14b 3 *Wirtschaftsbaracken*
14c *Abortsbaracken*
14d 10 *Unterkunfts- und Kammerbaracken*
14e 2 *Baracken für Brennmaterial*
14f 1 *Revierbaracke*
14g 1 *Truppensauna*
14h *Umzäunung (Holzzaun)*
14k *Splitterschutzgräben für die Truppe*
15 *Lagerhaus*
16 *Zufahrtstrassen und Parkplatz*
17 *Strassenbefestigung innerhalb des Lagers*
18 *Kanalisation und Kläranlage/Graben E, F, H, I*
18a *Ringgraben und Planierung*
19 *Wasserversorgungsanlage*
20 *Kraftstromanlage*
21 *Zuführung der Starkstromleitung von Birkenau*
22 *Telefonanlage*
23 *Alarmanlage*
24 *Einfriedigung/Zaunbau*
25 *Drahtzaun innerhalb des Lagers*
26 *Transformatorenstation im BW 9*
26a *Transformatorenstation im BW 19 BA II*
26b *Notstromanlage*
27 *Gleisanschluss vom Bahnhof Auschwitz*

28 *Kochkessel und Heizöfen*
29 *Feuerlöschteiche und Zisternen*
30 *Krematorium I*
30a *Krematorium II*
30b *Krematorium III*
30c *Krematorium IV*
31 *Bäckerei*
31a *Großbäckereianlage*
32 *Entwesungsanlage*
32a *Entwesungsbaracke im Zigeunerlager BAII*
33 30 *Effektenbaracken*
33a 3 *Baracken für Sondermassnahmen Typ 260/9 BAII*
3 *Baracken für Sondermassnahmen Typ 260/9 BAIII*
34a *4 Kammerbaracken BA II*
34b *4 Kammerbaracken BA III*
35 *Wasseraufbereitung*
36 *Truppenlazarett*
45 *Hauptinsgemein*
47 *Materialtransport*
48 *Abfertigungshalle für Transporte*
49 *Bekleidungsmagazin*
50 *Gemüselagerhallen*
51 *Lebensmittelmagazin*
52 *Feuerwehrgebäude*
53 *Gerätelager*
54 3 *Baracken für Sondermaßnahmen (Ungarn)*
66 *Kartoffelhalle*
77 *Hundezwinger Birkenau*
98 *Luftschutzdeckungsgraben*
159 *Flugzeug-Zerlegebetrie*

Source: 'Aufstellung der Bauwrke (BW) fur die Bauten, Aussen-und Nebananlagen des Bauvorhabens Konzetrationslager Auschwitz', dated 31 March 1942, 502-1-1 267, pp.3–13. 'Erlauterungsbericht zum Bauvorhaben Konzetrationslager Auschwitz O/S', dated 15 July 1942, RGVA (Russian State War Museum), 502-1-220,pp.1–52. 'Tatigkeitsbericht der Bauleitung KL und Landwirtschaft', dated 14 September 1943, RGVA (Russian State War Museum), 502–27, pp.1–8.

Appendix 11

Departments of the SS Main Economic and Administrative Office (SS-Wirtschafts und Verwaltungshauptamt; SS-WVHA)

The WVHA was made up of five main departments (*Ämter or Amtsgruppe*)

Amt A, Personnel – Finance, Law and Administration
Amtsgruppe A, among other things, discharged the responsibility for financial matters of the SS, including those relating to its concentration camps.

Amt B, Payroll and Supply
Amtsgruppe B, among other things, was responsible for the supply of food and clothing for inmates of the concentration camps, and of food, uniforms, equipment, billets, and camp quarters for the members of the SS.

Amt C, Buildings and Works
Amtsgruppe C, among other things was charged with the construction and maintenance of houses, buildings, and structures of the SS, the German police, and of the concentration camps and prisoner of war camps.

Amt D, Concentration Camps
Amtsgruppe D, which prior to March 1942 was known as the Inspectorate of Concentration Camps, was responsible, among other things, for the administration of the concentration camps and of the concentration camp inmates.

Amt W, Business – Economics
Amtsgruppe W, among other things, was responsible for the operation and maintenance of various industrial, manufacturing, and service enterprises throughout Germany and the occupied countries. It was also responsible for providing clothing for concentration camp inmates. In the operation of the enterprises under its control, this Amtsgruppe employed many concentration camp inmates.

Appendix 12

Architects of Genocide

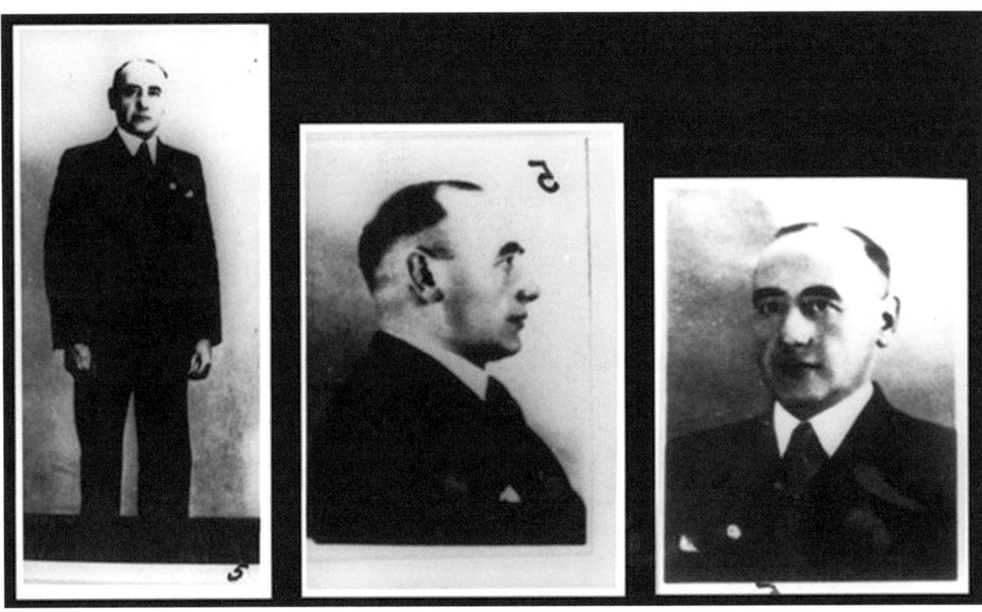

SS-Sturmbannführer **Karl Bischoff** (9 August 1897–2 October 1950)
Bischoff was an architect and engineer. He served at Auschwitz as chief of the Central Construction Office of the Waffen-SS and became chief of construction of Auschitz-Birkenau. In October 1941 Bischoff arrived in Auschwitz, where he became chief of the Central Construction Office of the Waffen-SS and the Police Auschwitz in Upper Silesia (*fori. Zentralbauleitung der Waffen-SS und Polizei, Auschwitz O/S*). It was Bischoff who planned the expansion programme of Auschwitz by creating a PoW camp which later evolved into the planning and construction of the crematoria at Birkenau.

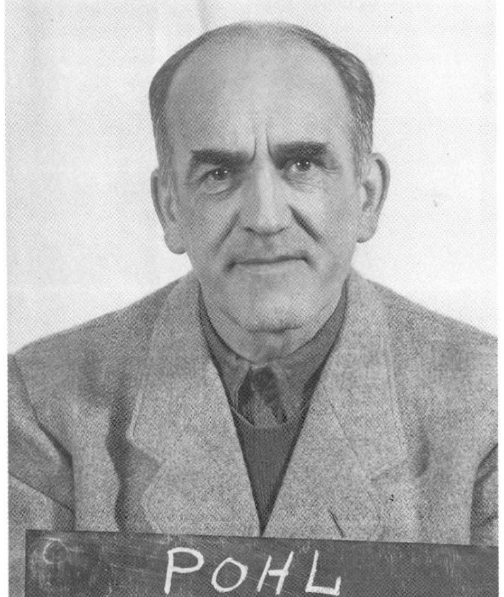

SS-Obergruppenführer **Oswald Ludwig Pohl** (30 June 1892–7 June 1951)
Pohl was head of the SS Main Economic and Administrative Office and head administrator of the concentration camp system. In January 1942 Himmler consolidated all of the offices for which Pohl was responsible into one, creating the SS Main Economic and Adminstrative Office (*Wirtschafts- und Verwaltungshauptamt*; WVHA). Pohl became a key figure in the holocaust and worked very closely with *SS-Reichsführer* Heinrich Himmler. He held four powerful departments which placed Pohl at the top of many of the decisions that were made in the construction and murder of the Jews at Auschwitz. In total he controlled the 20 concentration camps and 165 labour camps where he directed all SS and Police building projects. He was in charge of all SS economic enterprises and signed off many of the important plans that saw Auschwitz-Birkenaua become the largest killing in factory of all time.

SS-Obergruppenführer **Hans Kammler** (26 August 1901–1945)
Kammler was in charge of civil engineering projects across the concentration camp system, notably Auschwitz. He held the command in Office D within the Main Economic and Adminstration Office and also oversaw the V-weapons programme and emergency programmes towards the end of the war. When Kammler joined the Main Economic and Adminstration Office, he became *SS-Obergruppenführer* Oswald Pohl's deputy, where he worked with *SS-Gruppenführer* Richard Glucks of Office D, and was also named chief of Office C, which overlooked the construction of all the concentration and extermination camps. Kammler became heavily embroiled internally in all major project works in Auschwitz and oversaw the construction of the crematoria.

SS-Untersturmführer **Fritz Ertl** *(31 August 1908–2 November 1982)*
Ertl was Deputy Head of the Central Construction Management of the Waffen-SS and Police at Auschwitz. It was Ertl that designed the barracks at Auschwitz-Birkenau. However due to limited budget many of the prefabricated buildings were converted from army horse stables for the camp barracks. Later in the construction of the camp he was temporarily assigned to the administrative head of the construction management in Auschwitz, which was the Central Construction Management of the Waffen-SS and Police. Ertl resigned from the Auschwitz Central Construction Office at the end of January 1943.

Kurt Prufer (21 April 1891 – 24 October 1952) Prufer was a German engineer who worked at the company JA Topf & Söhne JA in Erfurt, and was responsible for the construction of the crematoria at Auschwitz. From 1939 onwards, the Topf & Söhne Company worked very closely with the SS, including Karl Bischoff, and willingly received orders from the Reich Security Main Office (RSHA). From its inception Topf & Söhne supported the SS requirements in order to make the killing machinery at Auchwitz possible. (Hauptstaatsarchiv Weimar, J. A. Topf & Söhne, Nr. 252, Bl)

SS-Unterscharführer **August Schlachter** (January 25 1901–10 April 1996). Schlachter was a German architect who worked as a construction manager in a number of concentration camps. In 1940 he headed the new SS Construction Department KL Auschwitz/Upper Silesia from May 1940 to November 1941, and was responsible for setting up the main Auschwitz camp. He also created the central construction management of the Waffen-SS and Police Auschwitz in December 1941. However, in spite of his career, Schlachter was regarded by Rudold Höss as a 'provincial architect from Württemberg, a narrow mind with little drive'. As a result, he was transferred to Natzwiler at the end of 1941 as a construction manager.

SS-Obersturmführer **Werner Jothann** (18 May 1907–death unknown). Werner was a German civil engineer who led the central construction management of the Waffen-SS and Auschwitz police from November 1943. Initially, in early 1941, he was assigned to the construction management of the *SS New Construction Department KL Auschwitz/Upper Silesia*, which expanded the main camp. Later that year it was integrated into the central construction management of the Waffen-SS and Auschwitz police under the command of Karl Bischoff. In March 1942 Jothann became responsible for the construction of the Krupp AG detonator factory and the district heating plant and was leader of the Waffen-SS construction department. At the beginning of April 1943, Jothann replaced Fritz Ertl as Bischoff's deputy. At the beginning of November 1943, he took over control of construction management in Auschwitz and was entrusted with managing the business as head of the central construction management. He even commissioned the Topf and Sons company to overhaul the furnaces at Auschwitz-Birkenau and had a vent installed in a gas chamber for the Hungarian shipments.

SS-Obersturmführer **Walter Dejaco** (19 June 1909 – 9 January 1978). Dejaco was an Austrian architect who worked in the Auschwitz concentration camp as a construction manager in the central management of the Waffen-SS and police Auschwitz. From 6 June 1940, he became a member of the *SS Neubauleitung* Auschwitz and later that year he headed the planning department there. As a construction manager, Dejaco was extensively embroiled in the planning, construction and maintenance of the gas chambers and crematoria at Auschwitz. Hans Kammler, in a personal report, described him as a 'qualified construction specialist'. Between 1943 and 1944 Dejaco was deputy head of the construction management in Auschwitz, now known as the Central Construction Management of the Waffen-SS and Auschwitz Police. From mid-May 1944 he attended a three-month special course in construction at the SS leader school of the Arolsen Economic Administrative Service, but then returned to Auschwitz, where he was deployed until January 1945.

Notes and Sources

Published Material

Breitman, Richard, *The Architect of Genocide: Himmler and the Final Solution*, The Bodley Head, London, 1991.

Broad, Perry; Broad, Rudolf; Kremer, Johann Paul; Höss, Rudolf, *KL Auschwitz Seen by the SS*, Auschwitz State Museum, 1998.

Buchheim, Hans, *SS und Polizei im Nationalsozialistischen Staat*, Duisdorf bei Bonn: Selbstverlag der Studiengesellschaft fur Zietprobleme, 1964.

Cesarani, David, *Eichmann: His Life and Crimes*, Vintage, 2005.

Dicks, Henry, *Licensed Mass Murder: A Socio-Psychological Study of Some SS Killers*, London, Chatto Heinemann, 1972.

'Dienstaltersliste der Schutzstaffel der NSDAP', Stand vom 1. Oktober 1934. Berlin, *Personalkanzlei der Reichsführer-SS*, 1935.

'Dienstaltersliste der Schutzstaffel der NSDAP', Stand vom 1 Dezember 1936, Berlin, *Personalkanzlei der Reichsführer-SS*, 1937.

'Dienstaltersliste der Schutzstaffel der NSDAP (SS)', Stand vom 1 Dezember 1938, mit Berichtigungsheft, Stand vom 15 Juni 1939. *Biblio Verlag*, Osnabruck, 1987.

'Dienstaltersliste der Schutzstaffel der NSDAP (SS-Oberstgruppenführer und SS-Standartenführer'), Stand vom 9 November 1944, Berlin, 1944.

'Dienstaltersliste der Schutzstaffel der NSDAP (SS-Oberststurmbannführer und SS-Sturmbannführer'), Stand vom 1 Oktober 1944, Berlin, 1944.

'Dienstaltersliste der Waffen-SS. SS-Obergruppenführer bis SS Hauptsturmfuhrer', Stand vom 1 Juli 1944. *Biblio Verlag*, Osnabruck, 1987.

Dixon, Jeremy, *Commanders of Auschwitz: The SS Officers Who Ran the Largest Nazi Concentration Camp 1940–1945*, Schiffer Military History, Atglen, PA, 2005.

Dwork, Deborah and van Pelt, Robert Jan, *Auschwitz – 1270 to the Present*, W.W. Norton & Company, 1996.

Eisenbach, Artur, 'Operation Reinhard: Mass Extermination of the Jewish Population in Poland', *Polish Western Affairs*, 3 January 1962, 80–124.

Fitzgibbon, Constantine, *Commandant of Auschwitz*, Phoenix Press, 2000.

Friedrich, Otto, *The Kingdom of Auschwitz*, HarperCollins, 1982.

Gutman, Yisrael and Berenbaum, Michael, *Anatomy of the Auschwitz Death Camp*, United States Holocaust Memorial Museum, Indiana University Press, 1994.

Harris, Whitney R., *Tyranny on Trial: The Evidence at Nuremburg*, Dallas, Southern Methodist University Press, 1954.

Hilberg, Raul, *The Destruction of the European Jews*, Chicago, Quadrangle Books, 1960.

Höhne, Heinz, *Der Orden unter dem Totenkopf: Die Geschichte der SS*, Gutersloh, Sigbert Mohn Verlag, 1967.

Höss, Rudolf and Paskuly, Steven (ed.) *Death Dealer: The Memoirs of the SS Kommandant at Auschwitz*, Prometheus Books, Buffalo, NY, 1992.

Kogon, Engen; Langbein, Hermann; Rückerl, Adalbert (eds), *Nazi Mass Murder: A Documentary of the Use of Poison Gas*, Yale University Press, New Haven, 1993.

Kommandant in Auschwitz, Deutsche Verlags-Anstalt, 1958.
MacLean, French L., *The Camp Men: The SS Officers Who Ran the Nazi Concentration Camp System*, Schiffer Publishing, 1999, Atglen, PA.
Neufert, Ernst, *Bau-Entwurfslehre,* Bauwelt-Verlag, Berlin 1938.
Pressac, Jean-Claude, *Auschwitz: Technique and Operation of the Gas Chambers,* The Beate Klarsfeld Foundation, New York, 1989.
Rees, Laurence, *Auschwitz – The Nazis and the Final Solution*, BBC Books, 2005.
Reitlinger, Gerald, *The Final Solution: The Attempt to Exterminate the Jews of Europe, 1939–1945*, New York, Beechhurst Press, 1953.
——, *The SS: Alibi of a Nation, 1922–1945*, Arms & Armour Press, 1981.
Rothkirchen, Livia, 'The Final Solution in its Last Stages', *Yad Vashem Studies on the European Jewish Catastrophe and Resistance* 8, Jerusalem, 1970, 7–29.
Sehn, Jan, 'Oboz Koncentacyjny i zaglady Oswiecim', in, *Biuletyn Glownej Komisji badania zbrodni niemieckich w Polsce*, Vol. I, Warsaw, 1946.
Setkiewicz, Piotr, *Voices of Memory 13: The SS Garrison in KL Auschwitz*, published by International Center for Education About Auschwitz and the Holocaust. Auschwitz-Birkenau State Museum, 2018, p.174.
State Museum-Auschwitz-Birkenau, Auschwitz in den Augen der SS, Staatliches Museum Auschwitz, 1997.
Steinbacher, Sybille, *Auschwitz: A History*, Penguin Books, 2005.
Sydnor, Charles W., *Soldiers of Destruction: The SS Death's Head Division 1933–1945*, Guild Publishing, London, 1977.
Tenenbaum, Joseph, 'Auschwitz in Retrospect: The Self-Portrait of Rudolf Hoess, Commander of Auschwitz', *Jewish Social Studies* 15, July–October 1953, 203–36.
van Pelt, Robert Jan, *The Case for Auschwitz: Evidence from the Irving Trial*, Indiana University Press, Bloomington/Indianapolis, 2002.

Documents

A Letter Written by Schlachter to Rudolf Höss, 30 August 1940, [Osobyi Archive, Moscow] 502/1. File 214, 91f. [United States Holocaust Research Institute, Washington D.C, microfilm RG 11.001M.03, reel 34].
Affidavit by Rudolf Höss, 5 April 1946, at Nuremberg, (ND: 3868 – PS, NA Microfilm M.1270, Reel.7).
A letter to Rudolf Hoss from Kammler, 18 June 1940, box BW ½, file 1/9. [Auschwitz Museum].
Excerpted from a memorandum dated 27 April 1942 by Dr. Erhard Wetzel (a lawyer), who was serving as desk officer in the Reich Ministry for the Eastern Territories.
Memorandum from Gestapo Headquarters, 15 June 1944. Trials of War Criminals Before the Nuremberg Military Tribunals - Washington, U.S Govt. Print. Off., 1949-1953, Vol. IV, p. 1166: Office of US Chief Counsel for the prosecution of Axis criminality APO 124A, US Army Interrogation Division. Translation Document No.3868-PS. Affidavit of Rudolf Höss – 5 April 1946 [Reproduced from the holdings of the US Holocaust Memorial Museum Archives]
National Archives of the United States, Washington DC Microfilm T–1270.
National Archives of the United States, Washington DC Microfilm A3343 Series SO.
National Archives of the United States, Washington DC, *Captured German Record Group 242 (RG 242)*, Microfilm Series T–74, T–81, T–120, T–354, T–501, T–580, T–581: *War Crimes, RG 238 N1* Series (Microfilm T–301) NG Series (Microfilm T–1139).
Noakes, J. and Pridham, G. (eds). *Nazism: A History in Documents and Eyewitness Accounts, 1919-1945, Volume II*, Schocken Books, New York, (c)1988 by the Dept. of History and Archeology, University of Exeter. ISBN 0-8053-0973-5 (vol. 1), 0-8052-0972-7 (vol. 2). Document #690 on p.979: Institute für Zeitgeschichte, Munich: Akten der Parteikanzlei [microfiche] Rudolf Höss Aufzeichnungen.
Oswiecim, and Brzezinka, Microfilm A.0132 Reels 1–10.

Plan of Auschwitz-Birkenau, 6 January 1942, box BW 2/6. [Auschwitz Museum]
[PRO] UK Public Records Office documents Ref: F0371/57649 Dated March 1946 relating to Foreign Office communiqués to the Polish delegate on the War Crimes Commission to hand over Rudolf Höss to the Polish authorities to face trial.
Records created and inherited by Government Communications Headquarters (GCHQ) Division within HW General Records of the Government Code and Cypher School. HW 16 Government Code and Cypher School: German Police Section Decrypts of German Police Communications during WWII [Public Records Office].
Records of the SS officers from the Berlin Document Centre.
RSHA Statistical Tables, coll. NS 19, file 3979, 3, 11. [Federal Archive Koblenz]

Auschwitz and Yad Vashem Document Sources

Auschwitz-Birkenau State Museum

Page 6 – Auschwitz Document E.
Page 9 – AUSCHWITZ PMO Archive (No File Reference). Drawing commandant's house [drawn September 1944 by Haftling 121643].
Page 29 – AUSCHWITZ PMO Archive (No File Reference). Drawing shows fence posts.
Page 32 – AUSCHWITZ PMO File BW 11/1 P/1.
Page 33 – AUSCHWITZ PMO File BW 11/1, Page 3.
Page 34 – AUSCHWITZ PMO Neg No. 20818/1.
Page 35 – AUSCHWITZ PMO BW 11/1.
Page 56 – AUSCHWITZ PMO File No Reference (Horse Stable Barracks Drawing).
Page 60 – AUSCHWITZ PMO File BW 2/6. Neg No. 21135/4.
Page 67 – AUSCHWITZ PMO Archives (No Reference).
Page 72 – AUSCHWITZ PMO File BW 2/4. Neg No. 21135/3.
Page 83 – AUSCHWITZ PMO File BW 306–30c. Neg No. 20946/6.
Page 84 (Top) – AUSCHWITZ PMO File 306–30C/23.
Page 84 (Bottom) – AUSCHWITZ Neg No. 2094617.
Page 88 – AUSCHWITZ PMO File BW 30/26, Page 21.
Page 89 – AUSCHWITZ PMO File BW 30/30, Page 21.
Page 90 – AUSCHWITZ PMO File BW 2/11. Neg No. 21135/8.
Page 92 – AUSCHWITZ PMO File BW 30/34, Page 100 Volume II Höss Trail (Page 64).
Page 93 – AUSCHWITZ PMO File BW 30/34, Page 101.
Page 94 – AUSCHWITZ PMO File BW 30/34, Page 102.
Page 95 – AUSCHWITZ PMO File BW 30/36, Page 31.
Page 96 – AUSCHWITZ PMO File BW 30/28, Page 66.
Page 97 – AUSCHWITZ PMO File BW 30/36, Page 34.
Page 98 – AUSCHWITZ PMO File BW 30/36, Page 27.
Page 123 – AUSCHWITZ PMO File BW 30/27.
Page 124 – AUSCHWITZ PMO File 30/25, Page 7.
Page 125 – AUSCHWITZ PMO File 30/28.
Page 128 – AUSCHWITZ PMO File. Neg. No 20583.
Page 129 – (Top) AUSCHWITZ PMO File BW 30/43.
Page 129 – (Bottom) AUSCHWITZ PMO File BW 30b–30c/23. Neg Nos 2634 and 20818110.
Page 130 – AUSCHWITZ PMO File BW 30/43, Page 34.
Page 132 – AUSCHWITZ PMO File BW 30/27, Pages 11–12.
Page 133 – AUSCHWITZ PMO File BW 30/34, Page 42.
Page 134 – (Top) AUSCHWITZ PMO File 30/34.
Page 134 – (Bottom) AUSCHWITZ PMO File 30/43, Page 19.
Page 138 (Top & Bottom) – AUSCHWITZ PMO File Blueprint Haftling 15592 (Rudolf Kauer), Watch Tower Drawings (No Reference).

Page 141 – AUSCHWITZ PMO File Drawing *Blockführerbaracke* for BAIII in Birkenau (No Reference).
Page 142 – AUSCHWITZ PMO File BW 30/43, Page 20.
Page 143 – AUSCHWITZ PMO FILE BW 30/25, Page 14.
Page 143 – AUSCHWITZ PMO BW 30/43, Page 24.
Page 143 – AUSCHWITZ PMO BW 30/43, Page 23.
Page 146 – AUSCHWITZ PMO File BW 30a/7. Neg No. 20922/9 & Neg No. 20922/8 (Huta Drawings 109/15 of 24/09/43).
Page 147 – AUSCHWITZ PMO File BW 30a/19. Neg. No 20922/1.
Page 181 – AUSCHWITZ PMO. Neg No. 21032.

Yad Vashem Holocaust Remembrance Center Document Sources

Page 21 – YAD VASHEM – Drawing 1 March 1941. Drawing Auschwitz Birkenau (No File Reference).
Page 44 – YAD VASHEM – Drawing 7 October 1941. Drawing Fritz Ertl and approved by Bischoff (No File Reference).
Page 45 – YAD VASHEM – Drawing Birkenau dated 14 October 1941 by Haftling 471 (student Alfred Przybylski). (No File Reference).
Page 46 – YAD VASHEM – Drawing Birkenau Brick Barracks. Drawing *Construction Management of the Waffen-SS and Auschwitz Police* (No File Reference).
Page 53 – YAD VASHEM – Drawing Guardhouse for PoW camp (Guardhouse for PoW Camp) (No File Reference).
Page 54 – YAD VASHEM – Drawing Haftling 538 (5 November 1941. Façade, cross section and plan view of the Birkenau gate building entrance) (No File Reference).

Further Sources

Page 25

RGVA (Russian State War Museum), 502-1-11, pp.37f. (KL Auschwitz – construction projects second and third year of war economy, Kammler writes).

Pages 48–50

1) Bischoff outlined a report in order to plan for the new construction of the Waffen-SS PoW camp at Auschwitz "O/S" (Upper Silesia, which contained list of the *Bauwerke* (*Kostenüberschlag für das Bauvorhaben: SS Unterkunft und Konzentrationslager Auschwitz*, 31 October 1941. RGVA (Russian State War Museum), 502-2-97, pp.3–6.
2) (*Erläuterungsbericht zum Vorentwurf für den Neubau des Kriegsgefangenenlagers der Waffen-SS*, Auschwitz "O/S" and *Kostenvoranschlag für den Vorentwurf über den Neubau des Kriegsgefangenenlagers der Waffen-SS*, Auschwitz "O/S". RGVA (Russian State War Museum), 502-1-233, pp.13–30).
3) *Kostenüberschlag für das Bauvorhaben: SS Unterkunft und Konzentrationslager Auschwitz*, 31 October 1941. RGVA (Russian State War Museum), 502-2-97, pp.3–6.

Page 61

Letter from Pohl to Central Construction Office Auschwitz of 2 March 1942. RGVA (Russian State War Museum), 502-1-319, pp.210f.

Page 62

Erläuterungsbericht zum Vorentwurf für den Neubau des Kriegsgefangenenlagers der Waffen-SS, Auschwitz "O/S" and *Kostenvoranschlag für den Vorentwurf über den Neubau des Kriegsgefangenenlagers der Waffen-SS*, Auschwitz "O/S". RGVA, 502-1-233, pp.13–30.

Pages 81–3

SS-Gruppenführer Oswald Pohl approved the proposals listed (Letter from Pohl to Central Construction Office Auschwitz of 2 March 1942. RGVA, 502-1-319, pp.210f.

Pages 83–4

Interrogation of Richard Böck, 2 November 1960. Preparation of the Frankfurt Auschwitz trial, ref. 4 Js 444/59, vol. 29, pp.6881–6883. The original report published by G. Rudolf in the journal 'Aus den Akten des Frankfurter Auschwitz-Prozesses, Teil 4' *Vierteljahreshefte für freie Geschichtsforschung*, 7(2) (2003), p.228.